Emotional Logic and Decision Making

Emotional Logic and Decision Making

The interface between professional upheaval and personal evolution

Christian Bourion

Translated by Andrea Soulis

First published 2001 in France by Editions ESKA
This edition published 2005 by
PALGRAVE MACMILLAN
Houndmills, Basingstoke, Hampshire RG21 6XS and
175 Fifth Avenue, New York, N.Y. 10010
Companies and representatives throughout the world

PALGRAVE MACMILLAN is the global academic imprint of the Palgrave Macmillan division of St. Martin's Press, LLC and of Palgrave Macmillan Ltd. Macmillan® is a registered trademark in the United States, United Kingdom and other countries. Palgrave is a registered trademark in the European Union and other countries.

ISBN 1–4039–4508–X

This book is printed on paper suitable for recycling and made from fully managed and sustained forest sources.

A catalogue record for this book is available from the British Library.

Library of Congress Cataloging-in-Publication Data

Bourion, Christian, 1945–
    [Logique emotionnelle, English]
    Emotional logic and decision making : the interface between professional upheaval and personal evolution / Christian Bourion ; translated by Andrea Soulis.
       p. cm.
    Includes bibliographical references (p.) and index.
    ISBN 1–4039–4508–X (cloth)
    1. Decision making. 2. Emotional intelligence. I. Title.

HD30.23B677 2004
153.8'3—dc22   2004054939

10 9 8 7 6 5 4 3 2 1
14 13 12 11 10 09 08 07 06 05

Printed and bound in Great Britain by
Creative Print & Design (Wales), Ebbw Vale

To Jade and Robin

It is only with the heart that one can rightly see.
What is essential is invisible to the eye.

1946, A. de Saint-Exupéry

Contents

List of Exhibits

List of Questionnaires

Why "Self-Management"?

Until very recently, we willingly used the term "career" to characterize the professional path of young men and women at the end of their educational studies.

Today, the business world has changed radically; it has become both more flexible and more demanding. The "self-management" model fills that gap between the diploma and the (previously) quasi-fatal path that the diploma gives rise to. After the diploma, graduates need to begin work on their personal development and to equip themselves with the special strengths needed to manage their professional development successfully.

In terms of personal development, the young graduate just beginning in a profession has, above all, the responsibility to learn, to understand and to change.

Yesterday he was living in a world protected from failure, today he must learn to manage his errors and enter into the long process of disapprenticeship.

He will reconstruct himself several times in the course of his professional life.

In terms of professional development the graduate, even one who has been hired by a large firm, must often invent his job description and create his post in order to be in a responsible and profitable job position. Sometimes, as the ultimate step, he is driven to free himself and create his own employment.

The most popular form this takes these days is the creation of an activity, having short-term potential within a structure above and beyond the individual – that is to say within the firm itself.

In the near future, a more radical change will occur: the explosion of employees in high-level positions: work-sharing systems among several companies, contracting out of work managed by a third party association of freelance workers, limited project assignments within normal management contracts...

The individual will be the supplier of expertise, of know-how, in permanent interaction and constant transaction with his professional environment.

In brief, professional life has become its own métier requiring that one becomes, above all, a "self-manager".

Emotional logic, which will be presented on the following pages, describes one of the windows of change: understanding how we react in project situations in order to increase self-knowledge, increase understanding and improve contribution.

Without a doubt, the personality will become the first tool of the "self-manager".

Happy reading.

From Economic to Emotional Man

Over the course of the last half century the approach to decision-making, under the substantial influence of financial economic models, has resulted in a vision centered around brain functioning. From the decision-tree approach and actualization tables to the current approach, a true paradigm change was produced. Coming from a position of suspicion that virtually eliminated the actor and his subjectivity, the new models reintroduced him into the process, fully describing his choices in all their complexity, his contradictory centers of interest, his multiple interests, desires and secret behaviors, as well as personal jealousies and private paranoias.

In this rather slow progress[1], it was, above all, the Nobel Prize winner H. Simon who made major inroads in inventing the Limited Rationality Decision-maker, a sort of "yes, but…" response that his students, particularly March et al. (1972), would transform into a "no, but…" with the famous garbage can model that definitively closed the door on the rational model as the explanation of the way decisions are taken. Mintzberg in Canada had already begun to increase his attacks on this approach that he considered far from reality, but which was affecting the training of young managers, in particular with his question introducing the concept of the double functioning of the brain: "Why are some people so smart and so stupid at the same time?" In effect, even with limited rationality, Simon's decision-maker remained pharmacologically treated in order to stay devoid of undue emotion[2]. A Frenchman and the "new grid" (Laborit, 1974) gave birth to the **Emotionally Active Decision-maker**. In 1988, Ned Herrmann contributed a synthesis of this controversy by demonstrating in his work *The Creative Brain*, that not only do the rational and emotional processes coexist deep in the brain, but that there are yet two others, and that these four processes, more or less antinomic, more or less complementary, intervene simultaneously in decision-making.

In this series we have attempted to create a model of emotional logic aimed, first of all, at the teaching and preparing of future managers (business and engineering schools, executive business programs, etc.) but also at those engaged in behavioral research.

The first of our three works, *Emotional Logic,* describes the interaction between the decision-maker's internal and external environment in the context of challenging situations, hierarchical situations, situations of failure, irreversible situations and situations of success. The work goes beyond the framework of "occupation of manager" to tackle the "occupation of self". In particular, it sheds light on the process by which people must either enhance and increase their qualifications, or find themselves idle within the organization.

The second, *The Daily Business of Management,* describes ways of reacting to others, classifying these behaviors according to whether or not they provoke more complicated problems than the ones originally needing resolution. The work then highlights the more efficient of these behaviors. It concludes with a mini-test, more in fun than strictly evaluative, which exists also in CD-ROM.

Decision Logic responds to the following questions: How does our brain inform itself? How to formulate true problems? How to find creative solutions? It answers the questions: How to calculate risk? How to self-actualize? How to decide?

The Epistemological Position
of This Work

*This work develops the role that emotions play throughout the
action process. As useful guides and profound sources for choice,
emotions can also imprison the actor. More often, they play a
determining role in the apprenticeship process, in adaptation and in
mental blocking. Their way of operating, apparently irrational, in fact
obeys a rigorous logic. We define the model: emotional man or the
Emotionally Active Decision-maker (E.A.D.).*

1. Objectives

The objective of emotional logic is the description, explanation and understanding of the internal indicators that inform the decision-maker on the
interaction between his external and internal environment during the
choice process. Although it is the external indicators that reign primordial
when all is well, it is the internal indicators that become essential in
periods of crisis or failure. Just as economic crises must be guided
correctly in order fulfill their transitional roles, crises of the internal environment following inevitable failures or irreversible situations, also constitute a means to progress if the decision-maker understands their meaning
and sense.

2. Hybridization

Emotional production has often been mentioned in the research of **biology**
(Laborit, 1955, 1968, 1981; Krafft, 1985), **pharmacology** and **medicine**
(Kübler-Ross, 1986), **physics** (Costa de Beauregard, 1963; Prigogine,
1979), **psychology** (Goguelin et al., 1968; Lowen 1987), **psychiatry**
(D.S.M. 4, Bergeret, Kernberg, 1979), **general psychoanalysis** (Bettelheim, 1972; Donnars, 1982; Israël, 1989), **general semantics** (Korzybski,
1953; Bulla de Villeret, 1973; Saucet, 1987), **sociology** (Boudon, 1979),

economics (Meignez, 1971; Fourastié, 1973; Scitovki, 1976), **philosophy** (Blondin, 1983; Laborit, 1984), and above all in **organizational theory** (Dubreuil, 1924; Mayo, 1933; Lewin, 1935; Likert, 1958; Argyris, 1957; Woodward, 1958; Herzberg, 1962; Patton, Etzioni, 1964; McGregor, 1966; Drücker, 1967; Likert, 1969; Rousselet et al., 1970; Martin, 1976; Crozier, 1977; Nuttin, 1980; Frances, 1981; Levy-Leboyer, 1984; Hermann, Sandra, 1989; Dufour et al., 1990; Alvesson and Willmot, 1992; Pitcher, 1994; Clegg, Palmer, 1996; Villette, 1998 and Mintzberg, 1976, 1982, 1986, 1990). In management science, its essential role was updated in 1958 by March and Simon, who established that action is the result of more or less rational interaction between the **internal** and **external** environment and goals, but a description of this internal environment was neglected. This apprehension shows itself first of all in the over-simplified **"satisfaction–frustration"** continuum, where several dimensions are taken into account, notably **"dependence"** and **"stress"** (Chanlat et al., 1995). Today, our knowledge of the affective relationship maintained with the organization is constantly increasing and **the growth and deterioration of self-image are recognized as being in direct relation to organizational changes** that affect the individual, whereas the feeling of directing one's own life is identified as the best remedy for personal devalorization. The increase in professional and personal rifts have contributed to highlighting this role.

3. Status

Emotional man is an actor of proximity. By that we mean that he fulfills several roles. He reacts, and in order to succeed, he must make choices and judgments. While he doesn't possess any special supreme powers, he does possess a particular area of responsibility and independent resources. He hasn't undergone a lobotomy nor is he treated pharmacologically as is the Limited Rationality Decision-maker. He is not permanently narcissistic (Lowen, 1987) as are the "yuppies", nor is he like the young dynamic American managers of the 80's who deny all possibility of feeling. He feels joy or pain according to his successes or failures. He learns from his mistakes, but this apprenticeship puts him in a zone of effort that causes him, sometimes deep, suffering. He is also afraid of death, thus anxiety accompanies him and intervenes in his choices. The irreversibility of certain situations forces him either to change, or to grieve over the loss of certain projects.

He experiences his sense of belonging to the hierarchy with ambiguity, for the security it brings is tempered by the stress with which he is forced to live, and his wish for autonomy. His decisions are the product of intrapsychic conflict between his values, his objectives and the resources at his disposal.

Director, manager, executive, father (or mother), husband (or wife), member of a sports club – all point to the multiple statuses of proximity that our subject alternately occupies today. We have chosen to employ the words "actor", "executive" or "manager" to simplify our discussion, without losing sight of the totality of these diverse memberships that react to, and interact with, each other.

4. Descriptive Tool: The Emotional Program

An emotional program is a group of enumerated items that describe "segments" of action and attempt to clarify situations where these programs would have a tendency to set themselves off. There are approximately 50 of these described in the text.

Understanding the impact of emotional action on decision-making supposes that one is able to describe at least several elements, the ideal being able to identify and describe all elements for any given situation.

An emotional program is completely characterized if:

1. The "trigger" situation is specified – the situation entering in contact with the actor by an intermediary stimulus.
2. The emotional production that is provoked is specified (a single feeling or a complete range of feelings).
3. The psychological elements that permit us to diagnose whether a particular person will have the tendency to trigger one or another type of emotional production are specified.
4. The action or influence that the emotional production has on the decision or the behavior is described.

5. The Nature of the Illustrations

Among our illustrations or examples are numerous testimonies of proximity issues in different organizational domains (work, family, the couple, leisure activity, sports, the military, T.V. commentary…) and not exclusively within a business enterprise. The sports examples are many as the competitive model has often been brought forward in organizational procedures and also, because of being an unwavering follower of numerous sports, this author often finds himself in the position of "participating observer". All testimonies should be read "between quotes", and the author doesn't appear unless the testimony has been previously published (conferences or public interviews). Only the dates of the interviews will be noted, unless the "evidence" has been taken directly from the author.

In addition to personal testimony, several references are made to news stories, surveys or certain television film sequences as the televisual universe is today an integral part of the universe of proximity. In this case, the date and the broadcast are specified in order to facilitate access to INA (The French National Audiovisual Institute) classification.

Testimony and surveys may not have a strictly scientific value, but they do have a strong emotional and intuitive value and some of these form the basis of the research. These "eyewitness" testimonies are displayed in the text in a different font.

6. The Domain of Emotional Logic

Emotional logic is a logic describing the feelings and behaviors of the actor as seen in situations of deterioration, crisis and change. It is a logic of retroaction. When the external environment is stable, when the contingencies of action supersede the weight of structure[1] and when the external indicators are legible and stable and the results reassuring, the gap between explanations given by the rational model and the emotional model is slight and we stay within the domain of rational logic.[2]

Yet, when the external environment deteriorates, when the indicators are illegible or at least threatened by rapid change or slow deterioration, or when the weight of the structure crushes the contingencies of action, the rational model no longer explains the essential, for the internal indicators become the true source of situation definition, choice and strategy. We "pass" into the realm of emotional logic.

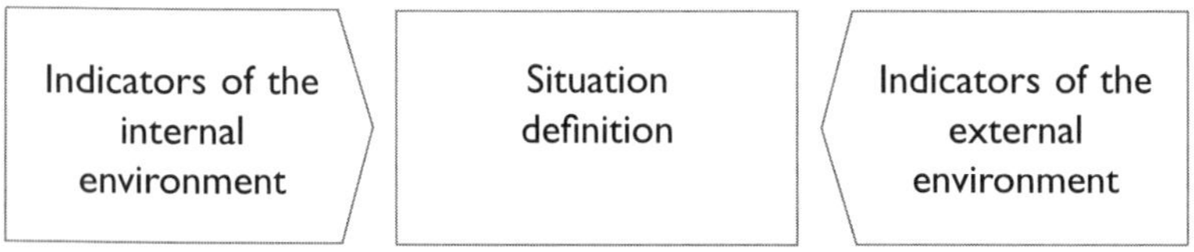

Indicators of the internal environment	Situation definition	Indicators of the external environment

Exhibit 1   Interface

7. Presentation of the Emotional Model: The Double-Entry Table

The limited rationality model established that the definition an actor makes for a given situation is confined to the domain which, in general, is restricted by his internal and external proximity (March and Simon, 1958).

If the **situation definition** seems to conform essentially to the situation, one could say that we are in rational logic. To illustrate this, take the example of the water temperature of a pool and imagine two possibilities: the water is 14 degrees or it is 28 degrees (centigrade). If the water is 14 degrees and the swimmer says "it's freezing", or the water is at 28 degrees and the swimmer says "it's perfect", he has defined the situations according to a rational logic and there is only one possible representation:

Exhibit 2 Single-entry table. The rational model		
The situation	14 degrees	28 degrees
The situation definition	"It's freezing"	"It's perfect"

Now, let us suppose that this pool belongs to the swimmer's boss, that the swimmer is afraid to offend him and that he has just been invited to take a swim. If the water is 14 degrees, one can imagine that he will say "it's very refreshing" even though he finds it "freezing". We would say that the situation has been defined according to a logic of submission to authority (Chapter 3, section 9) in the sense that his boss is proposing a very disagreeable task that consists of having to swim in freezing water and that he, without a doubt, will willingly accept, either because accepting appears easier than refusing or because it seems a good way of proving that he is capable. Finally, let's suppose that the water is 28 degrees and that the swimmer says "It's freezing", simply for the pleasure of disagreeing with his director. We would say that the situation has been defined according to a logic of resistance to authority (Chapter 3, section 11). If we introduce

Exhibit 3 Double-entry table. Mixed model: rational and emotional logic		
Actor's Response	**Water Temperature**	
	14 degrees	28 degrees
"The water is freezing"	Rational logic	Emotional logic of resistance to authority
"The water is perfect"	Emotional logic of submission to authority	Rational logic

both these logics, there is no longer one but two possible situation defini-tions for each case. We can represent this in the double-entry, four-case table in Exhibit 3. This publication is comprised of a great number of such tables that aim to introduce emotional logic. The "measures" of rational logic appear on the north-west south-east diagonal, and the others stem-ming from emotional logic are developed on the other axis.

With this table, we introduce the idea that, viewed separately, rational and emotional logic only take into account their particular portion of reality.

8. Presentation of Results

Emotional logic describes the interaction between the situation and the psyche, or if one prefers, between the actor's external and internal envi-ronments. It is a logic of process and not of structure. There are a number of reasons why we have retained situations (situated in the external envi-ronment) and not personalities (situated in the internal environment) as determinant variables.

First of all, models explaining behavior using the structure of the personality are most often taken from observations made in medical offices and are not necessarily the best to demonstrate what takes place in organizations. In fact, they rely on one implicit variable: emotional production, and if we manage to redefine that, we wouldn't need to know the structure of the personality except in those situations where behavior loses all connection with the real-life situation.

Next, emotional logic is a logic, and not a pathology, and in this sense it is a result of interaction and of exchange. To make personality structure the determinant variable is to work within a closed system model in order to explain behavior. What is needed is an open model that includes closure in the form of a limit and not the inverse. In our hypotheses, it is thus the situation, even a situation subject to a "distorting" definition, that will furnish the essential explanation.

Finally, using the personality as a basis, brings about a tautological reasoning; "He's acting crazy, but that's expected, since he is crazy!" This reasoning doesn't come from a position of understanding, but from a posi-tion of justification, whereas to make the hypothesis that the actor possesses an ordinary structure, and to try to explain observed behavior presents a true problem that could have significant limits. Our chapters correspond to varying situations and shows the principal processes observed in these situations.

8.1. Gratifying situations

In these situations, the actor learns by "capillarity". He improves and updates his expertise, stretches it a little and then applies it to a previously unknown situation. This situation then becomes known, and permits him to acquire new knowledge, expertise, etc. In these situations, the actor "enjoys" himself. Emotional logic intervenes but doesn't call into question the limited rationality model.

8.2. Aversive or challenging situations

These are at the heart of emotional logic, in the sense that from the start the actor is afraid. He is present at the deterioration of the situation and very quickly finds himself in psychological conflict. "Should I intervene?", "Right away?", "Should I wait?", "Should I do nothing?", "Will this resolve on its own?" or "There's nothing I can do, I should just drop it", "I'm getting out of here!" This situation escapes all rational explanation, and enters the domain of the Laboritien model.[3]

8.3. Situations of rupture or of "getting ahead"[4]

Only these situations truly involve decisions. Situations of proximity resolve themselves little by little by "capillarity" of know-how and not by "don't yet know how". Challenging situations are imposed by the environment. There is the choice to react or not. Situations of rupture, or of getting ahead, impose a choice *ex nihilo*. The voluntary change of employment, the choice of first employment, voluntary relocation, voluntary rupture of family ... buy, sell, construct ... It is in this domain that the emotional model most strongly contradicts the rational model. Our work is not yet finished in this area and the results will be presented in a publication on decision logic.

8.4. Hierarchical situations

These are marked by a triangulation between the situation, the actor and his superior, and constitute the domain containing the most serious of human psychic conflicts: the "avoidance–avoidance" conflict. These are also at the heart of the arbitration of "submission–resistance". The continual development of companies of inhuman size increases the validity of this logic.

8.5. Situations of failure

In introducing the logic of guilt or emotional collapse, these situations impact on the emotional, on the personality, on apprenticeship of the "trial and error" type, and on integration by disapprenticeship.

8.6. Irreversible situations

These represent a logic completely apart, the logic of accepting limits, and describes the more dangerous emotional processes which can serve to aggravate the situation.

8.7. Situations of success

The logic of success is its own logic that clearly differentiates itself from that of victory. It often rests on the capacity to acquire a sense of the life that is lived.

For questions of presentation, we have named these chapters, hierarchical situations, challenging situations, situations of failure,... but in reality, it is not about the situation, but about the definition the actor makes of the situation. In other terms, the chapters describe the interaction "internal environment–external environment".

9. The Corresponding Questionnaires

The questionnaires – there are approximately 30 – are above all pedagogical tools: they introduce an interactivity between the actor and the reader that can be used for a better understanding of the concepts, or to allow the readers to relate the concepts to their own lives. The use of questionnaires by training personnel is hereby authorized by the author with the proviso that the source be cited.

10. Research on Emotional Logic

Emotions do not have meaning *ex ante*. They are simply agreeable or disagreeable sensations; it is the brain that, *ex post*, gives them meaning and produces feeling. Traditional exploratory methods, which remain the dominant method, are founded on the existence of information existing a priori – which a questionnaire gathers – and must surrender their place to a confirmatory method[5] that permits an understanding of this reality. In the confirmatory approach, the researcher establishes his model, beginning with the intuition coming from his own osmosis with his domain, then subjects his model to verification *ex post*. The method, which has become common practice in marketing, is still rarely employed in human resources. A certain humility must be imposed, however, for while it is probable that quantification, even confirmatory, is not easy in the emotional arena, state of mind could be respected by proceeding in a qualitative manner and in keeping one's interest only on those situations belonging to the past. One way is by using open-ended interviews, being careful to center these interviews on the visible part of the iceberg (behavior), asking the subjects to begin by describing those series of events experienced in situations and only afterwards refocusing the interview on the feelings felt. One must also keep in mind that the subject being questioned will find it difficult to go beyond the qualification of agreeable/disagreeable, at least if he hasn't yet made sense out of his experience. All research of this type is not only dependent on the capacity to verbalize emotions, but is also dependent on cognitive dissonance which pushes the subject to justify and rationalize his past choices.

The point in keeping **experimental situations** in a laboratory is to maintain a high level of rigor by avoiding direct subject questioning. Even given the possibilities of "live" recording that empowers the laboratory, in particular the work of direct brain photography, one must not lose sight of the great difficulty that this type of situation provokes. If in order to study **submission to authority**[6], this procedure was used, it is precisely because the volunteers who agreed to take part in Milgram's study were, de facto, submitting to his authority, then one must expect that **the Milgram effect**[7] is in place and constitutes a source of disqualification of the experiment. To the extent that the procedure is the object of the study, it should take place outside the presence of authority if it is to be considered scientific. To compensate for this problem, one can imagine going on site to film and record the situation. In that case, it is **the Mayo effect**[8] that will falsify the results to the great despair of researchers. Due to the single fact that the subjects bring to the situation a certain level of interest, their feelings can modify their experience, strong feelings could arise that may be translated into behavioral modifications, such as the desire to do well, that do not usually correspond to normal conditions[9].

If the previous remarks lead to the exclusion of an observer, or non-participant, because by his status he modifies the experience of the observed and that this modified experience is itself being observed, then the model that we have developed shows the most advantage – in being based, first of all, on the situation[10] (apprenticeship, trial, hierarchy, failure, disapprenticeship, success …) and **of allowing a mixed approach**; it is, above all, possible to define, with the desired rigor, the situation that will be the object of the research; following that, *ex post*, to study the persons having had this experience, without having to disclose the true object of the research. It is then possible to conduct totally nondirective interviews with these participants, who due to their professional experience, are susceptible to having experienced the situations that are the subject of the study. When the interviewee mentions one of the situations that particularly interests the interviewer, the interviewer can probe more precisely by exploration or confirmation, the processes which are the object of the research.[11] As an example, in the exploratory phase of a failure situation, the question would be "What were you feeling?" In the confirmatory phase, the question would be "Did you feel guilty?" The subject's own emotional logic would skew the given responses following the procedures envisioned previously (Exhibit 4). The best guarantee is to establish a relation that both excludes the subject's propensity to either please the researcher or, on the other hand, forces him to be on his guard, to defend or try to enhance his image in front of the researcher.

Finally, it is possible to **willingly immerse oneself** in a milieu where the object of the research, the situation, may occur. This is a way of living with the status of observer-participant on the condition that it lasts long enough for the observer to lose his status of observer in the eyes of the subject and become an ordinary participant[12]. This method has two advantages: one of direct observation, and the other the ability to gather for himself the experiences which, for someone who is introspective, could help in the formulation of hypotheses[13].

Exhibit 4 Difficulties in information collection		
Actor's Response (did you feel guilty?)	**Failure situations**	
	Subject felt guilt	**Subject did not feel guilt**
Says yes	Rational logic	Hawthorne Effect; want to disappoint the researcher because he enjoys the interest taken in himself
Says no	Defense mechanism (forget, rationalize, etc.) Wants to give a different image of himself	Rational logic

11. The Teaching of Emotional Logic

The official approach, that of management programs in human resources, uses **file logic**, a judicial model, uniquely treating only that part reducible to a file containing numbers and evaluations (selection, pay, promotion, career management, work conflicts…). These are the tools necessary for file management by the specialized Human Resources departments following the now classic plan:

- obtain human resources
- conserve human resources
- develop human resources
- industrial relations[14]

In a parallel development, a movement within the teaching field created **structural logic,** tackling the question of behavior as stemming from personality. At the heart of this there is generally a test, permitting a certain sense of self-recognition within a typology. This influence, or movement, had at its source old classifications (emotionalism, activity, secondarity) that had been reviewed and corrected in an attempt to better approach work attitudes. Certain advertise general objectives, such as self-knowledge, means to personal progress, specifically using the analogy of an instruction booklet (the better you know your computer, the better it can serve you), and also knowledge of others, instrumental in increasing tolerance. In this school of thought, we cite the typology test (promoting, analyzing, facilitating, controlling); the work of typology indicators of Myers-Briggs[15] (Extraversion, Feeling, Sensing, Judgment), adapted by P. Cauvin and G. Cailloux[16] from the concepts of C.G. Jung, using 16 types in all[17], that permit definition of dominant behaviors, stemming from the transactional analysis of Taibi et al. (1994)[18], with the strongest test centered on work attitudes (empathics, workaholics, perseverers, rebels, dreamers, promotors…) whose primary interest was to describe behavior in situations of both strong and weak stress, descriptions that we cannot find elsewhere. The H.B.D.I. of Ned Herrmann and Vuillemin[19], describes how the actor uses his intellect, and defined a complete series of adaptations developed by small firms, "inspired" more or less legally, by the work of H.B.D.I., the Pontia test for example. Other work, more rare, attacks the objective of emotional education, to become "emotionally correct", using, among others, common psychiatric classifications (paranoid, schizoid, depressive…) or explaining how to minimize weak points (Goleman, 1995). This work is often that of consultants or journalists trained in psychopathology.

The third approach, to which we adhere, develops **situation logic.** In this we include the **communication** or **negotiation** that carries out a transverse approach centered around the obtaining of agreement in which personality structure, emotional production or management culture play a more or less important explanatory role. The work on **stress** management essentially develops situation logic and can no longer be ignored today seen from the global dimension of the problem – but the word "stress" increasingly hides a multiform reality, having as its only connection that of the suffering of the person who is the object of the study. We prefer the concept of **emotional production** that allows us to refine the underlying process.

Today, "emotional logic" is not yet part of teaching in the traditional training of our future economic, commercial or even political managers. As a result, recent behavioral developments such as self-motivation of adult workers, the deterioration of mental health of young people (gratuitous violence, record number of motorcycle road accidents, record number of suicides), the use of alcohol by younger and younger teenagers, the use of tranquilizers by entire populations, are not yet truly understood. The internal environment – the psyche – not drawn upon by management science, risks being treated as the environment was by the economic sciences 30 years ago: they proposed solutions without concerning themselves with the consequences, thus giving birth to the mechanism of retroaction[20] that paved the way for the interference of "boomerang" effects (Solzhenitsyn, 1974[21]; Nizard, 1991[22]).

To progress, one must first coherently organize the research contributions from different fields that concern **the actor in a project situation**, for the logic of action can be found in different scientific domains. Then a "science of decision" division can be established with the human resource management specialization that integrates the emotional dimension and organizes transversal teaching addressing operational managers (future engineers, team leaders, heads of services or sales …) who rarely follow a specialization in H.R.M. We have named the specialization "self-management", inheriting the concept from that of the "Outstanding Personal Enterprise" (Castagné et al., 1988), itself taken from the Canadian school of "small business".

12. The Practice of Emotional Logic

The practice of emotional logic resembles the American film technique of "traveling". The camera is positioned in the place of the actor, and describes what is happening in his exterior field of vision seen from his interior field. It is thus a tool that aims to describe, explain, understand and standardize the resulting message: "Here are some guidelines if you should find yourself in this situation." This material aims to encourage each person in the analysis and investigation of knowledge of his own emotional production in, above all, difficult situations. The hypothesis implies that there are no "good" or "bad" managers, there are only managers who pay attention to who they "are" or rather who they "are not", and there are managers who don't. Only emotional production can inform them about themselves and make each false step a chance to progress. Several researchers have shown, and this has already been affirmed by numerous directors, that to understand that knowledge itself has its proper limits is the necessary condition to efficient management. The hypothesis of emotional logic is to consider the first tool of a manager is his personality and that the young manager just starting out should begin by learning how his personality interacts with, and impacts on, problem resolution. Of course, this didactic step has limits because only experience provides a human being with a vision of his own reality. Nevertheless, experience is not the only necessary condition, as it is the capacity of the interpreter that will make up the sufficient condition, and that may be notably improved by the comprehension of "emotional logic". In conclusion, if I had only one chapter of this book to read, my preference would be that of the analysis of irreversible situations. Today, each professional change is accompanied by deep personal upheaval. No one exists who can be sure of avoiding the changes his future may bring, but to understand how it could come about is what permits the transformation of a situation of rupture/split into an occasion of personal development.

The Concept of Emotional Production

Emotional production is considered a "soft" subject and, as such, is not much cared for by the exact sciences. Nevertheless, even given this attitude which falsely simplifies survey results, and even despite measurement difficulties, the concept is being introduced little by little in the work of decisions in, and arbitration of, difficult situations. This troubles the classical models, which preside over employment market descriptions, and seriously questions the caricature of the "emotionally correct" candidate in recruitment agencies.

1. A Defense for the Introduction of Emotional Production in the Field of Decision Theory

Emotional production of the human nervous system is comparable, in its information function, to the production of the instrument panel of a modern aircraft. It is, first of all, composed of signals[1] which when correctly interpreted, inform us about the **external environment**: compass (direction, objectives), ventimeter (difficulty level, turbulence), barometer (will the action taken translate into an ascent or rapid descent?), etc. It is also made up of signals[2] informing us about the **internal environment**: oil pressure (a measure of the necessary energy needed), engine temperature (risk of overheating), tachometer (speed level), fuel gauge (distance capacity), oil level, etc. This information production plays a determinant role in piloting and indicates permanent adjustments between the two environments. Emotional production creates both suffering and joy for the actor. It can represent an **objective in itself**, with the objective of attitudes and behaviors being to give birth to certain of its elements. For example, risk could be sought after for the level of pleasure that it creates. It obeys, in fact, a triple cybernetic logic of interaction among goals, emotions and situations (Fraisse, Piaget, 1963). The different internal/ external environment mimics that of exteroceptors and interoceptors. In our epistemological position, the internal environment is read by the actor on the same level as the external environment, and this reading is a source of meaning, even if it is only translated into a sense of intuition. Internal and external environments are equally important. A pilot who doesn't take into account potential landing difficulties inherent in the landing itself may damage the wheels of the machine, and if he doesn't take care of the machine he could damage the engine... In the 60's, economists did not include the environment in their modeling. Today, at the dawn of the 21st century, management sciences find themselves confronting the same problem. Should the logic of the internal environment of the actor – his psyche – continue to be neglected, leaving him to run the risk of acquiring the status of a garbage dump where managerial activity puts any refuse that it doesn't know how to treat?

Emotional logic contains the key to numerous phenomena which are too often reduced to their visible, measurable and sensational dimension: the exorbitant cost of functional illness, aberrant use of tranquilizers, scandalous rise in young suicides[3], permanent increase in violence, increase in the frequency of strikes and gratuitous defacement of public property, the rise of the extreme right – social expression of adult rebellion. Those who end up paying the heaviest price – in the absence of emotional ecology – are the middle managers (all types of department heads, directors or salespeople), and of course, the unemployed. In order to finance its responsibilities, the state increases pressure, and wage costs and taxes are doubled for the organization. The overloaded organization passes on its burden to its ever diminishing workforce and this workforce transmits this burden to its nervous system situated at the forefront of the chain. And it's a wonder that we are surprised at the increase in stress!

▶ "The Paris office regularly asks us to fire someone. After having streamlined the excess fat, we are now being asked to attack the muscle of our organization and it's not stopping. We will not be able to do our work correctly. There is never enough time." *(Manager of a large automobile group declaring excellent 1999 financial results)*

▶ In March 1999, the announcement of a planned 10% reduction of staff (15,000 employees) literally launched a 10% increase in Sony stock shares.

On the other hand, the measurement of this is difficult[4] and leads us to believe that this operation may remain an area of ignorance, but perhaps not for long. The research allows us to think that one day it will be possible to interpret images of mental states as well as emotions.

▶ During an interview with the director it is explained to a manager that, after an unsuccessful 3-month trial period, he is not well-fitted to his managerial post and he agrees to put in his resignation. Given that we possess the instruments to measure the duration of the interview and even to tape the points made by each one, if we add to that the possibility to accurately measure the consecutive reduction of energy in the following days by blood analysis, and also the energy consumed by the process of grieving which will take place, and which is the sine qua non to start up again in another position in another enterprise, we would still miss all direct measurement given the current state of our knowledge.

▶ "In 1997, anxious to know the evolution of stress on a population of 250 students that we bring each year on an off-site seminar" (rafting trip), we brought together a multidisciplinary team of doctors and psychotherapists under the direction of Professor Krafft's laboratory, who proceeded to regularly take saliva samples, after having asked each volunteer to brush his teeth with a sterile product. The experiment used a recent discovery that established that stress secretes a particular molecule that can be isolated in saliva and that constitutes the best measure of stress today."

2. Scientific Status

2.1 Its existence

It is said that the misanthrope and megalomaniac Louis II of Wittelsbach, King of Bavaria (1864–1886), was looking to escape his boredom by trying to establish if the natural language of children at birth was Latin or Greek… Having brought together a group of newborns, he ordered the wet nurses to take care of the infants, but not to utter a single word. Soldiers, taken from their regiment for the occasion, were under orders to shoot any nurses who disobeyed this directive. The results were predictable – all the babies died.

Louis II of Bavaria had so many enemies in his government that it is impossible to establish if the above story was defamation or truth. If this story is true, this "experiment" furnishes proof that affective nourishment is as important as physical nourishment for the newborn. In the course of his famous Hawthorne experiment for General Motors, Elton Mayo (1946) discovered the existence of worker self-motivation was equally due to an obscure emotional variable that persisted, despite the reworking of the measured variables (suppression of all material advantages)[5]. Another experiment conducted with Wistar rats in the laboratory of behavioral biology of Professor Krafft (University of Nancy 1) also showed this incidence of emotional activity. Three groups of cages were organized: the first group where the rats were "coddled", the second where they were tortured and the last, where nothing at all happened. It was in this last group that the mortality rate was the highest.

2.2 Its place

Even after having spared no effort to break loose from the introspective method in order to establish methods of research which would finally be considered scientific, classic psychology is still mistrusted. We owe a great deal of work to the practice of doctors, homeopathologists, psychotherapists, psychiatrists and psychoanalysts in this area. In the same manner, doctoral candidates in human resources management remained suspect for a long time, as this constitutes a "soft" subject to which it is difficult to apply exploratory or confirmatory analyses (LISREL), but whose use represents an unquestionable norm of quality in the area of management research today. As a result, production is not a specific subject of research with a few notable exceptions (Diel, 1947, 1956). However, in the last few decades, due to increasing rupture and upheaval in both personal and professional situations, numerous researchers are finding it more and more difficult to pass over the role played by emotional production in their observations. As of 1990, the term "suffering" has been used to define organizations (Dejours, 1990). In 1991, the Ottawa thesis (Paquet, Gélinier) illuminated the gap between the two visions of the organization – roughly speaking, between those described within a clinical domain, and those using scientific models – and attributed to the scientists who control the financing of the research, the birth of a process of autocensure and the elimination of the qualitative aspects that have become second nature to doctoral students. In 1994, the theme of the 4th colloquium of the AGRH[6] in France, "The Sciences of Action", opened the door to recognition for this production, and gave way to increased communication in this domain. By the end of 1995, a public debate between scientists and sociologists defined the suburbs as "a place of pain", thus abandoning all other criteria except the emotional one, that being the only one to globally demonstrate organizational deterioration. In 1996, J-F. Chanlat, in his inaugural class held up, among the great questions between the social sciences and management sciences, "the questions of domination and pain"; "We are forced to note that this question has often been relegated to the sidelines, if not totally withdrawn in the interests of a concept that is more harmonious in terms of functional interests and visions of power" (Chanlat, 1997, p. 91). In 1998, Marie-France Hirigoyen reported on moral harassment and violence, giving evidence of emotional manipulation in the workplace.

And when will we see a definition of the enterprise as a "place of professional growth"?

2.3 The study of organizational process and decision-making

In the course of the 1970's and 80's, the field of practitioners published an impressive volume of prescriptive works indicating how to make decisions. Studies published by researchers describing how to effectively make decisions are less numerous (March, Simon, 1958, 1969). As of 1959, William Foote Whyte became one of the first to be interested in emotional production in the context of the organization. He wrote that organizations must be analyzed in terms of interaction: "interpersonal contact, activities or tasks and **feelings**". He defined the latter as "the way in which individuals experience the world around them" (Silverman, 1970). At the beginning of the 60's, March and Simon acknowledged that it is on a subjective basis of the personality that decisions are taken: "Members of an organization arrive in that organization with a pre-existing structure of preferences – a personality, **if you will** – upon which they work out their decisions" (1969). We can see, with the use of the "if you will", to what point this concept is considered burdensome. March and Simon recognized the existence of this production, but write that they do not need it to understand the organization. It wasn't until the **famous garbage can model** that emotional production was recognized by organizational theory as the vital "flow" that feeds the process of problem resolution (Rojot, Bergmann, 1989). In 1988, Ned Herrmann published the results of his 10 years of research in his voluminous 450-page work, *The Creative Brain*, where the entirety of brain production (logical, organizational, emotional and creative) is analyzed systematically and in which he developed a test, the "H.B.D.I."[7], which allowed him to make precise descriptions of 6000 managers. It is a revolution. Several theses have been defended, or begun, on the subject, a dozen articles published and, for the moment, none contradicts the research.

2.4 Study of the action process

2.4.1 The concept of satisfaction

Following the work of Mayo, the research on work productivity after the war centered on the concept of satisfaction as underlying that of emotional production. The abundance of published works is witness to the gap between the results from observation, and the predictions of the theory: observation of **emotional misery** within organizations, and interrogation on its nature (Durkheim, 1893; Lewin, 1935; Argyris, 1957; Woodward, 1958; Friedmann, 1963, 1964; McGrégor, 1975; Likert, 1969; Lawrence and Lorsch, 1974; Crozier, 1977; Mintzberg, 1976, 1982, 1986, 1990; Dejours, 1993).

2.4.2 The concept of motivation

Within the practitioners' field, the trend resulted in a broader concept but still without ever defining it, and even today we discover that no satisfactory definition exists. All efforts that have been made run into the fact that the element which motivates humans is subjective: **"If I am motivated, it is because I am able to discern my desire, my wishes, my needs and my wants. No observable objective element can be related to this situation"** (Maslow, 1968). Like commercial models, which show an impressive level of sophistication, numerous theories reason in terms of satisfaction. This logical and rational representation of reality contributes to masking a fundamental phenomenon found among executives: the process of self-motivation at work.

2.4.3 Facts contradict theory

To illustrate Sievers' remark, the following several examples show that traditional concepts do not manage to take behavior into account.

The famous work by Milgram (1974) carried out at Yale University between 1950 and 1963, shows that man can agree to stay in an extremely frustrating situation, accepting to live with interior conflict – even reaching the outer limits of what is tolerable to him – illustrated by the fact that he agrees to carry out those tasks that would otherwise be repugnant to him (for example, something carried out against an innocent person) simply because he feels respect towards the giver of the order. Doctor Nijole Kurdirka shows in his thesis that it is the same, even if these acts are against the subject himself (Milgram, 1974, p. 9). On the other hand, because of the hate or scorn felt for an authority, some men feel a sense of heroism in resisting this authority despite the worsening of their conditions in prison or extreme pressure which (Charansky, Amalrik, Boukosky)[8] sometimes goes as far as the death of the subject. Bettelheim (1972), in writing about his detention in a concentration camp, says existing models do not take into account behaviors that contribute to making a good life or a good man, "ego is not a weak servant of super-ego". The deeds which allow a person to stay in a materially very uncomfortable situation, or to leave an extremely comfortable situation for another more frustrating one, are numerous. How can we explain, using the classical models, why a manager who complains daily about his work becomes depressed when he retires? Why does a wife, having lived with an abusive alcoholic husband, also become depressed when he returns home from the rehabilitation center cured? Why do a couple – seemingly calm and stable – begin to tear each other to pieces as soon as a dinner guest arrives? Why does the suicide rate of young Algerians fall during Ramadan and why is the mortality rate of senior citizens much lower during holidays and on Sundays? Why are doctor's strikes (in Israel) accompanied by a drop in mortality? Why do the inhabitants of shantytowns find it difficult to leave? Why, in government jobs, do dynamic and effective employees have more problems with their chain of command than those who are inactive? Why do high-quality, but lifestyle-changing products have a negative effect on the buyers? Why do people remain angry at the "bearers of bad tidings"? Why do well brought-up young people get involved in a sect that will destroy them in a few weeks, without their realizing it? Why do abused children often defend their torturers and deny the facts? Why do otherwise sweet and friendly adolescents, burn up several cars one night without being either drunk or on drugs? We could continue, without end, to cite those situations where it is impossible to overlook emotional logic. Even if we bring in emotional production, models founded on the need for love, and the research on personal development, the explanations are self-evident: these people survive in extremely frustrating situations because the situations themselves are a source of rare emotional production such as the **feeling of being needed**, or having self-respect, or serving a respected authority figure, or the feeling of being diminished. Behavior that continues in a frustrating situation can be explained by the existence of **a "hidden" production**, the cessation of which provokes a collapse of the psyche. Ramadan and other holidays serve to tighten affective bonds, dynamic and the new things worry and create fear, whereas a feeling of dependence prohibits rebellion. The suburbs are sources of intense emotion: there is always something to fight or to love…

All research that concerns man and that doesn't take into account the affective or emotional dimension constitutes a hazardous scientific simplification. If it obtains results, it is because the neglected variables are in co-dependence with the measured variables.

2.4.4 Calling the models into question

According to Allport (1955), the "stimuli–response" model becomes ridiculous and untenable if we focus on people engaged in self-realization… The source of their action is interior rather than reactionary. In 1968, Abraham Maslow was among the first to denounce the studies on work satisfaction, noting that these constitute a narrow and inadmissible reduction of the causal relationship between work productivity and personal satisfaction. 2): The satisfaction–efficiency link; a poorly postulated problem". In 1990, an article of Bukard Sievers appeared: "Motivation: ersatz significance" (Chanlat, 1990, pp. 337–61). The author writes that the only worthwhile concept in this area is that of Maslow's (self-actualization), but at the same time, he writes that "it will never truly be recognized and used in the domain of management…"

2.4.5 The search for broader models

This was done by researchers who were outside the influence of behavioralism. In 1958, Leavitt showed – in studying one, two, then a full group of workers – that behavior depends on not one but three elements. He distinguishes between cause, motive and goals. Nevertheless, his schema remains focused on the extinction of need. In 1968, Maslow proposed the first concept to definitively move away from previous research: that of **self-actualization**. In 1976, Scitovsky established, with the aid of a questionnaire, that the absence of suffering or pain is not a necessary prerequisite for the experience of pleasure and that intense pleasure is perfectly compatible with great pain.

In 1983, Robert Blondin published the largest enterprise study in this field. He shows that the research on satisfaction, and that of happiness, has no interconnection. He clearly demonstrates that the emotional production that creates a state of "happiness" can exist, and can be stimulated by an extremely frustrating situation.

2.5 The study of self-actualization

At the junction of organizational and personal development, there are several works that employ emotional production to measure satisfaction. We have used the research of Lindsey, Rogers, Maslow, Alderfer and, in Japan, the thesis of Chuichi Murai (1957). For these researchers, emotional production represents a central object of research, and the research specifies the organizational conditions for this production. In 1956, Lindsey showed that repetitive mechanical tasks can play a positive role. A machine, operated by a patient in a psychiatric hospital, can result in astonishing patient progress without human intervention (this machine feeds a starving cat, drop by drop, and is clearly visible behind a glass). This experiment, however limited, introduces the affective concept – **the feeling of being needed** – in the study of organizational process. An opening is achieved, as it is established that repetitive or difficult work could be a source of emotional production which cannot be avoided, and which actually contributes to its development. "Even a machine can help if confidence plays an important role" (Rogers, 1978). In 1957, Chuichi Murai's thesis and the observations via Tokyo Shibaura Denky (*Encyclopedia of Management*, 5.22.4) showed that among the various factors that impact on motivation, most are linked with the emotional production that they produce:

1. The feeling that the work we do is useful.
2. The occasion to show our ability at work.
3. The satisfaction that we draw from our work.
4. The pride we draw from our work.
5. The degree of knowledge and ability that the work requires.

In 1968, A. Maslow published his fundamental work *Towards a Psychology of Being,* establishing a new concept: "the paroxysmal experience" that no longer belongs to the family of satisfaction concepts and that develops a completely new idea centered on self-modification and the resulting emotional production. In 1976, Scitovski takes stock of existing work which establishes "the conviction, within man, to create different goals in his life and to obtain more satisfaction in the achieving, than in their achievement".

3. Managerial Status

3.1 Its place in the decision-making process

The status given to emotional production differs according to the object and the evolution of the organizational process; in the analysis phase of external reality, it is ruled out because it interferes with the analysis and prevents the discovery of an adequate solution. The most widely sold book on management, the work of the engineers Kepner and Tregoe (1972), proposed a method that blocked all harmful effects of emotional production, using a process of analysis that employed a rigorous method of situation definition. On the other hand, at the level of choice, it reappears as fundamental, for it avoids the potential clash between personal values and the necessities of the situation. It supplies an implicit reference in so many decisions that seem to have been taken in a opposite direction from what would have been predicted by scientific objectives.

In the decision-making process, not only is an external reality involved, but taking into account the consequences of this reality for the actor, emotional production represents the primary reference as the object is no longer the organizational situation, but the actor's situation. It represents a guide since the actor's objective is, specifically, to reduce the pain that his emotional production brings.

3.2 Its true place in the employment market

With the new conditions created by stagnation and unemployment, it becomes difficult today to refer to the classic hypotheses which hold that the relationships between the population of management candidates and that of enterprises, are uniquely regulated by market function. The candidate reacts with the market up until the moment when he finds a suitable proposition. The enterprise, on the look-out for the best possible quality, simplifies its human resources management to portfolio management.

Young managers function according to other precise schemas – first of all **the objective is to escape the job market**. To go out into the job market – responding to a job announcement – is already a failure situation and is something to be avoided. Following that, the work of the employed – from the moment of hiring – represents itself the apparent objective of the transaction (salary, hours, diplomas, experience…). But if we examine more closely the factors that will be the most active in the choice taken, one sees that the internal environment of the candidate, as it is expressed in his words and behavior, constitutes a determining factor in the decision. We could make the hypothesis that, behind the apparent objective of the transaction, is hidden an implicit goal that is much more complex.

Finally, the job market stipulates the existence of an ordered relationship between the existence of a post *ex ante*, that justifies the search *ex post* of the candidate. But daily experience shows that it is not rare that the opposite occurs: "someone of value" is noticed in the organization, often in the course of a short-term contract, an internship, a consultancy project or temporary work, and because of the behavioral qualities of the candidate, the company begins to look for the necessary resources to create a post that would allow the candidate to remain with the enterprise. An irrational step? In any case, there is less risk, for the guarantees supplied by usual selection means are patently insufficient when it comes to learning about the "human machine", and the false sense of security stemming from legislation that insists on the seemingly "ordered" relationship increases recruitment error.

3.2.1 Self-motivation of job candidates

Emotional production is the true source of the phenomenon of **self-motivation**. It guarantees a great portion of organizational activity, especially if this activity is geared towards a sense of responsibility. The recruitment market has developed a system of objective tests that all but rejects self-motivation. In fact, we will show (Chapter 2, section 6) that certain affective deficits that reduce test scores, are the principal source of emotional production motivating a large proportion of professional activity in defiance of all other satisfaction.

3.2.2 The job's emotional coefficient

The definition of a post should contain a measure of its emotional coefficient that indicates the pressure that the employee will sustain during his work. The systemization of steps or levels of this type would be extremely valuable, not only for the company's health plan, but also for the implicit recognition of a factor that is generally ignored today: psychological tension.

An example of a series of levels of psychological tension for a receptionist's job follows (the aggravating factors are put in parentheses):

1. The employee is in permanent contact with the public, either face to face or over the telephone (in an administration whose very essence is stressful – like the Internal Revenue Service).
2. The employee is in permanent contact with the public and is obliged to remain smiling and pleasant even though the public has expressly come to complain (plus noise levels, air drafts).
3. In addition to receiving unhappy clients, the employee must accomplish certain computer tasks demanding high concentration (plus a serious and strict hierarchy and late opening hours).

3.2.3 Work time and attendance time

In fact, the manager sells his **actual attendance** to an organization, the contents of which are particularly vague and could include production of required work, production of non-required work, production of rest time, **emotional production**, information production, reaction to the organization's culture and values, acquisition and development of potential, etc. It can be noted that in the case where the employee or manager begins to stay longer than usual at work, he "brings" with him all sorts of other personal preoccupations that will interact with his work, as has been described in March's garbage can model. Within organizations, we can cite various testimonies where the emotional dimension would be primordial:

▶ "At S… nothing changes whether you work or not; what counts is not to make mistakes and to be nice with everyone. Once you have spent all your energy on that, there is nothing left over for work."

▶ "Within the university, a dean can't apply himself to the development of his organization. For those professors who accept to take on more responsibility, he has no means to remunerate them and, in fact, it could ruin their careers if more responsibility translates into less time dedicated to research."

▶ "In 1995, a French politician said that the trouble today is that he must dedicate all his time to producing information for the media and that there is very little time left to work. Jacques Séguéla showed that if one wants to win an election, it is best to introduce a good dose of emotion within all this information production. The American television audience prefers first to see a pastor cry in front of 10,000 of his own emotional disciples, recognizing his flagrant offense of adultery, in order to forgive him."

▶ "At the end of 1998, the President of the United States increased his public excuses concerning his private life, in the hopes that it would inspire forgiveness on the part of his people. He conserved more than 60% of the election poll, despite the targeted campaign to denounce his illegitimate sexual relations."

Again, we could continue to cite examples, illustrating the importance of emotional production as an object of study to understand and to insure the workings of the organization.

Written work on motivation has contributed to establishing the illusion that the organization has the power to motivate its members. Now it appears that the **individual motivates, above all, himself** and, from that point, the individuals who possess this capacity should be pursued, for it is far from evident that organizations possess some secret to compensate for this deficit, if there is one.

3.2.4 The emotional dimension of dismissal

The empathy of the industrial conciliation board who experience their interventions according to Karpman's emotional model, gives the impression that the employee has nothing to lose and everything to gain. Having a good lawyer, and presenting his dismissal as a product of a decision based on personal rather than professional considerations, he has every chance of transforming failure into opportunity.

> ▶ We can cite cases, in the past rare but today much more numerous, of employees who have made this into a type of sport, coming before the board with successive dismissal cases, as occurred in certain countries at a different time when the liberal indemnity laws[9] allowed a woman to be definitively financially independent after only two divorces.

3.2.5 The essential criteria in the choice of a management candidate

At hiring, the evaluation of this implicit dimension is essential to the managerial function. If, in effect, two candidates are capable of supplying the same quantity and quality of work, but one of them **complains about, and constantly criticizes**, the organization in its corridors and contributes to rumors by speaking ill of the hierarchy, and the other one is loyal and concentrates on finding solutions, is it reasonable to think that the organization is indifferent about its choice and the two candidates have the same hiring "value"? (Reichheld, 1996).

Exhibit 5 Emotional appreciation of an employee			
Internal environment	External environment		
	Efficient	Less efficient	Has become inefficient
Loyal	A rare and highly valued employee	Valued employee	Tolerated employee
Disloyal	Disliked employee	The company is ready to pay compensation if he resigns	The company fires him without consideration

3.2.6 Tomorrow, we will all be "independent workers"

If this prediction is true, each one of us must manage our own successful enterprise (Castagné et al., 1988). Self-managing our energy, our emotional logic will become fundamental, much more so than today.

4. The Contribution of the "Emotional Production" Concept

If something irrational intervenes in processes as fundamental as decision-making or motivation, does any reason exist not to try to understand its logic?

4.1 In theory

The school of psychoanalysis offers some useful work that originated in the clinical domain. It refers to observations concerning the "sick" where, by definition, behavior would be seen through a highly rigid personality, and makes the concept of "structure" the model best adapted to a descriptive approach. At work, where action and results more or less govern the maintenance of the membership status, an employee must adjust and it is no longer the structure but the interactive process of apprenticeship and of transformation that are essential. The emotional investment – that is either joy or pain – is at the heart of the apprentice-ship process.

The company only survives due to the existence of its clients, and there we also have the notion of structuration and of segmentation, domi-nating the model at the time where a certain stability still existed in the behavior of the client. In the case where the client is able to respond quickly, and modify its reactions, the concept of process become essential, and understanding that this is not the object of this volume of work, it is probable that emotional productions provoked by the end product will play a primary role in these models.

Finally, economics and management are more than sciences, as they govern the same domain where man survives in interaction with his envi-ronment. In this interaction, the gaps – increasingly numerous between economic norms and those which the actors can accept – give birth to a "pressure-cooker" on which emotional production serves as the warning light and a tool for integration.

▶ A dichotomy of behavior exists with students that is well known by teachers. Certain students behave as "consumers" and others as "producers". The behavior of the first group oscillates between compliment, silence and criticism, giving an external status to the training. In a general manner, the satisfaction of needs model describes this behavior which is situated at one end of the continuum. At the other extreme, the behavior of the second group is involved in a productive approach, giving an internal status to the training. This second group does not hesitate to engage in all sorts of frus-trating efforts, because it is realized within the framework of self-actualiza-tion. The emotional logic model takes into account the behavior of the second group.

4.2 In practice

4.2.1 The stability of motivation

Emotional production represents a source of either reinforcement or personal destabilization depending on one's nature. For example, a manager hasn't shown much energy at the workplace recently, and the explanation given is his lack of involvement. Most of the time, however, it is some other mechanism in question. Following some personal event, this manager may find himself to be a victim of an emotional production far from what he is able to handle and most of his energy has been mobilized to support this. Usually, the bad period will pass, the destructive production stops, and the manager finds his energy once again totally available for his work and may even has a surplus of efficiency resulting from the experience.

4.2.2 The sources of creative effort

The behavior of Bernard Palissy is so out of the ordinary that we still hear of it today. In 1994, we met Roland Moreno, inventor of the "smart" card which made him a millionaire. He testifies to the same behavior: to have sacrificed all during 10 years, to concentrate on what he values more than anything else – his invention.

▶ I am astonished by the attitude of those that apply for trademarks. They are involved in that work and nothing else. A trademark is like a child, you have to lavish it with care in order for it to grow successfully. *(R. Moreno)*

Obviously, this attitude is not rational, as the creator sacrifices his present to the creation, in other words, to an uncertain future. The emotional model accounts perfectly for the logic of his approach.

4.2.3 Understanding the protected sector

The economy operates on two levels. While the exposed (private) sector finds itself highly focused on its external environment, and cannot afford to have moods, the protected (government/public) sector and functions (which accounts for more than 50% of the active French population), operates in a closed system and emotional logic plays a determinant role. To illustrate this difference, we quote the fact that during World War II (an exposed period) psychological consultations lessened. It wasn't that everyone was suddenly in a much better emotional shape, but rather that they had other preoccupations and as Laborit says "a nervous system is first of all made to react!".

5. The Nature of Emotional Production

It must be said that throughout this text, we have, in fact, abused the language in our choice of words. In reality, we are not only speaking of emotions, but also of feelings, these last being a set of emotions that produces a sense. If we return to the analogy of the instrument panel that introduced this work, the red flashing light is emotion and the information that we gather from it is the feeling.

> **Emotional Production =**
> The sum of the felt emotions + the sense attributed to these emotions

Exhibit 6 Definition of emotional production

Emotion, then, is above all, an operation of memorization. If there is no emotion, there is no long-term memorization. Of course, one can learn by rote, but it is forgotten just as quickly. As the years pass, we can still remember our school desks from elementary school without necessarily remembering the seemingly unending classes. More often it is the incidences that made us laugh or angry that will stay with us. There is one exception, that of an emotion resulting from an intense joy that that we do not remember: the orgasm! Try to remember the sensation and you will see, it is impossible.

5.1 In what part of the brain is emotion developed?

According to the research and hypotheses of Mintzberg (1976) and Laborit (1981), the seat of emotion is situated in the right hemisphere of the brain, some studies specifying the limbic zone surrounding the hypothalamus. Emotions would be produced by the hyperthalamus, but controlled by the amygdale. A subject without an amygdale shows his emotions uncontrollably, and has a crisis when an unknown element invades his private domain. The neocortex represents the area where emotions acquire sense. In today's circumstances, it is prudent to consider this latter location as a convenient metaphor to describe the **process of creation of sense**. INSERM's electroencephalopatic mapping shows that numerous brain zones simultaneously begin to "turn red" on the screen when a subject is executing some simple task. Thanks to magnetic resonance, researchers believe that it will soon be possible to interpret these mental images as emotions (Sulloway, 1979).

5.2 The nature of emotion linked with action

According to Stanislas Grof (1975) there are four basic emotional "matrices":

- **The first** is received by the fetus' cortex. It is very pleasant and will be felt, and sought after, throughout life. It is found again and again in numerous situations which Grof enumerates: "happy love relationships, vacations in wonderful places, artistic creation of a high esthetic value", etc.
- **The second** is imprinted on the cortex when the mother's uterus first begins the contractions necessary to birth. It reappears in "situations that put survival in danger, imprisonment, brainwashing, lack of affection, threatening situations, oppressive atmospheres, humiliation", etc.
- **The third** is the most painful. It is imprinted on the cortex during the final birth process. It reappears in situations of "struggle, combat, hazardous activities, military service, turbulent air flights", etc.
- **The fourth** is imprinted on the cortex in the infant's first moment of contact with its new milieu. It is positive, and will reappear in those "situations in which one is victorious, such as surviving an accident, overcoming obstacles with hard work, episodes of tension and struggle that end up as brilliant success, natural situations such as a sunrise, the beginning of spring, the end of a storm", etc.

▶ "During our training, we systematically questioned women who have given birth by caesarean, about 30 cases. The results are unanimous: the parents questioned state that the babies that were delivered by caesarean before the third phase of delivery show more stable behavior and are less anxious.[10]"

5.3 How is sense production developed?

How does the pilot learn to interpret the flashing on the control panel? By teaching and experience, of course. As far as the interpretation of the emotions that give rise to feelings is concerned, the process is not as simple. In fact, the "subject–situation" interaction begins at birth, and a precocious start on this process could make for impossible or false "labeling". If one considers the transformation process, one can say that two "principles" of experience assimilation are at work: the pleasure principle and the reality principle.

▶ "Joanne is 3 years old, she wants to "make soap bubbles"; I tell her she must go outside for that, because soap bubbles are very messy. But to go outside, she has to put on her shoes, which she doesn't like to do. She abandons her soap bubble project because the idea of all the effort needed to put on those shoes cancels out the pleasure of making bubbles. The reality principle has been set against the pleasure principle."

5.4 Emotional production not yet symbolized

Since the work of Freud, when we encounter a situation where sense is not accessible, we say that "event-emotion" remains in the unconscious. We understand that by the following process: it is inscribed in long-term memory in a primitive form that contains only one level of information: the situation on a continuum of "agreeable–disagreeable". These successive memorizations build up a "reservoir" for future symbolization. It seems that if emotion is memorized without being symbolized by language, it has several consequences:

- It is possible to perceive the existence of these memorizations, as they can be written indirectly in language, or directly in the body which will serve to express a nonidentified problem. This "ersatz" symbolization will be largely taken from medicine's "functional" symptoms.
- The oldest are the most important, as they occur in a virgin psyche. To illustrate this paradox, Boris Cyrulnik (1993) uses the following metaphor: "at the time when parchment was rare and costly, monks would scratch the surface of text clean in order to write another. Using light diffraction, it is possible see the traces of the original manuscript... as these first imprints record better on a virgin skin where all circuits are still possible" (p. 198)
- They have a strong influence on behavior; for example, a situation resulting in guilt feelings – rejected in the unconscious by the process described in the preceding paragraph – represents an inexhaustible source of energy employed to diminish the pain of that "feeling" which the subject will permanently ignore.

5.5 Classification of emotional production

In the following pages, we distinguish the nature of emotional production given a situation in which a manager may find himself. The situation definition belongs to Herbert Simon; it is a mental representation.

5.5.1 "A" type production

The situation is difficult, but gratifying:

- the euphoria of management,
- the feeling of competence.

5.5.2 "B" Type production

The situation is deteriorating and becoming an ordeal:

- fear,
- feeling of threat,
- worry,
- stress,

indicating that the situation escapes the manager in question, either because he lacks information and is in a situation of information deficit, or because the warnings were registered but not interpreted, or because he doesn't possess the program execution experience that would permit resolution, or because there is a gap between the resolution capacity of the actor and the situation he is in and must react to.

5.5.3 "C" type production

Situations linked to an intermediate hierarchical status:

- anxiety and inhibition of action,
- the feeling of dependence,
- the feeling of powerlessness,
- the feeling of abandon,
- the feeling of alienation,

indicating that the actor finds himself in a double bind: the obligation to be a member of the organization in order to earn a living, coupled with loss of autonomy.

5.5.4 "D" type production

Failure situation:

- denial and the search for the guilty party,
- the feeling of guilt,
- emotional breakdown,
- disapprenticeship.

Faced with failure, the actor has two possibilities: to accept or reject it. Rejection results in its reappearance by a recurring phenomenon, whereas acceptance brings about disapprenticeship and adaptation.

5.5.5 "E" type production

The situation becomes irreversible:

- negation,
- anger,
- religious prayer and superstition,
- depression,
- letting go.

The image that the actor has of himself, as well as the belief that he can react in this situation, must be abandoned. He is engaged in a process of disapprenticeship of action, and transformation of his way of seeing things, in order to assimilate the impossibility.

5.5.6 "F" type production

Situations leading to success:

- feeling of existence,
- the feeling of validation,
- the feeling of belonging,
- the feeling of being in control of your life,

constitute the production most sought after, even if it sometimes comes with a price attached, a price for breaking rules and/or perhaps a price of some material sacrifice.

Emotional production exists because psychic activity is reflexive. It is what makes up the individual and the image that he has of himself (Korzybski, 1953). Negative production corresponds to the formation of a skewed self-image, just as positive production corresponds to the formation of a refocused self-image. Type "E" production is accompanied by an abandonment of an impossible self-image. It thus represents a difficult road, but allows access to type "F" production.

CHAPTER 1

Gratifying Situations: The Resolution and the Acquisition of Know-How

It's not that the situation to be resolved is easy, on the contrary, it could be extremely difficult. The feeling of gratification comes from a positive attitude vis-à-vis the situation to be resolved: a desire to do something, and an absence of fear to the extent that the actor has the feeling of being able to dominate the situation, even if the situation appears threatening. Thus, even a difficult, or threatening, situation can be highly gratifying. Using all his know-how and expertise, and using a process called "capillarity", he approaches these situations without difficulty and with pleasure. If the process of resolution is not optimum, it becomes so, little by little, and the procedure is backed up by the feeling of having been useful in the case of success. In the case of failure, it is supported by the feeling of having learned something new.

> A project that concludes resembles a birth; its gestation is the source of intense happiness, whereas its ending produces a feeling of emptiness.

The resolution of a situation supposes three conditions:

1. that a resolution exists;
2. that the level of resources needed is reasonable for the problem to be resolved;
3. that the solution doesn't create, at another level, one or more additional problems, that are eventually more difficult to resolve.

> ▶ To underline the capital importance of the third condition, which is usually ignored in specialized training, the French, mocking their superiors, explain that what is meant by "savoir-faire" is to brilliantly resolve a given problem, by simultaneously creating two or three other problems, for which no one, absolutely no one, is able to find a solution…

The situation to be resolved represents a "unit of value" for the manager. If the manager resolves more problems than he creates, he is an outstanding manager and if he creates more than he resolves (except for a beginning manager), he is a bad manager. But, if he doesn't create problems because he does nothing, then he is a useless manager.

Exhibit 7 Difficulties in information collection		
Creates problems	**Resolves problems**	
	Little	**A lot**
Little	"Decorative" manager	"High" level manager
A lot	"Trouble-maker" manager	A manager who must "improve" his emotional management

As a starting point, let us admit that a problem is the discrepancy between two elements: a norm and a result or event.

- the result or the event belongs to the past;
- the norm is the resultant consequence of what you believe should occur in a given situation;
- and the discrepancy originates from the difference between the norm and the result. It represents the problem. The solution must cancel out this discrepancy.

$$E = R - N$$

E : discrepancy in absolute value
R : result
N : norm

This discrepancy is the stimulus that reaches the actor.

- A supplier refuses to deliver because the bills have not yet been paid by the accounts department.
- The order is not correct.
- The supplier hasn't met the agreed deadline and manufacturing is late.
- The rate of returns is increasing.
- Turnover is decreasing.
- The secretary who's been working on these projects has left on maternity leave.
- The new person is not working out.
- The equipment has broken down and the after-sales service isn't reliable.

- The client's bill is increasing dangerously.
- The number of client complaints are increasing.
- Working conditions are not respected.
- Absenteeism is high because of a flu epidemic.
- Overdraft credit limit has been passed.
- There's an overstock situation.
- There's just been a work accident.
- The service budget has been cut by 20%.
- Our main clients are "discontinuing" our line.

▶ In situations that he is familiar with, the actor will want to react immediately. When he finds himself in such a situation, he is happy. All that's missing is the problem. He is in his element, it's what he likes to do and the more difficult the situation, the more motivated he is. In the area of sports or leisure activities, the typical example of these situations is seen by observing in action, teams leaving for a rescue mission in the mountains; even the dog, chained in the helicopter, is fidgeting out of happiness and impatience… For services, we can cite teams who throw themselves into the filming of a new ad campaign for a client that they don't want to disappoint. In the case of highway maintenance, we can cite teams and highway patrolmen who obey the same logic; I've seen equipment managers install new light signals at a non-stop pace. Even for road salting teams; waking up at 2:00 a.m., these men work all night long with passion and at a frantic pace. They feel truly needed and share a keen awareness that the economy of their region depends on their work.

1. The Application of Know-how

The work of Nobel prize-winner H. Simon has shown that the application of know-how is accomplished in two phases: the definition of the situation, followed by the application of an adequate program of execution, using a process limited to a rationale of proximity.

1.1 Situation definition

"Situation definition" is an indispensable phase. We don't know what the "situation" is: the decision-maker is rarely a direct witness, the information obtained often goes through three or four people before it gets to him and each actor involved gives a different version! While the situation belongs to the external environment, the situation definition comes from the actor's internal environment. It represents a simplified and distorted schema of the external situation as the actor's filter affects all "data" that enter into the decision-making process; knowledge and suppositions regarding future occurrences, available alternatives, objectives and values (cited by March and Simon, 1969).

Exhibit 8 Definition of the situation as a double product of the decision-maker's internal and external environments

Situation definition	Situation	
	Easy	**Difficult**
Easy	Correct evaluation	Feeling of being able to master the situation
Difficult	Feeling of not being able to master the situation	Correct evaluation

The definition of the situation results in a diagnosis: "this is what must be done…"

1.2 The application of an execution program

Simon specifies the possible activities of a manager in defining the two extreme situations on a continuum, of which the implicit variable is represented by the quantity of preexisting and available information in the actor's internal environment. In fact, rather than speak of situation definition, one might say situation "recognition" or "identification". Either the actor "recognizes" the situation and applies the know-how previously learned – we call that program execution – or he doesn't identify it and goes to look for a new solution based on search activity. This resolution activity is recognized as such and is put aside as soon as the new expertise has been acquired.

1. the individual finds himself confronted with a situation **that he identifies as being known**,
2. he starts up **an execution program**,
3. this activity is evaluated as satisfactory in relation to the norms, go back to step 1,

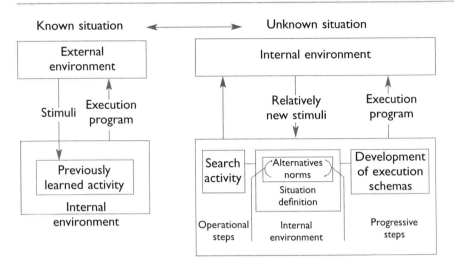

Exhibit 9 Simon's continuum

4. this activity is evaluated as insufficient in relation to the norms, go back to step 2, then move on to resolution activity if the discrepancy continues.

The notion of "execution programs" or simply that of "management programs" is taken up by Mintzberg for whom the occupation of manager passes, first of all, through the apprenticeship of these programs. How to work with your secretary? How to work with your superior? How to conduct a meeting with an unhappy client? How to recruit personnel?, represent just a few of the innumerable and daily management programs.

▶ Below is an illustrative example of a daily execution program for teachers. In principle, this program should take place in a context of a logic gratifying for the teacher.

▣ The stimulus that triggers the program is the arrival of a student in the professor's office, asking for an explanation of a bad grade (on a test, or paper…).

▣ The execution program is the following:
1. the professor listens to the request,
2. he looks for the paper and examines it,
3. he explains the system of criteria used in grading the paper,
4. he checks the application of the system in this particular case,
5. he asks the student if he has any questions,

6. he responds to the questions and goes back to step 3, if necessary, then moves directly to step 7,

7. he thanks the student and says goodbye.

■ But sometimes the actual execution of the program is far from the norm and renders the situation aversive, as well as resulting in an apprenticeship situation.

1. The student, under the pretext of needing to correct a typographical error in his paper, has gotten a hold of the professor's portable phone number from the secretary.

2. The professor receives the phone call in his car, without being able to consult the student's paper. He discovers that there is no concrete error, that the student has manipulated the secretary, and that he is just contesting the grade given and arguing that the comments made on the paper are not complete.

3. The professor re-explains to the student the difference between individually corrected homework, and the final paper which just receives a grade.

4. He suggests that the student looks at a corrected example which is available in his office.

5. The discussion becomes stormy and the student, whose name the professor hasn't gotten, hangs up on him.

We can see that the gap between the "rational" program and the "emotional" reality in the field is great. In this example, the student is highly stressed because the retake exam is being held that same afternoon. He becomes verbally abusive, and the professor himself is far from calm.

QUESTIONNAIRE I

Do you have many execution programs at your disposal?

Put a check in one column for each question using the key below:

1: I completely disagree
2: I mildly disagree
3: I'm not sure
4: I mildly agree
5: I completely agree

Connect the checks. The more your profile appears on the right-hand side, the more you have responded positively to the question.

	1	2	3	4	5
1. I have a driver's license.					
2. I know how to cook.					
3. I know how to use a computer.					
4. I know how to write a memo.					
5. I know how to write a legal-sounding letter.					
6. I know how to conduct an interview.					
7. I know how to run a meeting.					
8. I know how to do a lecture.					
9. I know how to write a budget.					
10. I know how to write.					
11. I know how to travel (train, subway, plane).					
12. I know how to ski.					
13. I know how to swim.					
14. I know how to shop.					
15. I know how to parachute jump.					
16. I know how to windsurf.					
17. I know how to raise a child.					
18. I know how to "pilot" a microlight.					
19. I know how to "pilot" a yacht.					
20. I know how to skin a rabbit.					
21. I know how to do electrical work.					
22. I know how to do plumbing.					
23. I know how to fix a car engine.					
24. I know how to spray paint.					
25. I know how to change a tire.					
26. I know how to reverse into a difficult parking space.					
27. I know how to talk to a banker.					
28. I know how to negotiate a pay increase.					
29. I know how to tape on a VCR.					
30. I know how to use a washing machine.					
31. I know how to take care of an animal.					
32. I know how to manage a budget.					
33. I know how to buy clothes.					
34. I know how to buy an apartment.					
35. I know how to choose credit.					
36. I know how to obey.					
37. I know how to make people obey.					
38. I know how to plant a tree.					
39. I know how to trim a rose bush.					
40. I know how to draw.					
41. I know how to love.					
42. I know how to make love.					
43. I know how to wash and put away the dishes.					
44. I know how to maintain a good relationship with those that finance us.					
45. I know how to discuss price with a supplier.					
46. Specialization, it's for the birds…					

2. The Acquisition of Know-how

The apprenticeship of know-how will appear as soon as the actor is confronted with a situation that is slightly different from those that he has previously encountered. The new program will be acquired "by capillarity", that is to say by direct contact with the new situation, using either what he already knows, or his training, or by trying to acquire programs that have been established by others.

2.1 Apprenticeship by capillarity

If the programs at the manager's disposition are insufficient, he must go into "resolution activity" mode. The manager, confronted with a situation, finds himself in an interaction between his external environment where the situation originates, and his internal environment. The internal environment is the "place" where his previously accumulated experience resides.

2.1.1 The starting point

The starting point determines the sector of intervention as the statistics show: the son's socioeconomic status is very often a function of the father's, and it takes many generations to make that "jump" from one professional milieu to another[1]. At the beginning, no one has a clear vision of their goals: "I want to earn a living" is usually about as far as it goes.

At this "first" contact with the unknown situation, the actor has absolutely no experience with the situation's terrain and he is thus in a zone of maximum risk.

▶ In Vietnam, when young recruits, called "fresh meat", arrived on the battlefield, the veterans avoided them, to avoid getting attached to them, for the recruits' lack of experience resulted in a life expectancy of a few days, despite the training received at the start.

▶ The mortality rate of individual or small enterprises is highest during the first three years. That is why some innovative minds[2] installed a system of "enterprise incubators" that supplied offices and training for these people during the start-up period.

2.1.2 The different "knowledge" of a situation

Acquired experience will slowly shed light on choices. It is not uniquely composed of situations where "I know how to do it". It also includes those situations corresponding to **"I know what I shouldn't do"**[3], to situations corresponding to **"I know that I don't know how"**, and also to situations corresponding to **"I don't know what to do anymore"**. Know-how is a product of situations that are treated efficiently. The "know what I shouldn't do" and the "know but don't know how to do it" are the products of situations treated with bad programs, and these situations are either aggravated or remain without solutions. Finally, if the situation is not resolved after the first attempt, it will continue to deteriorate, producing new information that will in turn be used to redefine an attempt to intervene and so on, undergoing entropy (Prigogine, Stengers, 1979), with the external environment producing supplemental information for the actor's internal environment (Costa de Beauregard, 1963). The energy spent by the actor on his actions – above all those not ending in success – also undergoes entropy that evolves towards its limit, a function of resistance to obstruction (Warden, 1926, cited by Sillamy, 1989), and could bring us to the "I no longer know what to do" phase. The "know-how" that professionals acquire will be greater if the post occupied permits a large range of experiences. Beyond that it is the succession of posts and functions that will provide the opportunity to accumulate know-how... or to accumulate the "know but don't know how to do it"; depending on whether the jobs are left in order to escape an impossible situation, or whether the jobs are left in order to find a new professional situation because we have done all that can be done in the old one.

2.1.3 The logic of solution construction

To construct a solution one must draw upon the well of acquired knowledge. To attack the resolution of an unknown situation, the manager doesn't work out the solution *ex nihilo* corresponding to a so-called optimum. On the contrary, he will draw upon the knowledge and know-how that he possesses, and putting it all together will obtain the beginning of a solution. This process is far from optimal, it is simply the only one possible. It obeys a rationale of proximity; starting with what we know how to do, or what we have. Effectively, the resources he uses are those at his disposal, or that he could make available, and his creativity will determine if he manages to adapt these to the situation or not. His professional road obeys **capillarity logic**, using what he knows how to do, and the resources that he has. Quality know-how permits one to penetrate an unknown socioprofessional milieu, and expertise of that milieu can allow the acquisition of new know-how. If this search is well done, the person betters himself and slowly acquires competence and self-confidence, which will allow him one day to understand that he has achieved his goal, but he will perceive this *ex post*. However, his voyage is not blind. His values will permanently serve in situation evaluations and keep them emotionally alive, either in the form of success – if the situations meet value standards – or in the form of failure if they do not. "Be happy with what you have" is a proverb that shows that values are neither fixed nor intangible. They undergo modifications and transformations as a function of the acquired experiences. If the situation goes well, the actor raises his standards and, in the reverse case, he lowers them. The risks of proximity could also drive an actor, guided by certain values (accumulation of wealth, for example) to take on other values, up until now dormant, that completely and immediately modify his progress. Accidents and serious failures play the same role, and could modify all the actor's values which have been abruptly confronted with a previously ignored reality (Chapter 4). Finally, at the end of this progress, should he come across a cul-de-sac, with the impossibility, not only to go further, but also to get out of the situation, the idea of living with this impossibility for the rest of his life could provoke vastly different reactions – the adaptation of which will be internal. When the situation stabilizes, the psyche should definitively let go of the dream and learn to adapt to an undesired reality (Chapter 5).

▶ Choices are made, little by little, in terms of the opportunities of proximity. An actor who is an expert in interview techniques could go from a "employee of a headhunting agency" to "the creation of a training school for admission interviews for administrative posts or top level schools". An ex-military person could throw himself into action training, but it is rare that a professor becomes a real estate agent[4].

▶ "Mountainbiking gave me a sense of balance that allowed me to tackle windsurfing. Windsurfing allowed me to acquire the feeling of the wind while staying on the water, and that gave me the desire to try hang gliding where I also succeeded. To believe that one can succeed ex nihilo in the latter sport is a mistake; there are too many variables to control where the slightest error is an accident and often, death."

▶ "I had started my graduate studies, and I got to know the university environment; they were looking for assistants, I took the exam and I am still there, 20 years later."

► "At the age of 16, I painted, but I didn't continue. One day in July, 1995, my daughter gave me a brick of clay and said "Papa, I think you would enjoy sculpture." I put it in the basement and two months later I took it out again. Today, in 1999, I have had 3 exhibitions and I create ceramic sculptures, one and a half meters high."

► "My parents were in psychology and they often discussed it. As soon as I turned 13, I began to listen carefully to their arguments and began asking myself if they were right. Today, I'm finishing my degree and I've also a masters in "neuroscience" that allows me to more easily "arbitrate" this subject." *(interview, February 23, 1999)*

► "I received my diploma in computers and I installed programs in medium-sized companies for a small group of consultants. The employees needed training and I loved doing that. Today, I've completely forgotten computers, but I am involved as a trainer in most areas of human resources, not without having redone a previous masters in which I excelled." *(interview, February 25, 1999)*

► "My father was in sales, and what impressed me was although he was intelligent, he always took decisions that slowly contributed to his ruination. Why does someone, who understands most things, do the opposite of what should be done? This problem greatly interested me and it is the reason I became interested in emotional logic. I noticed that he wasn't the only one to function on an emotional level, and that this problem was common in medium-size companies and in the large protected bureaucracies (administration, state monopolies...)."

► "We owned a restaurant, father and son, situated way out in the countryside near Romans. We were excellent cooks, but there weren't enough clients. I told my wife: "In Paris, the cultural life serves to attract clients, I'll put on a show during the meal." Everyone told me "It'll never work", and then when my grandmother learned it was to be a strip-tease, she was shocked: "but what will they say, these people just coming from church? she asked..." Today, our annual turnover is 26 million French francs. I created 82 employee positions, I had to enlarge our restaurant four times and changing the show (once a year) costs 4 million French francs." *(Channel 2, 2:40 a.m., March 3, 1999)*

2.2 Apprenticeship by training

When the gap is too great, a "jump" is needed in order to move from one activity to another, from one domain to another, and this can sometimes require preparation[5].

All training procedures consist of showing what must be done, and of putting the trainees in a simulated situation or in a situation resembling the real one, in which they must try and acquire a certain amount of know-how that will allow them to more easily succeed in the real situation.

The quality of an apprenticeship system is measured by its degree of realism. The farther it gets from the real situation that the actor must face, the more unsuitable it is.

In the choice to "jump" or not, emotion plays a determining role. It is the antagonist between leaving "known security" for a "hope for growth", taking the risk of failure and feeling self-doubt in the new situation: the antagonist between the mix of anxiety and pleasure, knowing that the increase of failure reduces the resistance to obstacles that is sometimes needed to overcome inhibition, and knowing that the increase of success strengthens resistance to obstacles and brings a feeling of personal success, two opposed notions that have nevertheless the commonality of coming from the same place: attempt and/or action! This dialogue between the psyche and its environment must become a competent and adapted dialogue for success to occur. Situations that involve a split with the past, give rise to alteration, a change with high real or emotional risk. The **rational** program of resolution activity is the following:

1. the individual is confronted with a new situation,
2. he deploys search and apprenticeship activity,
3. he establishes a resolution program,
4. if the research is simple, he raises the level of the norm to be achieved and improves the program,
5. the norm is lowered if the research is difficult,
6. he executes the resolution program,
7. if the program is followed by situation modifications evaluated as **satisfactory** in relation to the norms, return to step 1,
8. if the program is followed by situation modifications evaluated as **insufficient** in relation to the norms, return to step 6.

▶ Around 1983, before the sport became a craze, we had created a piloting school for teaching hang gliding to the young. We had introduced two simulations: the first consisted of teaching them to fly a few meters from the ground, the other to be attached to the plane on top of a Land Rover that was being driven at 30 km/h. In order to limit the risk of panic as much as possible, the first solo was preceded by a flight with dual commands. With these three apprenticeships, the aspiring pilot had the chance to acquire the true reflexes necessary in a real flight, and we were able to minimize the unknown character of the situation. But never did we give in to the temptation to have them fly standing – as did many at that time in the schools of Grenobloises de N… as it simplified the training for the trainer, but left out an essential survival reflex of the trainee: to lie down as quickly as possible in the trapeze in order to speed up…

QUESTIONNAIRE 2

Test your resolution capacity

Put a check in one column for each question using the key below:

1: I completely disagree

2: I mildly disagree

3: I'm not sure

4: I mildly agree

5: I completely agree

Connect the checks. The more your profile appears on the right-hand side, the more you have responded positively to the question.

		1	2	3	4	5
1.	I need to have two or three similar experiences before I feel I can manage.					
2.	I have absolutely no difficulty getting information that I need.					
3.	I find it easy to recognize my errors and to avoid them in the future.					
4.	Everything is meaning and symbol.					
5.	For me, life is a succession of situations that must be resolved and I do so very well.					
6.	When I don't know a situation, I don't hesitate to go see someone better informed than I.					
7.	I write possible solutions on the computer to help me clarify my ideas.					
8.	People say that I am a resourceful person.					
9.	The more experience you have in different areas the better you do.					
10.	Don't ask yourself "who is right", ask "which is right".					
11.	Opinions give sense to facts.					
12.	It is very important to continually ask yourself: "who should be aware of what I'm doing".					
13.	If you don't have an argument "against", you don't have an argument "for".					

3. Associated Emotional Production

"He enjoys his job."

A feeling of competence is associated with the application phase of know-how, whereas the acquisition of know-how is accompanied by a period of euphoria.

3.1 The feeling of competence

The feeling of competence is associated with situations that simultaneously bring into play problems to resolve, objectives to reach, aptitudes and the professional experience allowing one to confront problems rather rapidly. We will repeat many times that the difficulty is not the threatening or difficult character of the situation, but the feeling of not being able to handle it (Katz and Kahn, 1966; Laborit, 1981).

Exhibit 10 Emotional logic associated with know-how	
Situation definition	Threatening or non-threatening situations
I know how to handle this	Gratifying situation (Chapter 1)
I don't know how to handle this	Aversive situation (Chapter 2)

What feels good is attacking the situation, experiencing the "spice" of a challenge, adding in a touch of fear for there is always risk and, above all, the promise of feeling *ex post* strong gratification in the case of success, and the feeling of having completed the apprenticeship in case of difficulties met and resolved. These situations directly contribute to the person's personal development.

3.2 The euphoria of gestation

The feeling of euphoria, followed by a feeling of loss, as experienced by pregnant women, constitute the model of the emotional process that accompanies the acquisition phase of new know-how, of a new project, etc. This period, no matter how difficult, is accompanied by an emotional production that will support the enormous affective investment of the learner. Unfortunately, it will be followed by a feeling of emptiness.

▶ "I always need to be learning something; I get true pleasure from self-enrichment. It is true though, that sometimes, my knowledge is not always directly useful, but experience shows that it always ends up helping me to avoid a significant number of errors." *(March 3, 1999)*

4. Associated Emotional Conflict: "Approach–Approach"

In these situations, there is still some conciliation to be done with the internal state of psychic conflict. There is a choice that takes place between two ways of doing things. On must determine which one is best.

▶ A problem with the team: should it be a topic of discussion in a meeting or would a simple memo suffice?

▶ A problem with a collaborator: should a note be sent or wait to see him in order to speak about it directly?

▶ A speech to prepare: What tone to take? How to alternate humorous and serious?

▶ A request for the director: should ask for a formal meeting or just arrange to bump into him in the hall? etc.

The "approach–approach" conflict is the only one of Lewin's three internal conflicts (1935) to be considered gratifying, because even in the case of failure, one's potential is greatly improved by knowing how to choose between two programs the next time around.

5. A Brief Overview of This Chapter

5.1 Situation definition

The definition is the "internal version" of the situation, mirrored in the psyche of the manager.

5.2 The execution program

If you are confronted with a situation and you know what to do, you possess the appropriate program. The average manager possesses more than 200 of these. The most common of these are:

- know how to conduct an interview,
- know how to answer the phone,
- know how to write a letter,
- know how to conduct a meeting,
- know how to write a budget,
- know how to present and successfully manage a project,
- know how to obey,
- know how to command,
- know how to read an organizational chart,
- know how to write a memo,
- know how to work with your secretary,
- know how to work with your boss.

5.3 The acquisition of know-how

If you are faced with a situation that you are not familiar with, you must "invent" the solution. The activity is based on the "search" for information. Then with the aid of other advice obtained, and known programs that are slightly adapted, modified or assembled in a different manner, a solution is brought about. It is also possible to rely on the use of a training program.

5.4 Associated emotional production

These situations are gratifying, as they are about problem resolution and a feeling of competence or utility; or they could equally be about a sentiment of profound joy that provokes the development of a new project or the acquisition of new know-how.

5.5 The "approach–approach" conflict

In these situations the psyche experiences internal conflict with all its related pressure, but it is easy to overcome, because it is a simple result of the difficulty in choosing between two ways of doing things. Even if the choice retained is not the best, it will result in an apprenticeship, an improvement of competences that will themselves be a source of gratification.

CHAPTER 2

Aversive Situations: Challenge and Self-doubt

When a situation immediately creates fear, anxiety or distress, the logic of action becomes emotional. The first step is to ask oneself if it is possible to escape the situation, and, if that's not possible, it must be faced. But even in the latter case, the resistance to obstruction is not unlimited and the actor could – under the influence of persistent factors – be discouraged and left unable to continue.

Living is an occupation. (Jean-Pierre Cassel)

1. The Preliminaries

When it no longer works, read the instructions. (popular saying)

In defining a situation, we define the problem to be resolved, the objective to be achieved and the result to be produced. The challenge is born from the emergence of a situation of choice, for all choice, without exception, is a challenge. What to do? What not to do? How to do it? **Meeting the challenge causes entry into the emotional arena.**

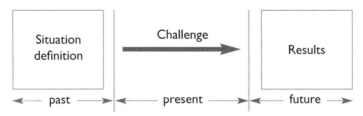

Exhibit 11 The challenge and the problem

The concept of challenge can be defined, first of all, in relation to the concept of the problem. A challenge, as well as a problem, results from a discrepancy from the norm, but is differentiated on two points. Whereas the problem indicates a past situation, the challenge indicates the future.

The actor will try to react to resolve the problem and that is the challenge. Later, although the problem is external to the actor, the challenge includes a psychological dimension. A challenge can also be defined as the discrepancy between the "program" that comes from the actor's internal environment and, we might say, the "plan" that comes from his external environment. The writer Bernard Montaud (1993) makes reference to an "invisible hand", specifying that the challenging situation, a source of apprenticeship, is a part of the "plan".

▶ Researchers who want to simulate a *problem* for rats, create a system that includes the manipulation of a pedal that delivers a morsel of food. The rat learns to use the pedal and thus resolves his problem of nourishment.

To simulate a challenge, and to put the animal in a situation of choice, the researchers electrified the pedal and the rat who wishes to eat learns that the feeding pedal provokes a electrical shock.

▶ A simple telephone call can be a challenge, so much so that the person asks someone else to make that call in his stead. In the same way, answering the telephone can be such a challenge that many people leave the answering machine on, even while they are in, in order to screen the calls.

▶ Responding to a job ad is often a very difficult challenge.

▶ Looking someone in the eyes can be a challenge more difficult than skydiving.

▶ A manager, even a high-level manager, can be incapable of having face-to-face meetings, choosing instead to put everything that he has to say in writing.

▶ Having to go to a meeting the next day can demand an inordinate amount of energy and could prevent the actor from sleeping the night before.

▶ Writing a memo that may "make waves" could require an uncommon amount of courage.

▶ Asking for a pay raise, saying "no" to someone, speaking in public, could all be challenges as difficult as firing someone or imposing a prison sentence.

1.1 Challenge and competition

When I look at myself, I am worried; when I compare myself, I am reassured. (Sacha Guitry)

Competition is a challenge that one chooses **willingly**. Competition, no matter its nature – organizational or sportive – is established in relation to two norms: the level of performance and the level of risk. The **level of performance** is a norm which permits qualification of the results, while the **level of risk** is the norm which permits qualification of the dangers brought about by the resources used, notably the life or health of the competitor. There are two major types of competition: competition with others and competition with oneself. Of course, the two types are always present within a challenge, but not in the same proportion. For example, if you compare tennis with bungee jumping, it is clear that the latter is uniquely a competition with oneself, and that the notion of performance is absent, whereas in the first activity, it is first and foremost about defeating one's adversary.

Situations that are easy will attract more people; the competition will be severe, and the risk of being beaten by an adversary will be higher. One way to escape this difficulty is to choose those much less frequented situations of risk, where the combat is above all with oneself. These risk situations are often chosen by those who dread competition with others, preferring competition with themselves. They have something to prove in a combat that remains interior. One could deduce two attitudes involved, for the first a more or less rational logic, and for the second a more or less emotional logic.

In the first attitude, only the external challenge preoccupies the actor. In the second attitude, it is the internal challenges that motivate him, and the norm is the norm of risk. He prefers to practice those activities with higher risks, but where the level of performance does not intervene in the same way.

Exhibit 12 Risk and performance		
Level of risk	Level of performance	
	Weak	High
Weak	Radio game shows	Tennis, swimming
High	Bungee jumping	Paris–Dakar Rally; Gulf War; Vendée Globe; job interviews; administrative exams

The rational competitor is attracted by the performance that can put him in among the first, whereas the emotional competitor, having a high negative valence for competition between people, will be strongly attracted by those situations that give him the possibility to conquer himself, to succeed at a new feat, for example.

1. The individual is engaged in a resolution program,
2. a series of events thwarts the program,
3. it sets off an intense emotional activity that we call "a challenging situation".
4. He can approach this situation by following two logics.
5. He makes his decisions being concerned either with conquering others or improving his own performance.

2. The Situation Deteriorates

Most of the time in an organization the challenge doesn't come from a deliberate choice, but from a situation that is deteriorating within our area of responsibility. These situations deteriorate over time, according to a principle of entropy, followed by irreversibility (Prigogine and Stengers, 1979), in a process that can be very generally schematized as follows:

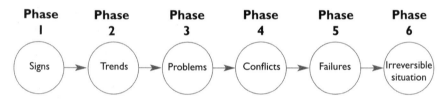

| Phase 1 | Phase 2 | Phase 3 | Phase 4 | Phase 5 | Phase 6 |

Signs → Trends → Problems → Conflicts → Failures → Irreversible situation

Exhibit 13 Deterioration of the situation

The signs

The discrepancy in relation to the norm is first of all revealed by signs. Their interpretation is difficult when they are few and isolated. In addition, if the situation has had nothing but success until now, the preliminary signs of the deterioration will be practically impossible to perceive. According to Thomas Kuhn (1962, 1970, 1983), the actor is "biologically" incapable of detecting changes at this level.

▶ The Swiss had 90% of the watch market. Today, it is below 10%. One day, an inventor perfected the quartz watch. He presented his invention to Swiss watchmakers who weren't interested, but he exhibited it anyway at the Zurich fair. That is how the now well-known "Mr. Seiko" entered into this story, for the researcher, being unaware of the interest in his discovery, had failed to protect it. In fact, do you know the nationality of the inventor? Try to guess...!

The trend

A trend appears when the deterioration of the situation produces more and more numerous, and converging, signs. Reacting at this level means accepting to do something that one hasn't ever done before and to be among the first to do it.

> ▶ "My father was an independent salesman. In the 70's, this milieu was composed of individualists and conservatives. They had little concern for the future. My father had gone to the United States, and what he saw persuaded him that hypermarkets would one day invade France and small, independent store owners would be crushed. Another trip to Sweden introduced him to independent collectives, a means to hold out against the conglomerates. He had taken me to see "Cité II" at Carcassonne, the "Casemates" at Grenoble, and the "GERICK" at Thionville, who were among the forerunners. He instigated meetings of town storeowners with the objective of developing an association with legal status ("G.I.E., groupement d'intérêt économique", an economic cooperative). He was never able to accomplish this and died in 1978. In 1990, when I happened to bump into one of the people who remembered my father's attempts, he began the conversation by telling me: "he understood everything, if only we had followed his advice while there was still time".

The problem

The manager capable of seeing and understanding trends is a "visionary", but he is more often up against the incomprehension of others. On the other hand, once the trend is rewritten as a problem, things are clear for all, and most managers will be in agreement about attempting a resolution. They may not be able to find a solution, or more simply, resistance may come from the employees of the enterprise, who, confronted with changes imposed by the solution, block it and push the situation so that it degenerates into conflict, failure and finally, precludes all possibility of going back and making amends.

> ▶ The deterioration of a situation at this level is well illustrated by the state transport organizations "Air France", "SNCF" (train transport) and the energy sector. In general, the "problem" comes from changes that are not exactly to the liking of the unions – or to the political powers – and set off conflict upon conflict designed to block the changes that would save the situation. These organizations are the only ones where the union (CGT) is very powerful. Many enterprises disappear in this phase (except if they are subsi-

dized), because the employees do not want, or cannot, question their union in order to allow the enterprise to overcome the problem.

2.1 Does the situation definition really come before its resolution?

Imagine two enemy tanks, face to face, but instead of firing, one of them proposes a meeting to define the situation...

The limited rationality model leads us to believe that situation definition precedes action or, at least, that action is the product of the manager's know-how which is part of the definition in question. It is probable that the manager, acting on his know-how, puts into action a response to the situation, S_t, that is a function of the accumulation of knowledge from situations S_{t-4}, S_{t-3}, S_{t-2}, S_{t-1}... which preceded it. In this hypothesis, it is only after responding that he will notice the gap between the desired response and the one given. This gap could result in an apprenticeship, a learning experience, that will give rise to a redefinition of the situation, intervening *ex post*, that will permit him to enrich his response for the next time. The program of apprenticeship for this gap is as follows:

1. the individual finds himself confronted with a situation,
2. he executes a resolution program,
3. the gap between the given response and the desired response is apparent *ex post*,
4. he discovers, by experience, how he could have acted in a more efficient manner,
5. he integrates his errors in his resolution program for the next time.

2.2 The search for information, a search for false security

The race begins between the definition of the situation and its deterioration.

First of all, it is discovered that the situation degradation in the external environment is "producing" information in the internal environment of the actor whose reading of the situation is improving. The starting point is practically imperceptible as it is located in a "sea of uncertainty". The end point is accompanied by the production of perfect information (evaluation, balance sheets...). It is noticed that afterwards, in the absence of intervention, there is a sort of convergence of the evolution of the three characteristics of the situation:

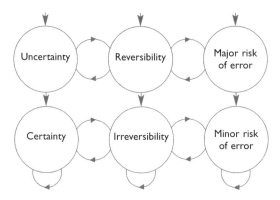

Exhibit 14 Increase of available volume of information results in deterioration

Phases 1, 2 and 3 (Exhibit 13) are reversible under the managers' decision pressure. The other phases are the more difficult. The persons in charge have an "aversive" attitude towards phases 1 and 2, for reasons of insufficient information, whereas to wait for phases 3, 4 and 5 is very risky. Internal conflict is linked directly with this "aversive" attitude – towards risk and uncertainty – and is most strongly opposed to the need to act in anticipation. If they want to escape this risk, they must have at their disposition a volume of information that would allow them to deduce from the situation the required action. The search for this information takes a great deal of time that would result in action taken too late for the stimulus and would represent a factor of failure linked to the aggravation of the situation. This aggravation will be greater because the difference between the speed of the degradation of the situation, and the speed needed to obtain data, will be higher. The managers find themselves in a bidding situation, American style. They take part in the "degradation" of the price, but they experience a conflict between the desire to "pay" the least expensive price possible and the risk of losing all if they don't intervene in time… On the other hand, the capacity to anticipate problems and to act before they manifest themselves, represents a factor of success, but, in this case, the manager is working with an abundance of **emotional, intuitive and irrational data**[1], and objective data is more reassuring. At the risk of creating a caricature, it is possible to imagine that a situation has produced a large volume of information, and now has left the arena of the actor and entered the arena of the observer. In other words, in this process of degradation, **that which is measurable and could be an object of research is – by nature – useless in the action arena concerned, because it is already outdated**. The actor will anyway learn to confront the situation,

but his apprenticeship does not pass through rational information; he takes
a **shortcut** – which excludes a conscious definition of the situation – using
a series of emotional "data" called know-how, intuition or reflex[2]. Everything happens as if rational information was the product of situation
entropy, to the point where the only true source that informs the actor, who
wishes to intervene before degradation, will be of an emotional nature.

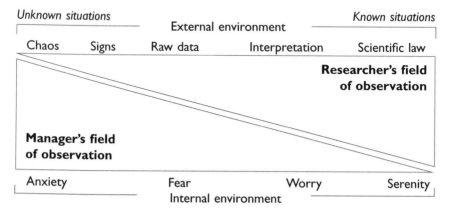

Exhibit 15 State of the search

2.3 The intervention of precaution or prevention suppresses the proof of its utility

Simon indicates that managers react to stimuli that condition the beginning
of the search activity, by giving the example of a fire alarm signal (Simon,
1974, p. 137). But the "stimuli–search" relation is found to be a function of
two completely subjective data comprised of the **level of vigilance and the
capacity to extract "sense" from "signs"**. Why does a manager react to
the first "stimulus"? In the case of eventual failure, it will be patent, but
because of the nature of anticipatory activity, a measure of its utility is
impossible. If the manager takes the risk to be, at worst, negatively sanctioned, and at best, have nothing happen, only a solid professional
conscience or a strong hierarchical support can incite such a precocious act
on his part. It is reasonable to imagine that the beginning of a search
activity is submitted to a delay that is cumulative with the precedent.

▶ "I was walking with my friend, in Senegal on the Atlantic coast, in the
Casamance region. We arrived at one of those pleasant fishing villages that
are along the coast. After a short period of observation-integration, we were

invited to join in conversation with three fishermen who were resewing their nets. We got to know and like each other. The fisherman invited us to go out on the sea with them the next day. I accepted. The Senegalese build boats of different sizes but always rather small. I had often seen them return, on the beach after the fishing and I observed them empty out their catch with all sorts of fish, including "guitar ray" fish or small sharks. At the same time, they take advantage of this to empty out the water that had accumulated during their fishing trip. A feeling began to weigh on me little by little. Without apparent reason, I no longer wanted to go fishing. It's indefinable, I began to dread it. Yet, it wasn't my first experience with air, land or sea travel that I had done in an environment supposedly not as secure as European travel. I'm a good swimmer and don't have any particular fear of water. I can't say I was scared, I know that feeling and that's not what I was feeling in this situation. Simply, I no longer wanted to act on the invitation. I had, however, made a promise vis-à-vis the fishermen and I want to honor my engagement, if only to keep my promise. In addition, how could I explain to my friend the reason for my withdrawal, I had actually no reason except a feeling not to go. Yet, I had to admit that this feeling existed and came from something even if I was ignorant of its origin. Despite the reactions that opposed my refusal to go out on the sea, I kept to my decision not to take part in the fishing expedition." (note from author: during the testimony, the narrator asked me if he did the right thing. It is impossible to say. But it is probable that his state of vigilance allowed him to record the non-verbal data that established some doubt in the confidence he could have in the fishermen…)

▶ The media reported on the steps taken by Ayrton Senna, according to other drivers, to try to cancel the race a few hours before his fatal accident. In fact, in this "conversation" that he had with the situation, he had the presentiment of danger, significant for Senna, who drove faster than the others. His advice wasn't followed by the competition because the danger was to himself – taking into account his emotional evaluation and his driving speed – and not for the others. He didn't listen to his intuition. We know what happened (see also 5.2.3.).

▶ There is a sort of myth that exists in the Durance: the Rabioux. It is an immense wave that is upstream from Embrun. I remember, having requested to leave the raft, when my team was preparing to go there for the second time, because the subjective evaluation of what I was feeling (drop of energy level due to the excessive physical demands that was necessary the first time) prohibited me from staying and throwing myself immediately for the second time into this adventure.

▶ In the 60's, companies had massively resorted to the use of consultants to evaluate their problems. They experienced quite a bit of failure because of this phenomenon, for the dialogue that the consultant had with the situation only rarely integrated emotional subjectivity, and the organizational subconscious of those who were responsible for the decisions made. Those who must act should be, at a minimum, associated with the situation because their own capacity will be integrated in the choice of solutions.

2.4 The level of self-confidence impacts on situation evaluation

When a manager is confronted with a situation, there are three entities involved; the manager, the situation and the relation that the manager has with the situation. The importance of this last factor is decisive.

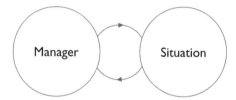

Exhibit 16 Interrelationship between the actor and the situation

Self-knowledge – and the knowledge of one's own emotional logic – is the predominant element in the efficacy of choices that will be made. The manager has a dialogue with the situation, he is the principal actor in it and if he poorly evaluates the emotional relation that he has with the situation, it could have dire consequences. Situation and personality integrate, and the taking into account of this subjectivity is a guarantee against risk of failure. If the manager underestimates himself or lacks self-confidence, and he occupies a role of responsibility in these situations that generate unbearable emotional production, he will be living with permanent pressure. If his personal and affective life often generate this type of situation, he is at risk of always being thinking of leaving... More usefully, we can inverse the propositions and say that his desires to personally or professionally leave are symptoms of a situation that distances him from his "center". When all is said and done, there are several possible reactions that are a function of emotional activity:

1. The actor confronts a challenge.
2. Go on to 3 and/or 4 and/or 5 and/or 6.
3. He perceives neither the importance nor the gravity of the situation and doesn't take care of it. Return to 1 or go directly to 4.

4. He perceives the risk, but doesn't wish to intervene too early, for he knows from experience that it will only bring trouble as long as it is not perceived by others and he is afraid of being wrong.
5. He doesn't have self-confidence and prefers to wait.
6. He acts on his instincts without defining them.

QUESTIONNAIRE 3

Test your capacity to anticipate

Put a check in one column for each question using the key below:

1: I completely disagree

2: I mildly disagree

3: I'm not sure

4: I mildly agree

5: I completely agree

Connect the checks. The more your profile appears on the right-hand side, the more you have responded positively to the question.

	1	2	3	4	5
1. It is said that you have intuition.					
2. Solutions seem obvious to you and you are astonished that others don't see them also.					
3. Better safe than sorry.					
4. You practice a high-risk sport where there is no room for error.					
5. You always try to leave an exit open for yourself.					
6. Security for you is having an extra string for your bow if it should break.					
7. When you board a boat you don't hesitate to put on the life jacket.					
8. It's better to avoid a fire than to put one out, even if the latter is more heroic.					
9. While driving, you anticipate road difficulties and adjust your speed accordingly.					
10. You expect others to make mistakes and you are never caught off guard.					
11. To win takes time.					
12. On a totally dry road, a smooth tire adheres better than a treaded one.					
13. In a fire, you must stay close to the ground.					
14. In an accident, the most important thing is to avoid creating a second one.					
15. In the city, most serious accidents happen at night.					
16. In winter, once you start salting the road or staircase, you have to continue – otherwise it's worse than having done nothing at all.					

The actor centered on the action doesn't have the luxury of being satisfied with sure and verifiable observation as is the researcher[3] who is responsible for observation; he must live with the obligation to act on data that is incomplete, inexact, contradictory, ambiguous, false... As a result, his emotional environment will be invaded by a range of diverse sentiments. We will analyze fear, the feeling of threat, stress and anxiety.

3. Associated Emotional Production

The Limited Rationality Decision-maker is a pharmacologically treated being who does not feel emotion in relation to the situations experienced, but who does have a memory. Laborit demonstrates that this is impossible, as emotional production plays a determinant role in memory. "The synthetic protein that accompanies this production is the source of long term memory" (Laborit, 1981). He invents the Emotionally Active Decision-maker.

3.1 Fear of the situation

Fear constitutes the simplest of emotions. Whether it is associated with a situation to resolve or with a meeting, and, actually, for the latter we speak of the feeling of threat instead. Fear appears as soon as the situation is defined and remains during the entire period until D-Day, when it will disappear most often during the action phase. The nervous system being made, first of all, to act, all emotional production will cease as soon as it can move into action. Afterwards, emotional production will reappear in the form of joy or pain according to the results obtained.

3.1.1 The feeling of not being able to control the situation

Fear does not originate from the confrontation between the actor and the unknown situation (leaving for an unknown country, change of job, first marriage or first separation), but from a situation that gives rise to a feeling of not being able to confront it, not knowing what to do, or from a situation that creates a feeling of not being able to control it, most of the time due to the presence of other actors in the situation who have the opportunity to oppose the solution. If the actor only experiences the feeling of not being able to confront the situation (first speech in front of a large audience, for example), it is in consciously preparing his task, and the contents of the speech, that will diminish the fear. In fact, Brownet Katz et al. remarked that threatening situations, where the subject feels capable of overcoming them, does not increase the release of the 17 hydrocorticides (Laborit, 1981). **It is not the threatening character of the situation that provokes the fear, it is the feeling of not being able to confront it.**

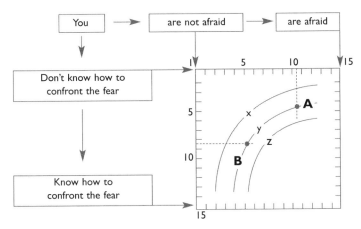

Exhibit 17 Law of Brownet Katz, Weiner et al.: fear as an inverse function of the possibility of situation resolution[4]

3.1.2 The overestimation of risk

Anyone finding themselves confronted with an opportunity must decide whether they will choose to seize the opportunity or let it "pass". According to the work of Abraham Maslow (1968), for each human being there are two types of forces at work; one of these is organized around a pole of resistance which holds on to security to defend against fear. These forces tend towards regression, by holding on to the repetition of the past through the creation of habits. The person caught in this system dreads risk as if he were a prisoner in a large invisible womb…

Exhibit 18 Fear as a product of the gap between the definition of the situation and the situation itself		
Situation definition	**The situation**	
	Simple	**Difficult**
Simple	Correct evaluation	Feeling of situation dominance: absence of fear; risk of underestimation
Difficult	Feeling of not dominating the situation: the actor is afraid; risk of overvaluation	Correct evaluation

He is afraid to try his luck, afraid to put in peril what he has acquired:

1. the person finds himself in the presence of an opportunity,
2. the situation definition establishes its threatening character,
3. this character sets off a violent feeling of insecurity;
4. this character sets off the fear of not being able to handle the situation,
5. the opportunity is not taken,
6. return to 1.

▶ "Physiological needs, needs for security, love, respect, information, are disturbing for many people. They create psychic difficulties and pose problems, especially for those who have had the unhappy experience of wanting to respond to these needs and not being able to" *(Maslow, 1968, p. 31)*

3.1.3 The underestimation of risk

When the actor carries out his informational evaluation at the end of a search activity, he does it following a biological process that allows the establishment of the situation by responding to a supplementary question with the answer: "I know this situation, I know what to do"; "I know this situation, I'm not afraid!" In doing so the **repetitive mechanisms of anticipation** could render a dangerous situation commonplace and contribute to failure. One is reminded of the proverb according to which if you cry "wolf" too often, people get used to it and will ignore the warning:

1. the person finds himself confronted with a threatening situation,
2. go on to 3 or 4 or 5,
3. the person has never encountered this situation before and feels no danger, go on to 6,
4. the person has already encountered this situation, is very afraid but is still drawn to it, go on to 6,
5. he has encountered this threat numerous times and no longer pays any attention to it, go on to 6,
6. he ignores the risk,
7. go on to 8 or the end of the program.
8. An accident occurs.

▶ In his first broadcast dedicated to natural catastrophes, Sylvain Augier (March 9) showed numerous cases where, even when warned, the population didn't react, despite the eruption of a volcano resulting in tens of thousands of deaths, whereas in another case, where they didn't know of the volcano, they instituted evacuation procedures anyway. When a specialized team came to study the terrain, prior to the installation of machinery, the team realized that the zone was the site of an old volcano and immediately put up an observatory. Sometime later, the announcement of a predicted eruption allowed them to sound the alert and the population was evacuated without a problem. In the first case, the population that had experience with this phenomenon had not believed in its gravity and were destroyed. In the second case, the population knew nothing of volcanic eruptions, were very afraid and accepted the evacuation. There were only a few casualties.

▶ Alain D., the driver of the train X2149, on the Bordeaux–Besançon–Bergerac–Soulat line, was approaching level crossing 3965, that of Porte Sainte Foy, when he became deathly afraid. The closer he approached, the more afraid he became. The tracks and the highway were parallel for 5 kilometers. The driver of the train could see cars overtaking him, and trucks crossing the state highway. It's difficult to know if he had passed beyond the beacon that was triggered 25 seconds before lowering of the gates. Several times in the past, the locomotive had come very close to a vehicle and one day a passenger who had been sitting on the folding seat, had jumped off the moving train believing an accident was imminent. Four days before, the barrier had been torn out. The fourth time since the beginning of the year. The driver was afraid, but he hesitated to slow down to 30 kph, as that would mean a delay of 2 minutes to Bergerac and he was being watched by his superiors, even though they declared (after the accident) that "we have never penalized someone who slowed down in this area". The hierarchy ruthlessly penalizes any slowdowns that result in delays. There had already been a collision in November '92. The "thermal" drivers at the Bordeaux station had passed the word: "To hell with the standard speed of 120 kph, on main line 395, slow down to 30 or 40!" But this was a double-edged sword, because the gate stayed down much longer, and a car driver, not seeing the train approach, could be tempted to pass through. In addition, the train was already 10 minutes late, having had to wait for the TGV (high speed train) to pass, which was itself 9 minutes late coming from Libourne. On September 8, Alain saw the semitrailer and sounded a very long whistle. It was noon, and the accident so feared had taken place. The tanker was torn to bits and its fuel set fire to everything around it. Thirteen dead, 5 of these rail workers, 43 hurt, 10 seriously. The firemen took 24 hours to release Alain's trapped body[5].

▶ We had just moved, and the guardrail on the staircase had been taken off in order to bring an armoire up to the first floor. My daughter was 2 years old, she was on the landing and I was on the ground floor, two meters below. She looked at me, smiling, and raised her arms and... let herself fall into space believing that I would catch her in my arms. I was so afraid! But she wasn't at all afraid, for a two year old, space doesn't have meaning yet, while jumping into her father's arms has a very positive meaning.

▶ On the other hand, during my training, I remember having seen someone, during the beam exercise proposed by Jacques Salomé, climb up on the beam, experience all sorts of emotional states with accompanying tears flowing down, because she was incapable of doing the exercise that she had chosen, which was to let yourself fall down onto a mattress which the rest of the group was holding out below the beam to catch you. For this person, to jump into open space, without a doubt, produced not only a high level of anxiety, but an incapacity to trust others. Maybe she had been betrayed sometime in her past?

3.1.4 How are first impressions established?

Memory of previous situations plays an essential role in the constitution of the valence of the situation[6]. The valence is not created by chance, it integrates a large quantity of data. For example, when you meet someone for the first time, you always feel something towards that person – either a weak or strong feeling – either positive or negative. In the case of immediate total aversion, this "feeling" is the product of multiple information accumulated during the course of previous meetings that were agreeable or… disagreeable. Given that, the emotional process of the "fabrication" of the valence of the first meeting is essential, as it integrates three series of data to produce a judgment on the relationship with this unknown person:

1. compatibility enters between the situation, the person and ourselves,
2. what we are, with all our faults, incapacities, ignorance and neurosis, confronts the situation,
3. and what the person met means to us, and what we may have with them in terms of relationship.

Finally, this first irrational judgment, if it is applied to the relational situation and not only considered as an attribute of the unknown person, is always the most complete. This first impression, integrated in the process geared towards establishing a value judgment, is always the best. But if we put ourselves in the process of objective selection, to choose a job candidate for example, one must avoid these first impressions like the plague. To give an example, during training for admission judges for Ivy League schools, the following advice is always given: "If, right away, as soon as he enters, the candidate makes you feel at ease, or, on the other hand, if you feel a strong aversion for him, don't question it, let someone else take your place as judge…".

3.1.5 How is the feeling of threat established?

Ex ante, "if that which we experience outside of ourselves agrees with the image that we have of ourselves, we will tend to perceive things without distortion. In the opposite case, we will feel **threatened**. The more disagreement there is between the Ego and that which we experience, the stronger the feeling of threat. We can respond to the danger by trying to integrate the Ego. That would mean a modification of the Ego: this modification would mean that one must begin a process that is long and more or less painful (suffering). Another solution consists of protecting the Ego against change by 'not seeing', by distorting or rejecting that which is outside of ourselves. We refuse to see what is inside of ourselves, specifically the aspects of Ego requiring a negation of reality." (C. Argyris, 1970, pp. 22–3)

1. The actor is faced with a new situation that doesn't agree with the conception he has of things,
2. this situation puts into question his personal achievements,
3. a feeling of threat arises,
4. go on to 5 or 6,
5. he puts into place defense mechanisms that distort situation evaluation in order to render it less painful (defense mechanisms that distort perception are repression, projection, rationalization, and in a certain sense, displacement).

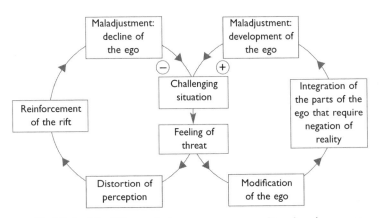

Exhibit 19 Effect of threat on personality development

6. there is a modification of achievements, suffering and the mechanism of disapprenticeship and the reconstruction of the personality.

In the major assessments made between items 5 and 6, the capacity to resist psychic pressure is decisive.

3.2 The pathology of fear

An obvious and observable example of this pathology in the life of a couple is where one is afraid of the good mood of the other. When one shows one's good mood, by singing or laughing, the other wonders: "Is he (she), by any chance, cheating on me?" In the professional milieu, the pathology of fear is recognized by the following:

1. the more the employee expects, without sufficient reason, that his superiors or colleagues will exploit or harm him;
2. the more he will doubt, without justification, the loyalty or honesty of his colleagues or superiors;
3. the more the employee will perceive hidden significance, humiliating or threatening, in innocuous comments or events;
4. the more the employee will feel resentful or not forgive any insult or scorn;
5. the more the employee will be reticent to trust anyone because he unjustly fears that any information given will be used against him;
6. the more the employee will easily feel scorned and be quick to react with anger or against the attacker, and we can say that he has emotional problems of the "paranoid" type.

Exhibit 20 Different logics of threat		
Internal environment	**External environment**	
	Normal situations in relation to risk	**High-risk situations**
Feeling of security	Suitable emotional production	Excess of self-confidence
Feeling of fear	Pathology of fear	Suitable emotional production

▶ I had just finished a conference on the management of proximity and I had shown, as a case study, one of the famous films of Peter Drücker. A young engineer from the National Polytechnic Institute, who had attended the class, came into my office. His face was fierce: he was big and powerful looking, he looked as if all his effort was concentrated on one objective, increasing the impression of strength. A big mustache and curly brown hair gave him a strange look, along with his large tortoiseshell glasses which covered his face. Immediately he said to me: "You have been to see my boss, you can't deny it, I know that you know him!" I knew right away not to contradict him. His attitude was triumphant, chin raised, a piercing look, eyes narrowed, the right hand gently pulling on the tip of his mustache. I had never faced a situation like this. The case study that I had shown was known throughout the world, but it seemed so much like what he was living through at the moment that he was persuaded that it was a result of video tape made from a conversation that had taken place with his own boss, a conversation whose goal was no doubt to fire him… It was my first year of teaching and I had not yet been in the presence of paranoia… I remember saying to myself: "How am I going to get out of this…?" Intuitively, I focused on the facts. I showed him the industrial packing of the video case study and the bill of sale. He seemed highly astonished, then, triumphantly: "Yes, but it's not coincidence that you chose this one and not another!" I am not in the habit of running away, but the discussion was destined for failure. I ended the meeting on a pretext of having an urgent appointment.

3.3 Stress

We speak of stress when the source seems to be coming from an organizational situation, and we speak of anxiety to highlight the interpersonal dimension. We will be treating the subject of anxiety in Chapter 3 section 5. Stress results from the interaction between the individual and the environment, notably due to too many changes in too short a time (Toffler, 1970). The role of the environment is preponderant, but personal equations exist when facing stress. Everyone does not react in the same way. Although the causal relation has not been established, we admit that stress is at the origin of hypertension. Numerous researchers have shown that if stress has a link with hypertension, it is because of the sympathetic nervous system. Ostfeld suggests that obesity and the excess absorption of salt could also be incriminated in certain cases (Laborit, 1981).

3.3.1 Family insecurity

The DSM 4 scales the seriousness of factors of family stress. The more durable circumstances are detailed in parentheses:

Level 1.   **None.**

Level 2.   **Mild:** a romantic break-up, a child leaving the home (family conflicts, professional dissatisfaction, living in an area of high delinquency).

Level 3.   **Average:** marriage, separation, loss of employment, retirement, miscarriage (marital problems, heavy financial problems, difficulties with a superior, single parent).

Level 4.   **Serious:** divorce, birth of a first child (unemployment, poverty).

Level 5.   **Extreme:** death of a spouse, diagnosis of a serious physical illness, rape victim (serious illness, personal or of a child, repeated sexual or physical trauma).

Level 6.   **Catastrophic:** death of a child, suicide of a spouse, natural catastrophe (hostage situation, experience in a concentration camp).

3.3.2 Professional insecurity

The following is a list, on a scale of seven points, of the different levels of on-the-job insecurity:

Level 1.   **Nonexistent:** tenured civil service worker; chaired professor.

Level 2.   **Weak:** personnel representative; union protected personnel; dismissal impossible.

Level 3.   **Mild:** management status with considerable seniority; dismissal would prove to be extremely costly.

Level 4.   **Average:** manager without seniority on a long-term contract.

Level 5.   **Serious:** non-management personnel, on short-term contract.

Level 6.   **Maximum:** intern, temporary worker.

Level 7.   **Extreme:** foreigner in an irregular working situation, under the table "salary", paid in cash.

3.3.3 Organizational insecurity

Argyris (1970) shows that stress appears in the following situations:

1. the capabilities of both the "giver" and "receiver" are not sufficient to meet the requirements of the enterprise;
2. the nature of the contribution brought or received by each of the

constituents is modified unpredictably, that is to say outside of the work project;

3. the available time to accomplish the work is too short or too long;
4. the resources necessary to accomplish a task have been radically reduced or added to;
5. new functions appear unexpectedly and spontaneously.

Two Harvard economists, Bloom and Freeman, have shown that the percentage of U.S. employees covered by retirement insurance (social security) went from 75% in 1988 to 42% in 1994. Merton supported the argument that personality changes of members of an organization come from factors determined by the structure of the organization (March and Simon, 1974).

Argyris wrote: "mental health (of which the first index is the stress coefficient) depends on factors linked to work". In 1993, Anne-Marie Toniolo, using with experiments conducted with Wistar rats, showed that even the structure of the "cage–tunnel–pool" gives rise to anxiety.

Whatever the technology, there are always some individuals who can control their anxiety and others who cannot.

3.3.4 The abundance or scarcity of information

Stress is essentially put into play by the emotional alert inherent in the waiting for action, and by the impossibility of controlling the situation.

▶ "In other words, the signals accompanying an informational deficit… by the fact of their novelty or their unpredictableness, are particularly apt to provoke the release of surrenal corticoids." *(Laborit, 1981, p. 105)*

QUESTIONNAIRE 4

To what degree are you subject to stress?

Put a check in one column for each question using the key below:

1: I completely disagree
2: I mildly disagree
3: I'm not sure
4: I mildly agree
5: I completely agree

Connect the checks. The more your profile appears on the right-hand side, the more you have responded positively to the question.

	1	2	3	4	5
1. I don't have a steady job.					
2. I am unemployed.					
3. I am divorced.					
4. Daycare for my children is not working out.					
5. I have a lot of professional responsibilities.					
6. I take care of numerous family or professional conflicts.					
7. I have lost people close to me (death of parents, children).					
8. While growing up, my father was an absent (or weak) father.					
9. It is difficult to be organized.					
10. I never have enough time.					
11. I work on computer.					
12. We are never well-informed.					
13. I walk quickly.					
14. I like violent sports that take a lot of energy.					
15. I am sometimes so angry I surprise myself.					
16. I often think of death.					
17. Everyone I speak to is equally important.					
18. All my tasks are equally important.					
19. I bite my nails.					
20. I know the Bach Flower Remedies.					
21. Lexomil is an allopathic medicine.					
22. Gelsemium is a homeopathic medicine.					
23. I lack time.					
24. I always want to be precisely on time for my appointments.					
25. I don't know how to say no.					
26. I don't like to cause pain.					

4. Associated Emotional Conflict: "Approach–Avoidance"

At the heart of strong psychological pressure is a difficult choice: either accept the situation or to flee the situation. The difficulty comes from the double nature of the emotional warning. It always contains two cautions: the first, the inadequacy of personal strength and second, the "violent" nature of the situation.

In this arbitration, the value system, the strength of the personality and the stability of the self-image will all play a decisive role.

4.1 Arbitration

The person may endure the situation, even though it is a source of suffering or repugnance, because he cannot do otherwise. If he has a choice and he still chooses to endure it, it is because implicitly, he thinks he can "hold on" and that his courage will make him "adult" in his own eyes, according to his own standards of behavior. He thinks it will enhance his self-image, but he takes the risk of "damaging" it, and also risks creating a pathological feeling of self-valorization based on the status of victim that the group has given him.

If he flees the situation, it is either because he believes he cannot confront it without running a considerable risk, or he believes he has nothing to gain. He runs the risk of making an error and may "bring" the source of the difficulty with him (if it is more internal than external) and to see it reappear in the next situation. He also misses the opportunity to learn something and may develop the feeling of self-devalorization based on the pathological status of the "incompetent" within the group.

The problem for those living through this conflict is to be able to answer the question: Am I up to this? Am I able to face this? Is it a good risk to take? This conflict is often out of proportion given the internal stakes which are much higher than the stakes linked to the external situation.

▶ "When I signed the contract to do this training, it was way in the future. It was an important challenge for me. But, little by little, as it got closer, my psychic discomfort increased and showed itself in worry and the temptation to escape the situation: "and if I cancelled because of the weather?" The arbitration was always at the last minute, and always the same: "I have to go, because I gave my word." At this precise moment, the temptation to escape disappeared and all my worry turned into positive concentration. There was no longer the choice to go or not to go, and a sort of peace descended and this was still 24 hours before the task, the evening before." *(interview with a consultant, January 16, 1999)*

▶ Facing a new job proposal, a manager will live through the same conflict, the same arbitration, and it will be as painful as the first time the problem presented itself. Should he keep his old job or should he "make the jump"? The resale of a first apartment – or first house – provokes the same conflict. It is the past and the future that are being hung in the balance.

▶ During the last few decades, two behavioral arbitrations have been reversed. Within the couple, women are more and more the ones asking for divorce, whereas with employment, immediately quitting a job that didn't please you, although not rare during the years after the war, today has become exceptional and many managers stay at jobs they don't like…

▶ Researchers have differing points of view regarding the way to manage intrapsychic conflict:

► The experiment done on rats at Professor Krafft's laboratory of biological behavior at Nancy 1 (Desor, Tonniolo) had shown that if you separate rats from their food by an obligatory "pool" crossing, one rat, incited by the group, will willingly plunge into the water and go looking for his food, even though it will be stolen from him when he returns. Measurements have shown that it is the "thieves" that are the most stressed. This fact can be explained by observing that the satisfaction of their needs depends on the action of the others, and that action, no matter what its nature, relieves stress, whereas wait and inaction increase it...

► For Laborit (*In praise of flight*), it is the flight that allows one to preserve mental health.

► For Maslow (*psychology of being*), it is "approach" that allows one to "grow up".

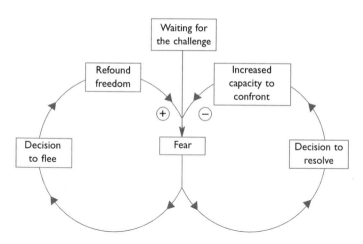

Exhibit 21 "Approach–avoidance" conflict

4.2 Pathological weakness

According to the DSM 4, borderline personality is characterized by insecurity and the instability of self-image. We know, today, that the love received in childhood constitutes one of the principal cements of self-image and the capacity to confront situations in adult life. It is this that will develop the sense of pleasure (or fear) in being with others. Experiments done with children have shown that those who are made to feel secure in parental love and attention will tend to choose games that are more complicated and risky (Fraisse and Piaget, 1963).

▶ "The essential characteristic of this disorder (borderline) is a generalized instability of self-image, interpersonal relationships and mood... An impressive and persistent disturbance of identity is almost always present. It is often diffused and is characterized by uncertainty concerning several fundamental questions such as self-image, professional direction... long term objectives, the adoption of a system of values." *(DSM III-R, 1992, p. 389)*

▶ A child, placed too young at the top of a ski run, will face a terrible choice. To descend or not to descend! If he chooses the second possibility, he will appear not to have controlled his fear, the fear that highlights the difference between the demands of the slope and what he feels are his capabilities. When a monitor orders him to descend and his submission to authority (3.9) makes him obey, he will experience a fright that may create a highly negative valence towards skiing, and he may hate this sport until the end of his days. The same process is set off when faced with the obligation to finish his plate when it's filled with a food he doesn't like.

---

5. The Practice of Counterfire

For certain actors, challenges represent an attraction, a promise of pleasure, without a doubt to fill a need or escape suffering or failure. They look for more and more difficult situations[7].

This fact is largely exploited by the film industry, among others *Apocalypse Now* (Coppola, 1979), *Itinéraire d'un enfant gâté* (Lelouch, 1988), *The City of Joy* (Joffé, 1993), *Platoon*... etc. People living through endemic affective deficits, put themselves voluntarily in high-risk situations and take on very difficult missions, i.e. leaving everything to live abroad, enlisting in the army in time of war, or practicing a high-risk sport.

In the psychoanalytic model it is called a death wish. But the emotional model allows us to support a completely different hypothesis, almost directly in opposition: the actor substitutes one situation for another; a situation of suffering that he cannot support, for a strongly aversive situation that will demand on his part a large amount of energy, but that he can "pilot". And, curiously, the suffering disappears and can even be replaced by other production, emotional, that is more positive and easier to master, like fear, fatigue or pain... In the case of success, it is possible that he'll be able to surpass himself, and do away with the emotional weak spot that was making him suffer.

1. In his present situation, the person is experiencing emotional production that is making him suffer.
2. He feels like a prisoner and a victim of himself, and he chooses to place himself willingly in more difficult situations.
3. Overcoming danger and risk provokes success and positive feelings and permits the reapprenticeship that will put previous failures into perspective.
4. He is aware of his capacity to succeed in something that he didn't believe himself capable of, and discovers the pleasure of piloting his own life. No return to step 1.

▶ During the 80's, I met some men, good company to be with, who were involved in hang gliding, although this sport was far from being safe. What astonished me was that in their lives, they were all involved in something that was very difficult (affective ruptures – grieving or separation – financial difficulties) and that they, more or less, consciously took on this very difficult sport in order to put their personal situations in perspective. I remember a wonderful moment, when for the first time, my machine, an "Azur", was swept up in an upstream air current, passing above the horizon, and I noticed that all that had preoccupied my every thought and every minute, several minutes earlier, and that had not given me one second of relief for months, seemed, all of a sudden, futile to me. A relatively minor experience, but it gave me a sense of perspective and the patience to wait out the end of a difficult period.

▶ In areas where it is very hard to "unlearn", as is the case for alcoholics, drug addicts or "special" children, certain "educators" apply the theory of counterfire, by placing adolescents in certain constrained situations, like expeditions, in order to give them the chance to overcome their difficulties.

▶ During the 60's, the interaction between the internal and external environment in organizational theory is reflected in the Palo Alto School: Jay Haley, Paul Watzlavick, John Grinder and Richard Bandler, John Weakland... Persuaded that the internal environment shapes its representations from this interaction, and that it is possible to help people modify them, the philosophy of the School dictates brief and, above all, operational therapy. The theory had been developed by J. Haley based on observing the work of Erikson. As soon as someone demonstrated their inability to get out of a situation on their own, where their involuntary behavior was continuing, even though it made them suffer and brought failure, Erikson set it up so that they would find the problem more difficult to keep than to get rid of. He rendered the pathological situation so painful that the patient would prefer to leave it, but it had to be done without the patient's knowledge – often under hypnosis – to avoid making him aware of it and to avoid him leaving psychotherapy. In Australia, a psychotherapist obtained results well above average in the curing of addicts by applying this theory of counterfire, but on a symbolic level (that is to say without risk). As an addict doesn't respect himself, he is not respected. The person continues to use drugs, but is submitted to the disrespect of all those around him. For example, someone else in the program would urinate on the addict... The treatment sets off, without fail, rebellion on the part of the addict and an awareness of the status he has given himself as an addict.

▶ In film, Bunuel illustrates this mechanism in the cult film, *Belle de Jour,* where Catherine Deneuve plays the role of a young, frigid woman who loves her husband, but who, to compel her body to "stop resisting pleasure", forces herself to prostitute for men whom she doesn't love. She is applying the technique of counterfire, in trying to "heal" a wrong with a wrong.

▶ In prisons, we find the same principle of behavior when the prisoners impose their own set of laws, so strict that the prison laws fade by comparison.

QUESTIONNAIRE 5

Test your capacity to anticipate

Put a check in one column for each question using the key below:

1: I completely disagree
2: I mildly disagree
3: I'm not sure
4: I mildly agree
5: I completely agree

Connect the checks. The more your profile appears on the right-hand side, the more you have responded positively to the question.

		1	2	3	4	5
1.	Do you force yourself to experience situations that make you are afraid?					
2.	Do you force yourself to watch a T.V. program that you truly hate?					
3.	Do you wish to cancel at the last moment, but go anyway?					
4.	Are you thirsty for new experiences?					
5.	Do you feel like a prisoner of your own behavior?					
6.	Do you feel like a prisoner of your own inhibitions?					
7.	Have you practiced high-risk sports?					
8.	Have you ever taken an appointment without knowing how it will end up?					
9.	Have you ever given an appointment without knowing what will happen?					

6.The Neurosis of the "Workaholic"

Numerous personality flaws, made up of chronic emotional deficits, are
the source of an inexhaustible desire to "fight" and not let go. Highly
successful careers, not only in the artistic domain, are linked to primary
deficiencies that only a permanent confrontation with difficulties will
compensate for. When there is an affective deficiency or a primary security
deficiency, there is suffering. Biologists have shown that the nervous
system, in reacting to this, produces the disappearance of negative
emotions, even if the action is completely useless. To act, to do something,
has a value, that in itself is independent of the results:

1. the person suffers from a chronic emotional deficiency,
2. she works, builds, faces the worst of situations, that she herself has
    constructed,
3. return to step 1.

6.1 The feeling of powerlessness

The feeling of powerlessness results from an incapacity to be loved, or
recognized, by people that the subject cannot allow himself to despise
(Peck, 1978, 1987). It gives rise to a powerful need for admiration. This
need feeds an inexhaustible motivation to always be on center stage.

1. the person feels powerless to make himself loved,
2. he spends an enormous amount of energy on charming his clients,
3. his commercial activity is a success,
4. return to step 1.

6.2 The feeling of helplessness

The original feeling of value is acquired in the first interactions between
life and the child. This fundamental flaw will feed a strong need, that of
feeling permanently useful. In order to experience this feeling, that will
consolidate the narcissistic flaw, the subject, when adult, will volunteer for
those tasks useful for his entourage, even if they are "degrading" and
rejected by others, and he will freely give himself over to the task.

1. the person is living with a personal narcissistic flaw,
2. this flaw produces permanent suffering,

3. he will volunteer for the most difficult of tasks, degrading or simply painful, and exert an enormous amount of organizational energy in his work,
4. he experiences a feeling of usefulness,
5. return to step 1.

▶ During some directed research in Professor Krafft's laboratory, a group of psychology students was asked to do a very unpleasant task – to inject a product in the stomach of one of the mice. If a student volunteered, he became the "slave" of the group for the rest of the year.

▶ In school it isn't rare, among students who have transferred in from other schools and therefore have something to prove, to find "hero–victim" behavior. For example, they may find themselves doing all the work for a group report, yet the report will be presented to the class by another student, a better speaker perhaps, but who had done no work.

▶ At the level of in-house company training, certain trainers[8] have developed the theory of manager–servant by drawing a hierarchical pyramid with the summit on the bottom, and the base on the top.

▶ As for religion, this approach has been well illustrated by the situation where Christ decides to wash the feet of his disciples.

6.3 The feeling of isolation

As early as 1959, Schacter (Fraisse and Piaget, 1963), demonstrated that anxiety stimulates a need for affiliation. The feeling of isolation and its influence on behavior can be observed experimentally in certain situations of transplantation far from home, such as in a war, a long mission abroad, prison, therapy groups (alcohol, tobacco and obesity treatment centers)… or Club Med.

We see that the feeling of isolation favors the acceptance of others' norms and the lowering of individual norms, in order to take refuge during a moment of isolation:

1. The person experiences a feeling of isolation,
2. He easily takes on the values of the group,
3. Return to step 1 or move on to step 4.
4. The person returns home,
5. He no longer feels isolated.

▶ Veterans, V.S.O.'s, ex-prisoners, returned G.M.'s, all testify to surprising changes, when upon returning home, they no longer have any interest at all in seeing the people with whom they have spent so much time during their stay. In effect, these people, being cut off from their homes, experienced a feeling of isolation that justifies their affiliative behavior and their search for friendship within that milieu. Upon their return, that feeling and behavior disappear.

▶ In the area of enterprises, failure at the end of a conflict creates a feeling of isolation and incites the search for alliance with yesterday's adversaries. Discord is forgotten in the need not to stay isolated in the face of greater dangers.

6.4 The incapacity to do nothing

Personality disorders, linked to permanent anxiety, often result in the person being ready to do anything, to help anybody, to always be ready to do a favor, because he cannot tolerate inaction. He cannot stay still. This person is on the permanent look-out for a source of action.

▶ "January, 1994. It was 10 p.m., and the bus was climbing the Avoriaz to take the group night snowmobiling, when it got stuck in the snow. The monitor suggested that the group continue walking for the time it would take to go get another, better equipped bus. Having a horror of waiting, I chose to go down with him and to get the snow chains out of my trunk. Thirty minutes later, we climbed back up, and pretty much in the same spot the new bus got stuck. I got off, and in a few seconds put my snow chains on the front wheels of the bus and we continued."

QUESTIONNAIRE 6

Do you face situations with courage?

Put a check in one column for each question using the key below:

1: I completely disagree

2: I mildly disagree

3: I'm not sure

4: I mildly agree

5: I completely agree

Connect the checks. The more your profile appears on the right-hand side, the more you have responded positively to the question.

		1	2	3	4	5
1.	I am best in difficult situations.					
2.	Do you feel you that fleeing is devaluing?					
3.	In a meeting, I always give my point of view, even at the risk of being looked badly upon.					
4.	When there is a problem I, first of all, try to solve it myself.					
5.	I always say what I feel.					
6.	If a request of mine has been denied, I continue to ask for it as many times as necessary, but change the wording a little each time.					
7.	If I start something, I finish it, out of self-respect.					
8.	They say when I have nothing to say you can cut out my tongue for it will no longer be of any use.					

7. Psychological Energy

Argyris (1970) has shown that psychological energy increases when the individual experiences psychological success, and it diminishes when she experiences failure. Following Argyris, two conditions are required to achieve psychological success:

1. People should give it value and aspire to experience a growing feeling of competence.
2. The organization should furnish work where people are capable of defining their immediate objectives, their own methods for achieving them, are able to self-evaluate their efficiency, and to continually grow in their competitiveness at work.

QUESTIONNAIRE 7

Test your psychological energy

Put a check in one column for each question using the key below:

1: I completely disagree

2: I mildly disagree

3: I'm not sure

4: I mildly agree

5: I completely agree

Connect the checks. The more your profile appears on the right-hand side, the more you have responded positively to the question.

	1	2	3	4	5
1. I often boost the morale of others.					
2. When I get to work in the morning, I bound up the stairs 4 at a time.					
3. I love what I do.					
4. When I'm tired, I change the activity and that refreshes me.					
5. In my leisure time, I prefer to act and produce (sport, activity), rather than passively watch T.V. or a movie.					
6. Life is beautiful.					
7. I am a believer.					
8. I make love often.					
9. If I have forgotten something, I don't hesitate to go back up to look for it.					
10. I am cheerful.					
11. People enjoy my company very much.					
12. I don't like to have nothing to do.					
13. I spend a lot of time on others.					
14. I like children.					

8. Resistance to Obstacles

The measure of the influence of failure on the psychological energy used to maintain a behavior was done experimentally in 1926 by C.-J. Warden (Sillamy, 1989). He had developed a machine, called an "obstacle cage", containing three parts: the one in the middle contained an electrified plank, whereas the other two extremes were situated in two compartments, one of which contained the rat and the other the "objective". The animal was put in and the number of attempts that it made to reach the "objective" before the activity was abandoned, was counted. A mother, separated from its young, exposed herself 22 times to pain in order to find them. Thirst produced 20 passes through, hunger 18, sex 13...

Examples of resistance in the face of obstacles:

> ▶ The most impressive testimony to obstacle resistance is that of Jerome, 22 years old, caught in a family "hell" concerning finances. He takes the bus, then walks, sleeps rough but always appears impeccable, knocks on the door of 131 enterprises in all the industrial zones around Poitiers. Hired for three days as an inventory assistant for one of these, he arrives early and stays 2 or 3 hours extra. At the end of his last day, the director calls him in, expresses his admiration and tells him that he has nothing available but one of his friends... and with that Jerome starts his sales career, earning 98% of sales in his first week. (interview, January 22, 1999)

▶ As pedagogic manager, I had taken on the project of developing an internal collection of manuals and works for the university that I belonged to. In 1994, I presented my project to the group of professors. A colleague suggested that the works should contain an international dimension, which was equivalent to a refusal, as it would be impossible at a first attempt and could only be achieved slowly. In fact, this project would mean a lot more work for those who participated, but if successful, would leave the others behind "in the dust"... 1995, I hadn't had my last word on the subject and I came back for another attack, but this time in front of a more restricted committee – the management committee – entry to which at least leant credibility to a quality project. Unfortunately, I made a mistake and presented a financial figure which terrified the financial director. Project rejected. Yet, I remained convinced of its importance. 1996, I had at my disposal a pedagogic budget and the principal needs of this area being fulfilled, I had the perverse idea to send a short memo: "the pedagogic budget will be reserved this year for the creation of a collection of manuals". No one reads memos, and those that do read them, believe in general that they are already endorsed. There was absolutely no reaction. The first manual came out and was a success. The following year, four works were published. The year after 25, and in 1999, 8 of them were accepted by four national editors and one international. The budget today has surpassed by 40% the budget that was refused in 1995, and we have just created a permanent position for the management of this.

Examples of abandonment in the face of obstacles:

▶ "The first project that I presented was refused. I then became involved in another project. At the end of three months of intense involvement, I presented it and it was also refused. In September, during a presentation for a third project, I discovered that a counter-project, solicited by the management, had been worked on by a member of my department, without my being notified. Disappointed and tired, I chose to withdraw my dossier and, after one year of obstacles, I asked to be discharged from the mission in question."

▶ "It was in 1982, I already had about 100 hours of microlight flying when I took my first lesson in an airplane. My error had been in calling a friend. During one full hour, he constantly reprimanded me, without a doubt because he was afraid, as I wasn't executing my turns very well, there were no foot pedals. I got out of the plane with tears in my eyes and I have never got back in the pilot's seat again. I believe I can say now that since that time, I dread all apprenticeships with a monitor. I prefer to manage on my own." (note from the author: the valence of apprenticeship has become negative)

▶ "I had done the 'wall' (rock climbing) during my youth, but the day of my first tennis match, my opponent kept me running from one side of the court to the other. He knew that I had never played before. I got to the balls, but in a state of disgust, I sold my rackets and never played tennis again."

▶ "It was my first language course in the 5th grade, and after a few lessons, the teacher asked that we write something. Mine was 20 lines long and I received a grade of 20 on it, my best friend – with whom there was some competition – had written 2 lines and received a 90. When questioned, my teacher told me that there were too many mistakes and I answered that had I only written two lines, there wouldn't have been as many errors, but he didn't want to know. I immediately asked to change my chosen language."

QUESTIONNAIRE 8

Are you resistant to obstacles?

Put a check in one column for each question using the key below:

1: I completely disagree
2: I mildly disagree
3: I'm not sure
4: I mildly agree
5: I completely agree

Connect the checks. The more your profile appears on the right-hand side, the more you have responded positively to the question.

		1	2	3	4	5
1.	Are you capable of going to an exam for nothing else but for the fact that you don't like to be caught?					
2.	If someone contradicts you, do you spend a lot of energy trying to get him to change his mind?					
3.	Your sink leaks, and this is the third time you've fixed it. Are you capable of doing it again for the fourth time rather than call a plumber?					
4.	If a girl (or a guy) turns down a date, are you capable of insisting until he (or she) changes their mind?					
5.	In your favorite sport, when you try something new, are you capable of doing it over again even though you have the feeling that you will never be able to do it?					
6.	If a salesperson refuses to give you a discount, do you insist until he accepts, even for 1% off, just on principle?					

9. Avoiding Challenge

The dread of aversive situations can be the result of either the incapacity to control them, or is pathological, as in the case of avoidance personality.

9.1 Laborit's experiments

H. Laborit showed the superiority of flight for rats placed in aversive situations. A cage had a double compartment with the door in a separating wall. A bell would warn the Wistars rat that an electrical current would pass through the floor of his box and immediately the rat would run into the other compartment. Taken back to the animal shelter, the rats ate, drank and copulated well and had no hypertension.

9.2 Flight, adapted to the situation

This type of flight results from the disequilibrium between the situation and what the manager can modify. In effect, if the challenge is out of proportion to strength or means of action, flight is a rational behavior.

1. the individual is faced with a challenge,
2. the risk is evaluated as excessive,
3. he looks for a program to allow him to escape the situation.

► A regional establishment had a paid director who ran a computer service that wasn't doing well because the head of the department, who acted very independently, had gotten into the habit of consecrating 80% of his time to taking care of the files for his hunting society. Everyone knew this, but no one said anything to the general director, for the department head was someone feared and dreaded. The ambiance was abominable and vacillated between fatalism and the magic hope that somehow things would work out by themselves. A high-level computer person was hired by the director of the establishment. She discovered the problem, but didn't say anything either because she feared that the ambiance would just get worse, as the department head, who was nice to her at the beginning was now, already, being extremely difficult. She left the company two years later...

► When I began hang gliding, if I ever forgot to check anything, however slight, during the take-off procedure, I would cancel the flight, not because there was danger from the thing forgotten, but because it was an indication that I had insufficient concentration.

▶ In the 60's, industries who developed compensation packages for volunteers in order to "trim" the staff, were victims of a particular phenomenon: high-quality workers who were sure to find jobs elsewhere left, whereas those who thought they would never find jobs again stayed.

▶ Flight from work is common. Absenteeism has gone up from 5% to more than 15% in 30 years, to cite one measure, but there are much more impressive cases than that: we report the case of a depressed postal worker, in whose home were found more than ten sacks of non-distributed mail. Repetitive strikes transform work boredom into an emotionally rich time. Certain job posts are submitted to such psychological pressure that it is impossible to keep to a traditional framework. Job rotation is instituted (certain police jobs or hostess/reception jobs), or vacations are longer (teachers).

People who are fired, or who quit, rather than submit passively, leave those situations where they cannot bring about improvements, and they do it because they have confidence in their ability to find something else much more interesting elsewhere. They accord themselves more value – following their own criteria – than those who choose to stay in place and passively submit.

10. Neurosis of the "Fugitive"

10.1 The haste to decide is a flight from internal conflict

> Beyond all illusion, lives a decision-maker facing his internal conflict. (Jarrosson 1994)

According to P. Drücker (1976) and S. Peck (1978, 1987), if everything is agreed to very quickly, it is probably due to a collective flight from the internal conflict provoked by the problem. The first decisional "reflex" is a response to something that worries us, and that we must get rid of. In these conditions, it is important to step back from the problem and to wait until all the managers concerned are called and asked their opinion. If we demand an immediate solution, it is because we cannot tolerate our discomfort long enough to analyze the situation.

▶ "Drücker also tells us that one of the most important things that he has learned in his life, was taught to him by an ex-president of General Motors: one day, an astounding project was proposed during a committee session and among the 50 people present there, no one could see any objections. After having questioned each one, the president sat down and said: you see, I can't think of any objections either to this project and in these conditions I suggest that the decision be postponed until next month." At the next committee meeting the project was turned down..." *(Effective decisions, 1976)*

10.2 The avoiding personality

According to Maslow, it is probable that this type of personality has not known psychological success, but for Laborit, it is the only way to preserve his equilibrium:

1. the individual faces a challenge,
2. the situation is evaluated, not as risky, but as disagreeable,
3. he looks for a program to allow him to avoid it.

▶ A study of two factories in which the majority of employees described the atmosphere as pleasant seemed suspicious: when we asked them how "pleasant" people behave and 90% declared: "Pleasant people are those who leave you alone and who you almost never see." *(Argyris, 1957)*

▶ "Avoiding-type personalities are easily hurt by criticism and are distraught at the slightest look of disapproval. These subjects are reticent about forming ties with others, unless they have a solid guarantee of unconditional approval. As a consequence, they have no friends. They have the tendency to avoid social or professional activities that could bring them important contacts... A generalized timidity brings about a resistance to do things outside of their routine. The subject often exaggerates potential difficulties, physical dangers or risks taken by an activity that is banal but that differs from their routine. They could, for example, cancel a trip because of strong rains that may make the road slippery." *(DSM-III-R, 1992, p. 396)*

QUESTIONNAIRE 9

Are you an avoider?

Put a check in one column for each question using the key below:

1: I completely disagree

2: I mildly disagree

3: I'm not sure

4: I mildly agree

5: I completely agree

Connect the checks. The more your profile appears on the right-hand side, the more you have responded positively to the question.

	1	2	3	4	5
1. I prefer to travel alone.					
2. Criticism hurts me deeply.					
3. I don't like someone if they don't approve of what I'm doing.					
4. I don't have many friends.					
5. In my leisure time, I prefer to practice sports or activities alone.					
6. I am extremely prudent.					
7. I fear accidents and do my best to avoid them.					
8. When I was young, my brothers and sisters hit me.					
9. I was always afraid in the yard at school.					
10. I don't see why I should do things that displease me.					
11. I prefer to stay at home.					
12. In life, one must avoid boring people and situations.					

11. Passive Acceptance of Challenge: Doing Nothing and Inhibition

The story of the donkey of Buridan, unable to choose between the carrot and the cabbage, is generally considered as the perfect illustration of the inhibition of decision.

11.1 The inhibition bundle

It has been shown that the brain has two particular bundles, isolated by Old and Milner (1954) and identified as the MFB[9] and the PVS[10]. One is the "activator" of action and the other is the "inhibitor" of action. If one is "debited" more than the other, the choice appears simple. If both are "debited" at the same time and in the same amount, the individual will appear as if paralyzed. Double debit is often the product of earlier failures that are superimposed on the current situation. Inhibition is thus the product of the simultaneous experience of pleasure and of suffering. An action is desired, but the acquired experience is negative and the person is afraid. He moves onto inhibition.

> ▶ According to Delgado, one can electronically activate the inhibitor bundle. A Spanish neurosurgeon was so sure of the location of inhibition that he went into the arena face to face with a furious bull, after having implanted an electrode in the rhinencephalitic amygdale of the bull's brain, permitting him, using a remote command, to instantaneously stop the bull's approach. (Cyrulnik, 1993, p. 133)

▶ The inhabitants of Nepal countryside say that during an encounter with a wild animal, you must speak to him, and look him straight in the eye. This will inhibit a part of his aggressiveness by setting off the inhibitor bundle in the brain. This last remark, made by academics, has saved many lives in the battle against tigers. The tiger, incapable of tolerating a stare, always attacks from behind. To reduce the risk of being attacked to zero, it is sufficient while travelling in these dangerous zones, to wear a mask on the back of the head on which two large eyes are drawn.

▶ If a pike is separated from its food by a glass, it will throw itself violently against the glass. After 3 days, the glass is removed and the pike, inhibited, will die of hunger, even though its food is within reach.

▶ The experiment of H. Laborit on Wistar rats is famous: a rat is enclosed in a cage without exit when a bell warns him that he will shortly receive electrical shocks from the floor. For a while, the rat explores the cage, looking for an exit. Then he no longer reacts and when returned to the shelter, he has lost his appetite, no longer copulates and has hypertension.

11.2 The wait

There is worse than worse, there is the waiting for worse. (Gilbert Cesbron)

The wait for a challenge or trial, coupled with the impossibility to act, provokes an almost intolerable emotional production in the person who is waiting, and this is even more so when the challenge concerns an important turning point in his life. This production is such that the challenge so dreaded can be wished for, and seen as a relief after a long wait.

Anxiety will be the painful feeling attached to this wait for a situation, an event or an object that one cannot yet classify as gratifying or aversive. It is thus linked to risk: this latter is a measure of the difference between the event *ex post* and what one imagined *ex ante*. In this prediction, there are two fundamental facts:

1. the fact of knowing if the new situation will be defined as gratifying or aversive,
2. the fact of knowing if the definition of the situation is connected to the true existing situation, or if it is the product of a bad interpretation from our nervous system.

▶ In May 1968, military personnel, all voluntarily enlisted, had to wait for several days to be called to intervene in a problematic situation concerning students. One of them declared: "If they had called us, I believe that we would have starting beating up on them like we were crazy, that's how much we were fed up and how much we had to let off steam…"

▶ Headhunters know not to make candidates wait: "D. couldn't receive him, and I had to do something to make him wait, but when D. was finally able to see him, he had already been waiting 45 minutes and he was clearly at the end of his rope. He literally hit D. in the face and left…" *(interview, February 2, 1999)*

▶ In 1976, Scitovsky cited a study from the Berlyne enterprise on convicts that showed that "uncertainty about the time left in prison constitutes one of the principal causes of moral suffering in a prisoner. Those that hoped to be freed soon on parole suffer a lot more than those who know that they are in for life.

QUESTIONNAIRE 10

Do you lack patience?

Put a check in one column for each question using the key below:

1: I completely disagree
2: I mildly disagree
3: I'm not sure
4: I mildly agree
5: I completely agree

Connect the checks. The more your profile appears on the right-hand side, the more you have responded positively to the question.

		1	2	3	4	5
1.	When my companion doesn't return on time, do I imagine the worst?					
2.	When I am kept waiting for an appointment, am I angry at the person?					
3.	I don't like long introductions.					
4.	I don't know how to eat slowly, without hurrying, even if I'm not hungry.					
5.	I don't like to arrive late.					
6.	I can break off a relationship with someone who is not on time for a date.					
7.	Punctuality is the courtesy of kings.					
8.	A road accident that stops me in traffic for an hour deeply upsets me.					

11.3 The feeling of injustice and discouragement

The beginner is self-motivated, driven by a pleasure principle, by his desires, beliefs and hopes. The quality of his organizational life is largely conditioned by an apprenticeship of resistance to frustration originating from the gap between the reality of the organizational environment and the imagined one that drives his internal environment. Pleasure principle and reality principle are in a permanent fight, with a resulting wish either to quit, or to patiently continue the apprenticeship of efficiency. Not only does the organization possess no means to motivate the beginner, but it supplies him with a veritable combat course that is comprised of a dozen daily reasons to be demotivated. The first source of discouragement, which will be felt all the more because he has worked so hard, is linked to the multitude of rumors about company decisions or incomprehensible behavior, where logic has absolutely no intelligent rapport with the desire to resolve problems, but seems destined to favor or protect the players. These conflictual knots are everywhere but, without a doubt, more powerful in societies where a large body of the members are protected and solidly implanted in the organization. Even outside of the context of action, the first challenge that awaits the young manager is the establishment of a solid resistance to the daily frustration that leads to a feeling of injustice. A manager who wants to survive in such a context must learn to act in the domain that is his own, and not let himself be immobilized by the sea of daily causes that weighs down the organization. He must admit that the organization is not a problem-resolving machine, but a place of conflict and of struggle for power, and that to succeed means to understand this and to use it to his advantage.

> ▶ An excellent salesperson, achieving on his own 50% of the sales figures in a very difficult period, observed that his colleagues were transmitting their own requests under his name, because they had noticed that due to his performance, the requests were more easily accepted by management. The writers of these requests would thank him facetiously for this.

11.4 The size of the group

A person alone comes more easily to the aid of another in difficulty. The larger the group, the larger the inhibition to help those in distress (Latané and Rodin, cited by Fraisse and Piaget, 1963).

▶ "I had taken my daughter to school, when a thick column of smoke indicated a fire starting in a house nearby. Parking my car, I ran immediately to help the obviously insufficient chain of four men who were taking furniture and clothes out of the house whose roof was burning. When the firemen arrived, we stopped and noticed that a group of 20 women were standing, a little farther away, looking at the impressive fire, commenting sadly, but not moving."

▶ J. Cameron's film *Titanic* tells of this dramatic behavior: when the lifeboats, filled with wives and their daughters, were half filled, the women remained inert in front of their husbands who were yelling and screaming at them, and their brothers who were dying in icy water just a few feet from them. One man, a sailor, after long hesitation, was the only one who, alone, saved six of these men.

▶ Collective catastrophes also create a factor of inhibition. We heard that a husband having been warned of a imminent flood in his village, had in turn warned the inhabitants who didn't budge.

▶ Certain speeches or the exaggerated behavior of a politician in front of a large audience works very well. When it is shown on television, in the intimacy shared by the family, he appears vulgar or at the very least, someone not to be trusted.

11.5 The religious influence

The influence is very strong in the Judeo-Christian ethic where challenge is often considered as having a divine origin. The Bible tells you to passively submit, as it is a test of faith. And yet, after the Flood, God had promised to no longer interfere in the affairs of men, and in this new alliance, human challenge was no longer of divine origin.

▶ It is written that "not one horse will fall on its head without God having wanted it so[11]!". Didn't Christ himself, facing the challenge of the cross plead in vain, without result[12]? Wasn't his attitude considered as an example to follow for all Christians? Isn't it written that if someone hits you on one cheek, you turn and offer him the other?[13] Or wasn't even Job ruined by God, uniquely to test his faith?[14]

11.6 Inhibition and survival

To illustrate the positive role of inhibition in certain situations, Jacques Donnars tells us that, in Nepal, he found himself in a situation facing a tiger with the wind not in his favor. His guide had said something impossible to translate, but whose sense was approximately "block your odors". Was this state of inhibition provoked by fear, by will or by chance? Anyway, the tiger passed them by without picking up their scent.

11.7 Inhibition and illness

> All that oppose a gratifying action, or who appease an innate or acquired need, put into play an endocrinosympathetic reaction, which, if it lasts, is harmful to the peripheral organs. This reaction gives rise to feelings of anxiety and is at the origin of those illnesses termed 'psychosomatic'. (Laborit, 1976, p. 27)

Inhibition is the ultimate defense mechanism; it is simultaneously positive and negative.

11.8 Inhibition and anxiety

Extreme worry, irrational fear and anxiety are not only a pathological phenomenon. It is linked to the human incapacity to control all situations of which the most powerful symbol is the confrontation with death. Anxiety is a painful situation of profound discomfort, determined by the diffuse impression of a vague, imminent danger, in face of which we are unarmed and powerless (Sillamy, 1989). The feeling of anxiety usually lasts a few minutes, more rarely several hours: weakness in the legs, sweating, palpitations, drop in blood pressure, stomach pains, diarrhea, backache and chest pains (DSM III-R, 1992). In this case, the person no longer recognizes the situation as the cause of this discomfort, unless all "signals" are on he can only be aware of the reflexive action of the sympathetic nervous system. The violent increase of anxiety is demonstrated by the fact that the person, surprised by this reaction, may begin to yell or talk, but only when they are alone. Anxiety is often at the source of many health problems – migraines and pains in the side – the easing of which is very welcome, indicating to us that, to use an appropriate term, we can breathe a little easier for the moment (Paucard, 1988). Anxiety could be "sought out" in certain situations: therapy, for example, destroys a system of defense against anxiety and suffering (Maslow, 1968). It does this so that the person can refind the path towards his/her "center".

In summary:

1. the manager finds himself facing a challenge,
2. he takes stock of the programs he has at his disposal to resolve the situation,
3. the execution programs are successful, end of program; or they are deemed inoperable and rejected, go to step 4.
4. the manager deploys resolution activity which is demonstrated by a high level of search activity,
5. the resolution activity is successful, end of program; or it fails, go on to step 6,
6. return to step 4 then move on to step 7, more or less rapidly in function of his **resistance to the obstacle**,
7. he inventories the programs he has to flee from the situation,
8. the flight programs are successful, end of program; or they fail, move on to step 9,
9. return to step 2 or 4 or 7 then continue on to step 10, more or less rapidly in function of his **resistance to the obstacle**,
10. he doesn't know what to do, and inhibits action,
11. this inhibition becomes an endemic state,
12. appearance of health problems.

QUESTIONNAIRE 11

Are you inhibited?

Put a check in one column for each question using the key below:

1: I completely disagree

2: I mildly disagree

3: I'm not sure

4: I mildly agree

5: I completely agree

Connect the checks. The more your profile appears on the right-hand side, the more you have responded positively to the question.

	1	2	3	4	5
1. I am often angry at myself for not having taken the first step.					
2. Sometimes I have the impression that life is passing me by.					
3. At the top of a ski lift, I have become paralyzed, incapable of pushing myself downhill.					
4. When I make love, I often feel no desire.					
5. I would like to dress in a different way, more colorful, but I don't dare.					
6. You mustn't shock people, it's not appropriate.					
7. I never speak in public, yet I have things to say.					
8. Be beautiful and shut up!					
9. I am capable of violent reactions that I, myself, don't understand.					
10. I have had a strict upbringing.					
11. My parents taught me to fear life rather than to be confident.					
12. I never know what to do with my hands.					

12. A Brief Overview of This Chapter

12.1 The challenge

Situation analysis allows one to be involved in a process of rectification. The manager has changed his status: from observer, he has become actor. He has gone straight to the heart of the situation.

12.2 Fear

Out of this face-to-face confrontation will be born a feeling of threat, a sort of "interior pressure". The actor must arbitrate: he accepts to endure this pressure in order to resolve the situation, or he decides to cut loose from the situation and flee.

12.3 The approach–avoidance conflict

This situation of choice turns into an internal state that we call interior conflict. In this choice (between staying or going), self-image and all strengths are analyzed and pass under review. Some, more solid than others, are less perturbed by this choice; they also have less to prove.

Exhibit 22 Ladder of dread

12.4 Psychological energy

Acquired through psychological success which pushes the actor to hold on and confront. Flaws of personality can also motivate the actor to jump in (or to surpass himself in order to rebuild).

12.5 Therapy of counterfire

Those who have lived through very difficult situations are better equipped than others. What others may consider insurmountable problems are considered as "peccadilloes" to them. The others, in order to harden themselves, must impose these situations on themselves. Facing an insurmountable situation, the best means to overcome it is to impose on yourself something even more difficult, but psychologically more apt to be mastered. That is counterfire.

12.6 The impossibility to act

Facing obstacles, some will give up, others will not, but all will go through a veritable internal block as if the scale was stuck at zero, with them staying in a position of inaction. It is the surest means of failing and of experiencing anxiety.

CHAPTER 3

Hierarchical Situations: Obedience

Begin with a confrontation with an aversive situation, add confrontation with the hierarchy, and you have a situation with double constraints, giving rise to all sorts of pathology. If the subordinate succeeds brilliantly, he finds himself in competition with his superior. Thus, the hierarchical situation is essentially conflictual, whether the subordinate succeeds or fails. The weight of the hierarchy is that much heavier when the actor is at the bottom of the pyramid, and the emotional conflict that results from the double confrontation is all the more profound if the gap between what is demanded by the situation, and what is demanded by the superior is great. Finally, emotional blindness, a product of isolation, grants both power and silence to the subordinate and increases this vicious circle. Reactions are varied, but facing an unacceptable order, 63% of subordinates will completely accept the principle of submission to an authority that they respect, while others will find some form of more or less active resistance.

> Life is not about climbing up the corporate ladder, it is about combining work and pleasure. (D. Boulanger, ICN, September 23, 1994)

In the preceding chapter, we examined challenging situations and how the actor tries to confront them. The relationship between actor and situation is one of constraint. The situation imposes its "law" and the actor tries to resolve the situation or to escape from it. The introduction of a hierarchy imposes a second constraint and adds to the "law" of the situation that of the hierarchy. Finally, because of emotional blindness, the hierarchical "law" is sometimes not congruent with that of the situation, bringing with it a risk of pathology. It results in an eternal struggle between the actor and his hierarchy that could range from active resistance to passive submission.

1. Material Situation Linked to Place in the Hierarchy

The hierarchy is a relationship of order, of classification of the actors in conjunction with a norm that has been rendered operational by a operative process.

1.1 The stakes of dominance

Access to resources is the first consequence of the attribution of a place on the human, or animal, hierarchical ladder. In the animal hierarchy, the resources are: water, food and females, available first to the dominant and then ex-dominant males. In the human hierarchy, access to resources also remains a determining element, the true power that an actor has at his disposal. They are simply more extensive: financial resources, for example, come first in the industrial and commercial world[1], but also in the political or entertainment arena, where sexual resources and access to sexual partners could represent serious power stakes. Information also constitutes an essential resource in different organizations. The possession of a diploma – guarantee of the individual's capacity – constitutes an almost required resource in today's organizations. Other actors are also resources and **the capacity to be able to act and modify the behavior of others** is a second source of power: having devoted friends, having the ability to organize individual work so that the collective objective is obtained, or being able to delegate work you don't want, etc.

Finally, the last source of power is that of internal resources – know-how, experience, knowledge, being multilingual, computer use, etc. Chapter 1 of this book developed the operational modes of acquisition of these resources that allow one to dominate in a **zone of ignorance or uncertainty** – the actor is indispensable there where the other actors need him (Crozier and Friedberg, 1977). Without experience, without friends, without a partner, without information, without a diploma and without money, the actor is highly diminished and loses his quality of being an actor, for in this case, he is no more than an observer…

1.2 The operative process

Hierarchical classification implies an operative process. The most widely used process today in France concerns higher education, **tests and competitive exams**, that – according to the quality of the school and academic placement upon graduating – determines the first job that's possible to obtain. A second process concerns the ownership of capital that allows you to protect your authority. In case of dissonance between the inheritance and the capacity to manage, failure is the result. The operative process in the latter case are the decisions and choices the manager makes. He is the owner of these decisions, he assumes the risk and he is the sole judge. Reality will sanction his decision and his heritage will allow him to take the consequences. The process of **promotion** that enables one to rise up the corporate ladder is based on results, but, in France, the door remains firmly closed by the higher-echelon schools that consider the level in question reserved for those who have first passed through its doors. It still exists. Finally, career change, and the ability to obtain higher-level posts, are a question of one's **personal network, or "address book"**... For other countries, the reader can refer to the work by G. Deloffre[2].

1.3 Revenue and hierarchy

In the U.S., between 1977 and 1987, the revenue of people belonging to the lowest 10% of income category decreased by 10%, the people belonging to the top 10% increased their revenue by 24.4%, and those belonging to the top 1%, increased by 74.2%. Between 1990 and 1995, salaries of 362 directors of the largest companies increased by 92%. (Chanlat, 1990, p. 30)

1. the more the means exist to climb up the corporate ladder,
2. the more the employee will find himself low in the hierarchy,
3. the greater the number of people in the company,
4. the more the employee will live with the anxiety of feeling dependent, and in certain cases, a feeling of alienation, impotence or abandonment,
5. the more he will live with distress, as he must inhibit action in order to survive these situations as well as keep his place in the organization.

2. Emotional Situation Linked to Place in the Hierarchy

2.1 Happiness and hierarchy

A number of American research reports, cited by Scitovsky (1976), show that increased revenue brings absolutely no increase in personal happiness (as estimated according to the subjects' own norms), whereas to rise above others brings about a significant increase in the response "very happy" to the question "how do you see yourself?" The number of people who classify themselves as "very happy" goes from 10% for those low on the corporate ladder to 80% for those high up on the corporate ladder. These results should be compared with those of Laborit (1981), who showed that only the individual placed on the top of the pyramid finds personal balance, whereas individuals placed somewhere in the middle are obliged to inhibit action, and the inhibition itself causes distress and blocks happiness.

2.2 Anxiety and hierarchy

In 1977 it was shown that hypertension is related to socioeconomic status and that it is three to four times more frequent at lower economic levels. For animals, anxiety is also a function of the hierarchical place occupied within the clan[3]. In general, the higher the place in the hierarchy, the less dense the corticoadrenal secretions are (Laborit, 1981).

2.3 Mental health and hierarchy

Kornhauser (1977) demonstrated that it was possible to establish an index of mental health based on six points: "anxiety", "hostility", "social partic-ipation" (in contrast to withdrawing into oneself), "self-esteem" (feeling good about oneself), "morality" (in contrast to amoral), and "general life satisfaction". He concludes that when workers are classified by their level of competence and the diversity of their tasks, the index given for mental health is in straight positive correlation with their hierarchical level (Argyris, 1970).

3. Alienation, Impotence and Surrender

3.1 Definition

If the activity of an actor is characterized by slow and progressive dwin-dling of energy and the low level of his earnings doesn't seem to satisfy his most elementary needs nor those of his family, he has the choice between working harder and putting his health at risk, or accepting an austere lifestyle dominated by money worries. He loses the character of "actor" and becomes a stake in the game, a piece of merchandise (Marx, 1938).

A series of experiments carried out with lab rats confirm the hypoth-esis: a cage, separated into two distinct parts, has an electrified floor with a voltage high enough to be extremely stressful for the rats. Each compartment is equipped with a special pedal switch, but only one is connected and will effectively cut the electrical current in both cages. Even though they are situated in two different compartments, each rat receives *exactly* the same amount of current, as they are on the same floor. Yet, only the rat that has access to the working switch remains in good health, whereas the other quickly establishes the absence of the possibility to act on the situation, and its health deteriorates.

> ▶ The person who feels alienated has the impression of literally being a stranger to herself. She doesn't feel as if she is the creator of her acts and behaviors. These acts are imposed on her, they have become the masters, she obeys them as if she were sleepwalking. The alienated person loses all contact with herself and with others; she no longer has any true relation with anyone.

3.2 Organizational sources

In 1964, Robert Blaumer attempted to study the power of alienation in an entire range of technologies. He put forth the hypothesis that certain technologies alienate more than others. Put more simply, he said that work in occupational industries (baker, shoemaker, computer technician) were the most satisfying, the least satisfying being those jobs in factory assembly lines (Silverman, 1970).

For Pearlin (1961), it is the psychological distance maintained between management and employees that would be responsible for the feeling of impotence, itself responsible for the feeling of alienation. He confirmed the feeling of impotence felt by personnel in a psychiatric hospital and showed that it had two causes:

1. it exists where there is a large distance between the positions of the authority figures and those of their subordinates,
2. it exists where the orders are communicated in such a way as to avoid or discourage any reciprocal influence (Argyris, 1970).

It has been shown elsewhere that the bureaucratic model results in a reduction of individualized relationships. We can thus support the theory that the feeling of impotence, both cause and source of stress in threatening situations, develops in those systems that strongly favor efficiency over personal relationships.

In certain government departments in Moscow, the telephone handset is only equipped with the listening end. The "microphone" part is reserved for those who give the orders.

3.3 Personal sources: the abandoning personality

> The investment of the Ego increases proportionately to the disinvestment in exterior objects or subjects. (Freud, cited by Peretti, 1981, p. 34)

The abandoner had to live through a large deficit of affection, at the age when dependence was total. Inhibition of survival took over and the abandoner could only conceive of himself as having no value whatsoever. How can you make him believe that he is the only person who counts when no one loved him as a child? It is the typical case where psychoanalysis founded on frustration doesn't work.

▶ "I remember immense happiness when my psychoanalyst agreed to lend me a newspaper I had started to read in the waiting room. With such emotion I photocopied the article and drove back across town to bring it back immediately. It was the first time that my substitute mother had concretely loved me." *(interview, March 26, 1999)*

3.4 Behavior, faced with alienation

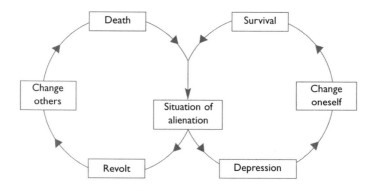

Exhibit 23 Dynamics of alienation

▶ "The depressed person is entrenched in his state of being; he is entrenched in his resignation. He could go on strike and show his disapproval but his depression is a solution of acceptance… When this solution is no longer tolerable, revolt arises: to revolt is to no longer accept his condition, to no longer accept to find himself in a path with no exit, to no longer know how to survive… Revolt is essentially anger, an anger that has become cold… a muted determination throws the individual into action sometimes towards others, sometimes towards himself… As long as the process is situated at the level of the neocortex, the intellect, nothing happens… When it arrives at the level of the archeocortex, the affective brain, impulses and more dangerous desires appear… When the limbic or reptilian brain is started up… it sets off instinctive motor impulses, violent and mute at the same time… Even if the logical brain decides to stop, the underlying mechanism doesn't follow suit… Revolt, different from revolution, will never begin (for it is looking on the outside for a reason for failure, while it is interior)… revolt knows that this inefficiency is pre-written in the act. It knows that the mechanisms that it has started up will lead to more serious failure, to death, or its symbolic equivalents." *(Donnars, 1984, pp. 2–24)*

Exhibit 24 Different logics of alienation		
Internal environment	**External environment**	
	Strongly alienating situation	**Weakly alienating situation**
Reject situation	Rational logic	Personality "in revolt"
Accept situation	"Abandoning" personality	Rational logic

1. The actor is alienated by his life, his scheduling, his work, etc. Go to 2 or 3.
2. The actor revolts against the environment by moving into action. Go to 4.
3. The actor is depressed but modifies his behavior, go to 5.
4. His revolt fails, and he feels even worse. Go back to 1.
5. His personal development allows him to modify his life and to take new decisions.

QUESTIONNAIRE 12

Do you feel alienated?

Put a check in one column for each question using the key below:

1: I completely disagree

2: I mildly disagree

3: I'm not sure

4: I mildly agree

5: I completely agree

Connect the checks. The more your profile appears on the right-hand side, the more you have responded positively to the question.

	1	2	3	4	5
1. Do you feel that no matter what you do you can't change your destiny?					
2. Whatever happens is God's will.					
3. Do you have long periods of emptiness, where you can't seem to do anything?					
4. Do you sometimes feel beaten?					
5. Does it make you anxious to watch violence on T.V.?					
6. Come what may…					
7. It's useless to vote, right or left it's the same thing.					
8. Only the right wing wants to change things…					
9. Why get divorced? In 10 years, the same thing would happen with someone else…					
10. I prefer not to think…					
11. If work is health, doing nothing will preserve it…					
12. This questionnaire is ridiculous, I'm not answering anymore, what is the use of this?					

4. Feelings of Dependence

The feeling of dependence is paradoxical, as it originates from a need that has been satisfied. To escape distress, the individual wishes to obtain external conditions of security. Once put in place, these conditions generate internal constraints which give rise to feelings of dependence. These show themselves sometimes directly, sometimes in the course of discussion when the person complains of the situation. But the behavior itself is witness to the need to be taken in charge by precise and repeated orders and instructions, and the person's attitude is witness to anxiety when faced with decisions he must make alone. The dependence could be identified by a type of emotional production normally referred to as "a beaten dog" or "blind devotion", very close to the "status of victim".

4.1 Organizational sources

According to Theodor Leavitt, dependence and hierarchy are two sides of the same coin. He stated that the distribution of authority as a function of the pyramid, results in the people at the bottom of the pyramid feeling probably more dependent on their superiors than the inverse. He also stated that the hierarchical system, in serving the necessities of the enterprise, causes feelings of dependence. Argyris ties dependence not only with the existence of the hierarchy, but with a certain attitude of the hierarchy: "the worker experiences the feeling of dependence and submission towards his superior especially when the superior keeps to himself all control over decisions such who will do what work, and who will be paid what salary" (1970, p. 70).

1. an actor belongs to a hierarchy,
2. this hierarchy possesses real or imagined means to affect him,
3. he experiences a feeling of dependence.

Affective dependence is common to all bureaucratic organizations that are founded on two principles (Trépo, 1973):

1. centralized decision-making that goes hand in hand with shortcutting the hierarchical echelon,
2. hierarchical levels and career paths founded on diplomas.

4.2 Personal sources

There are differences of intensity but not of nature between the "diagnosis" of the feeling of dependence, and the diagnosis of "abandonment disorders" affecting the personality. The behavioral criteria for the DSM 4 definition of the dependent personality nevertheless clarifies the nature of this feeling:

1. the more the employee is incapable of taking decisions in his daily life without being excessively reassured or given advice by others,
2. the more the employee lets his superior take most of the important decisions concerning himself (not to be confused with taking advice from others to reduce an information deficit),
3. the more the employee appears to be in agreement with his superior, even when he thinks he's wrong, for fear of being rejected,

4. the more the employee finds it difficult to initiate projects or otherwise do things on his own,
5. the more the employee will volunteer to do disagreeable or devaluing tasks to make himself liked by others,
6. the more he'll feel awkward or impotent when a close relationship is broken off,
7. the more he is frequently preoccupied by the fear of being abandoned,
8. the more the employee is easily hurt when he is criticized or disapproved of by others, the more the employee will feel dependent on structure.

Exhibit 25 Different logics of dependency		
Internal environment	**External environment**	
	Strong hierarchical pressure	**Weak hierarchical pressure**
Feeling of dependence	Appropriate emotional production	Dependent personality
Absence of feeling of dependence	Independent personality	Appropriate emotional production

QUESTIONNAIRE 13

Do you feel dependent?

Put a check in one column for each question using the key below:

1: I completely disagree
2: I mildly disagree
3: I'm not sure
4: I mildly agree
5: I completely agree

Connect the checks. The more your profile appears on the right-hand side, the more you have responded positively to the question.

	1	2	3	4	5
1. Do you find it difficult to express an opposing opinion?					
2. Are you the first to say hello even when you don't know the people?					
3. Do you have difficulty doing things alone?					
4. Do you prefer to work in a group?					
5. You don't hesitate to do something for others even when it's quite a lot of work.					
6. Do you have a tendency to give gifts too easily?					
7. Are you afraid of being abandoned by those you love?					
8. Does criticism hurt you deeply?					
9. It's better to have a desk job than a sales job.					
10. I can't tolerate being alone.					
11. The absence of my partner makes me very anxious.					

4.3 Dependent behavior

One of the important consequences of dependence is the ambiguous feelings vis-à-vis one's superior. The employee both loves and hates him. He loves him for what he brings (security), and hates him for what he prohibits (autonomy). In maintaining this permanent internal conflict, dependence can strongly affect the workings of an organization. It could cause tension between superior and subordinate, restrict freedom of communication and aggravate the worries of the subordinates, forcing them to question the attitudes of their superiors. In an atmosphere of dependence, all tasks are inevitably divided in two. The first is the realization of the task and the second is the pleasing of the superior. This second task could become of primary importance and will largely affect the first... Dependent situations – stressful to the point where the personality is slowly destroyed – requires that one flees the situation (Laborit, 1976) but the best way to discover that other possibilities exist is to be open to change (Blondin, 1983). The vicious circle comes from the fact that change itself consumes a high level of energy, and that at first, it increases stress. As a result, an independent man is more disposed to change than a dependent one, specifically because he accepts that change is necessary for the resolution of dependence.

▶ At an evening out with my co-workers, the boss arrived and the atmosphere changed; some avoided him, others spoke a little louder and a little faster... We briefly discussed the faults of others, but moved on quickly to the peculiarities of the boss which had become legendary; his moods monopolize conversation; the smallest statement on his part is cause for close examination to try to find a hidden meaning.

4.4 Dependence between the boxer and his manager

▶ "No one, but really no one, would say anything, if Robert Whathisname, the boxer, made more money than his manager... So why refuse to apply the same principle to business? Take him back into his laboratory and he would truly merit a raise in pay for the agony he endured for having tried to become a manager". (Peter Drücker, Video sur la prise de décision, 1976)

Epistemologically, the relationship between the boxer and his manager poses interesting problems. If he succeeds, the boxer is richer, and because of that, more famous, but he is still dependent on his manager. In order to

keep his resources, he must win, and to do that he must beat someone who
has done nothing to him. To get to that point supposes a total submission
to a superior authority who gives the order. The least feeling of guilt – in
the case of success – or fear – in the case of failure – and he will be desta-
bilized. He has to fight without thinking and has to be continually nour-
ished by the encouragement of his manager.

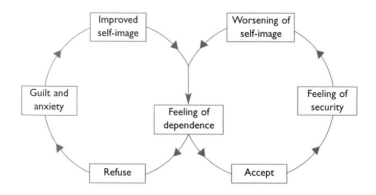

Exhibit 26 Dynamics of dependency

In summary:

1. The actor is dependent on people or situations that are not good for
   him,
2. go on to 3 or 5,
3. the actor submits to this dependence,
4. the actor ends up not being able to tolerate it.
5. The actor decides to escape these situations,
6. that increases his suffering because of the lack of a dependent situation, but it will disappear when he refinds his feeling of security,
7. the actor continues his personal and professional development.

5. Hierarchical Anxiety

Anxiety, linked to the exercise of power, was isolated by Elliott Jacques of
the Tavistock Institute in the course of his work with the London Glacier
Metal Company in 1948.

5.1 Status anxiety

According to Elliott Jacques, one of the principal factors of anxiety lies in the contradiction between the personality and the demands of a role. Within a hierarchy, one of the fundamental needs is to have a well-defined role, accepted by both the person and his colleagues. If there is confusion surrounding the limits of a role held by several people, or if one person holds multiple roles and these are poorly defined, frustration and insecurity surface (Scheid, 1980):

1. the more his status is poorly defined,
2. the less his status is accepted by others,
3. the more crosschecking of responsibility occurs with others,
4. the more the person will be anxious.

According to Aleznik, another factor of anxiety is linked to conflict between the manager's position of authority and his desire for friendship. When an individual begins to succeed and to make himself known, he loses his old friends and starts to be considered as competition:

1. the more the person experiences friendship in his professional framework,
2. the more he will have a position of authority in relation to his friends,
3. the more conflict there will be between what the position demands and what his friendships demand,
4. the more the person will feel anxious.

▶ What awaits the young beginner who leaves a friendly, horizontally constructed milieu (age, studies, sports, similar preoccupations between oneself and others) often comes as a reality shock when he discovers an organization that is vertically constructed (age pyramid, hierarchical levels, different cultural backgrounds and career motivations, from oneself or others).

5.2 The anxiety of competition

This anxiety is linked with the emotional production that is felt all along the ascent towards the top. A director who finds it difficult to adapt to this competitive environment will lose his effectiveness. The individual becomes anxious as soon as he begins to stand out. He can adapt to the situation using the psychological mechanisms of self-destruction to undermine his success and escape the painful emotional production that it generates. These self-destructive mechanisms can take several forms. They can be meant to avoid guilt feelings towards those that have not succeeded. They can be put into place to abide by the directions of the superego that prohibits pleasure (for example, a subconscious direction: "success must be something painful, difficult to achieve" is very common under the influence of the Judeo-Christian ethic). Placed in this situation, the actor diminishes the part he has played in his success (don't exaggerate, it was just luck, yes, but the next time I won't be able to do it...), or will do something so as not to benefit directly from his success (sharing, donations, delegation of the fruits of his success...):

1. the more the person succeeds,
2. the more this success will be accompanied by legible symbols,
3. the more this person will become anxious,
4. the more this person will do what he can to diminish or hide his success.

We have defined success as a process of personal construction at both the personal and professional level; it thus necessitates an inevitable and progressive change. Up to what point will the manager accept change, accepting to change himself? That depends on the emotional production that goes along with this change. If he finds himself prey to difficult emotional production, due to the gap between what he has become and the image of what he feels he should become, it could leave him seriously unhappy.

5.3 The anxiety of surprise

We offer this concept in order to describe the following phenomenon. A manager who no longer accomplishes his tasks himself, will nevertheless be evaluated on the accomplishment of these tasks by his co-workers. In the case of deviation from the norm, the quicker he is warned, the quicker he can take action to correct the discrepancy. **For a superior, there is no such thing as a good surprise.** A surprise is harmful and threatening, indicating an unexpected consequence of a decision. As a result, superiors must give instructions to their subordinates to inform them first, and as soon as possible, if something isn't going right. But most of the time, subordinates don't follow these instructions, or they do so too late. They themselves feel threatened when they must inform management about some discovery concerning unfortunate and unexpected results of a project that was important to the manager. They have the feeling that it could be dangerous to be the bearer of bad news, in spite of the fact that they are only obeying an instruction to bring the objective facts to their superior.

5.4 Relationship anxiety

The following is a list, on a scale of five points, of the level of insecurity felt in a relationship with a superior:

Level 1.　　　**Weak:** the superior seems to ignore the subordinate, greets him rapidly or absentmindedly, tries to avoid him in the corridors.

Level 2.　　　**Mild:** verbal summons from superior, without precise motive.

Level 3.　　　**Average:** state of conflict in a meeting, refusing to sit down, taking notes on the computer during interview with a co-signature at the end of the meeting.

Level 4.　　　**Strong:** given an innocuous post, relieved of responsibility, no sign-off authority, no financial budget allowed.

Level 5.　　　**Maximum:** written summons by recorded delivery, followed by redundancy with penalty for conflict.

5.5 The neurosis of the anxious personality

Anxiety describes an affective state characterized by a feeling of insecurity and a range of vague disorders. The term is often employed as a synonym for anguish or distress, but it is differentiated by the absence of physiological reaction (Sillamy, 1989). The DSM 4 defines generalized anxiety: "the essential characteristic of this disorder is fear, or unjustified and excessive worry (wait in dread) concerning two or more situations or events, for example, worry regarding something terrible happening to the children (when they are not in danger) or worry concerning their financial situation (without real reason), during six months or more, with the presence of these worries during one or two days". According to certain psychologists, all motivation comes from anxiety. Money is not desired for itself, but rather for the reduction of anxiety that it allows (Brown, 1953, Mower, 1952, cited by Fraisse and Piaget, 1963). Anxiety would be the sole human driving force centered around the ego. Certain adults, as children, were never really let go by their parents, never truly given precise and intangible parental rules. Their parents, in order to discipline, told them things like "if you do this … I won't love you anymore … ", sometimes resulting in adults with a terrible fear of the future …

Exhibit 27 Different logics of anxiety		
Internal environment	**External environment**	
	High anxiety-producing situation	**Low anxiety-producing situation**
High anxiety	Appropriate emotional production: stress	Anxious personality
Weak anxiety	Detachment	Appropriate emotional production: serenity

The weakness of the ego is clearly defined by Kernberg (1979) by one principal behavior (proposition 1) and by several affiliated behaviors (propositions 2 through 6):

1. predominance of defensive mechanisms,
2. lack of impulse control,
3. lack of tolerance for stress or anguish,
4. lack of the development of sublimation,
5. tendency towards primary thought processes,
6. weakening of reality checks.

Anxiety is often described as fear without legitimate object. The existence of an object sets off the defense reaction that suppresses the chemical activity that gives rise to anxiety. In the absence of a legitimate object, the action cannot take place and the system action inhibitor is solicited (Laborit, 1994). Anxiety thus remains firmly linked to information deficit in this case, but is all the more encompassing, because as the object does not exist, the information search is destined to failure. In this case, the anxiety has an endogene source, not open to being resolved through action. Such anxiety is said to be the uncontested source of certain lesions, such as stomach ulcers, and of hypertension (Laborit, 1974). In this case, anxiety is linked to the concept of neurosis (Guelfi, Criquillion-Doublet, 1992). Lastly, man knows he must die one day, and is in a chronic state of information deficit as to the date and the nature of the "event". He is highly concerned that no one, no other person, no machine, no computer could help him in this eventual confrontation. As long as man doesn't grieve for this lost power and accept this inescapable situation, the mortal nature of man will be the generator of high anxiety and of anguish.

In summary:

1. the more the actor finds himself with a poorly defined status,
2. the more there is confusion of responsibilities with others,
3. the more the actor is effective and wins,
4. the more he is in competition with others,
5. the more his success is exposed,
6. the more he is submitted to unexpected results or events,
7. the more he will experience anxiety.

QUESTIONNAIRE 14

Are you anxious?

Put a check in one column for each question using the key below:

1: I completely disagree

2: I mildly disagree

3: I'm not sure

4: I mildly agree

5: I completely agree

Connect the checks. The more your profile appears on the right-hand side, the more you have responded positively to the question.

	1	2	3	4	5
1. Do you bite your nails?					
2. Do you often have stomach aches?					
3. Is it difficult for you to fall asleep?					
4. Are you always thinking about your worries or things you have to do?					
5. Do you have backaches?					
6. Do you have eating problems, either you eat too much or too little?					
7. Do you rarely smile?					
8. Do people say you are serious?					
9. Do you hate surprises?					
10. Do you hate last minute changes?					

6. The Feeling of Belonging

A military career is a very particular human variety of the feeling of belonging: the more the group is structured (combat swimmers, parachutists, submarine personnel), the stronger the sentiment of belonging. (Cyrulnik, 1993, p. 101)

The feeling of belonging has a strong protective effect. In Toulon (France), a group of submarine personnel were closely selected according to physical and psychological criteria (difficulty in maintaining outside relationships) and were also among those that presented the least psychosomatic problems. In concentration camps, communists or Jehovah's Witnesses held up much better than those who did not "know" why they were there (Bettelheim, 1981, cited by Cyrulnik, 1993, p. 101).

QUESTIONNAIRE 15

Do you have a feeling of belonging?

Put a check in one column for each question using the key below:

1: I completely disagree

2: I mildly disagree

3: I'm not sure

4: I mildly agree

5: I completely agree

Connect the checks. The more your profile appears on the right-hand side, the more you have responded positively to the question.

	1	2	3	4	5
1. My society (or social group) is very prestigious.					
2. My organization is spoken highly of on T.V.					
3. It is very important that the objectives of the enterprise be reached.					
4. I have a lot of relationships with others in my organization.					
5. I've been in the enterprise a long time and we've become a group of friends.					
6. Our work means a great deal to us.					
7. There is not too much competition amongst us – just enough.					

7. Emotional Blindness

Climbing up the hierarchy gives power but, in extreme situations, can also isolate the manager by cutting him off from his own reality and by transforming his world into a closed system where the affective is at risk of being dominant. The process is all the more probable when the manager has a personality that does not easily submit to irrational behavior. In that situation, his value judgments, his diagnosis about his collaborators – normally resulting from a rational process evaluating their performance –

is slowly replaced by an affective process of evaluation, centered on the sympathy felt for the collaborator. From there, the risk of error is increased, except if the manager only feels sympathetic towards those whose work is truly efficient, and antipathetic towards those whose work is not efficient. In such emotional production, a very effective, but disliked subordinate runs the risk of losing his job, while those who know how to say hello with a smile are well received, and those who have a particular friendship with the manager are assured of their position, even if their work produces no results.

Exhibit 28 Different logics of value judgments		
Internal environment	**External environment**	
	Efficient	**Inefficient**
Friendly with the superior	Appropriate logic	Protected manager
Not friendly with the superior	Manager in danger of being fired	Appropriate logic

If these conditions are established, the subordinate who wants to survive must dedicate a large portion of his energy and time to "pleasing" his superior or, perhaps, given the organization's cultural situation, a large number of people. How much energy will he have left to actually do his work?

▶ On the other hand, the capacity to take the chance to keep to one's opinion at the risk of displeasing the manager, is illustrated perfectly in the film *Hommes, femmes, modes d'emploi* by Lelouch, where we see Bernard Tapie decked out in a horrible tie going to an administrative meeting where he must choose the person to be given a promotion to a post of director. Only the person who has the courage to tell him how horrible his tie is will get the promotion.

Exhibit 29 Daring to give one's opinion		
Internal environment	**External environment**	
	To be right	**To be wrong**
Keep your opinion	Rational logic	Counter-dependence on authority
Change opinion	Submission to authority	Rational logic

Richard is evaluated by his hierarchical superior based on a three-question test:
- is he efficient? the answer is "yes".
- is he capable of developing and of taking risks? the answer is "yes".
- is he friendly, nice? the answer is "no, he annoys me!".

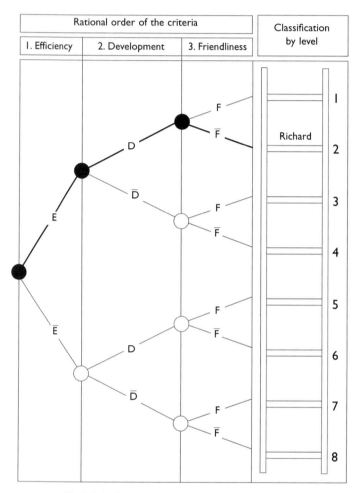

Exhibit 30 Rational evaluation of the subordinate

Suppose that Richard is evaluated on a scale of 8 points and the order of criteria places efficiency and development > friendliness. Looking at Exhibit 30, you see that Richard obtained level 2. Now suppose that the order of criteria has changed and friendliness > efficiency and development, meaning that the emotional dominates the evaluation, and using that order, Richard's rank is lowered to level 5 (Exhibit 31).

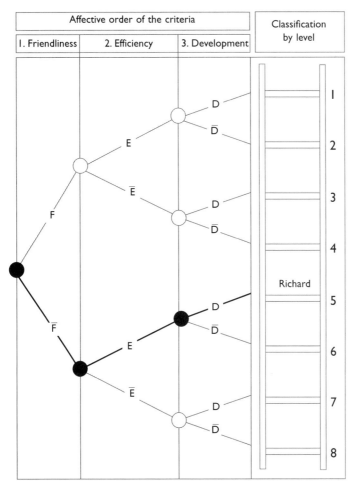

Affective order of the criteria			Classification by level
1. Friendliness	2. Efficiency	3. Development	

Exhibit 31 Affective evaluation of the subordinate

Exhibit 32 Evaluation of a manager by his superior				
	Rational logic		**Emotional logic**	
Domains evaluated	**Execution ability**	**Resolution ability**	**Execution ability**	**Resolution ability**
Questions asked	Does he know how?	Is he capable of taking risks and developing activities?	Is he nice to me?	Does he give me reason to worry? Does he make waves?

8. Emotional Conflict: "Avoidance–Avoidance"

The execution of an order obeys three distinct logical reasonings, depending on the degree of incompatibility between the given order and the values of the subordinate. The respect that the subordinate has for his/her superior is the variable that plays the essential role.

■ The intrapsychic conflict: "approach–approach"
This one presents little difficulty for the subordinate. He simply asks himself which is the best way to execute the order. His response is a function of his resolution capacity and his experience.

■ The intrapsychic conflict: "approach–avoidance"
This conflict is clearly more difficult to handle, as the subordinate asks himself whether or not he should obey the order. But it supposes a way to escape the consequences of the refusal to obey: quitting the job, for instance.

■ The intrapsychic conflict: "avoidance–avoidance"
The interior conflict that begins when a repugnant order is received is an "avoidance–avoidance" conflict, and it is one of the worst conflicts for, no matter what the choice, the actor will have to handle detrimental consequences. The situation of belonging to a hierarchy – one's country, family or organization – coupled with having to accomplish a painful or disagreeable task or simply one that is disapproved of, will always result in this type of conflict. The person may choose not to confront authority, and just do the degrading task, but he may also choose to refuse the task and then must confront the consequences of this refusal to submit. In the first solution, the confrontation with the superior authority is temporarily avoided, but, in fact, this confrontation will take place anyway, within himself, and will be impossible to avoid. In the second solution, the subordinate chooses to keep his self-respect and refuses to obey, but he will run the risk of serious consequences – possibly death. It is impossible to come out of this conflict unharmed; it is only possible to "minimize the damage".

▶ In the film *Sophie's Choice*, a sadistic Nazi officer gives Sophie the following choice: she could avoid the gas chamber for one of her children (she has a little boy and a little girl). She will struggle all her life to try to build a rationale for the choice she makes, but in the end, commits suicide.

▶ We were in a villa on the coast. I was about 15. A friend of my father's, a

Jewish man who had been tortured during the war, was talking with us. He had cancer and knew that he was dying. He left us with this message: "It would be good if no one was tortured, but you see, from the moment it begins, there are two possibilities, either you talk or you don't talk. And if you talk, you are no longer a man … ". I was very shocked by this remark, which seemed completely irrational. Torture being a means to take away someone's will, I didn't see how he could be responsible for his acts afterwards. I understood my error much later: it wasn't about any exterior judgement of someone, but it was that person himself who would judge himself no longer a man and it would be difficult to live with that image of yourself.

▶ *The Lost Poets' Society*[4] very clearly portrays the problem between a father – who is impossible to disobey – and a son who goes to a large military school, and is passionate about theatre. A professor of philosophy preaches to the adolescents the importance of self-respect and the young boy, in love with the theatre, sees at the same time the impossibility of going with his heart's desire and confronting his father. The pressure is so unbearable for him that he chooses to shoot himself in the head. The philosophy professor will be fired, because what they had asked of him was to teach the students obedience and not "carpe diem".

In the educational process, fathers who strengthen their authority – most often with their sons – in order to obtain the desired behavior on the part of their children, take great risks, for by doing so they put the adoles-

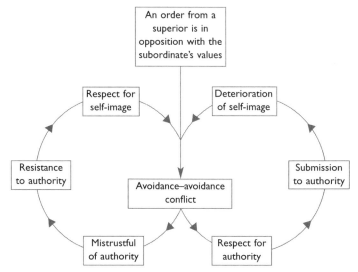

Exhibit 33 Dynamics of confrontation with authority

cents automatically in an "avoidance–avoidance" conflict. The program for this internal conflict is the following:

1. the more the person respects an authority,
2. the more this authority demands a task that the person doesn't approve of,
3. the more he will feel he is "doing something bad",
4. the more he will experience strong emotional pressure linked to the internal "avoidance–avoidance" conflicts,
5. but there is a strong chance that he will obey anyway.

9. Active Submission to Authority

In relation to the hierarchy, the actor has two opposing options. He can obey and submit, and be uncomfortable with the situation which is the case for 65% of subjects. He can also resist authority.

9.1 Experimental situations of submission

Milgram (1974) scientifically analyzed this situation in a series of experiments over a period of more than 10 years. Recaptured in the film *I comme Icare*, this experiment is very well known today. It took place as follows: Professor Milgram recruits his volunteers through an ad in the press. He gives them a false explanation of the experiment: to know if punishment helps memory. The naive candidate finds himself seated behind an impressive console where there are dozens of knobs marked 5 volts, 10 volts … up to 700 volts. The candidate reads a small list of words to someone (the stooge in the experiment) sitting on a supposedly electrified chair. The stooge keeps making errors and the candidate must punish him by sending off stronger and stronger electrical charges. Obviously, there isn't any electricity, but the stooge is a very good actor and his "pain" is so convincing that it is impossible to imagine that the torture is false. The true object of the experiment is to answer the question: "why would an individual agree to torture another, when the latter has done absolutely nothing?"

9.2 Real situations of submission to authority

In 1939, German forces crushed the Polish army in two weeks. Jews received an order to regroup in the larger towns and more than 10,000 Jews, completely submissive, obeying this order, arrived in Cracow every day. The Second World War was turning very quickly in favor of the Germans. Defeat wouldn't occur in France. The Vichy regime very quickly designated "interior" officials. Communists were the first to be incriminated, followed by Jews, freemasons and resisters (called "terrorists"). To drive out the "enemies of the state", all were denounced on a national scale. This was already being practiced on a grand scale in Germany where "heros" were made out of children denouncing their parents. The government showed "examples" by publishing an official list of 20,000 freemasons who lost all rights including the right to work. Two million letters of denunciation were sent by different writers. There are two conditions of submission to authority that aren't clear. The first point is whether the 2 million letters were written by people who knew that they were sending these denounced people to certain torture and death. The answer is yes for the communists and the resisters, as this list was publicly displayed. For Jews, there were no lists, they were simply no longer seen. Newspapers like *Je suis partout* (I am everywhere) did not hesitate to publish lists of names and addresses obtained by anonymous letters. The more the end of the war seemed uncertain, the more the informers increased and thousands of people would disappear in the few weeks before the end of the war. The second point that isn't clear is whether or not the psychological pressure felt by the informer was the source of his behavior, or if the informer was taking advantage of the situation for revenge. The trials after the war showed that most of the people had the feeling of obeying and doing their duty. One concierge alone had sent 80 people to the gas chamber with the best of patriotic sentiments.

The logic of submission is as follows:

1. the more an authority is respected,
2. no matter what the nature of the order,
3. the orders will, for the most part, be carried out.

9.3 Personal consequences

Stuck in the hierarchy, the subject will experience an "avoidance–avoidance" conflict, on the condition that he is conscious of the horror of what is being asked of him. He has only two possible choices and each one has serious consequences for him:

- either he obeys and "martyrs" someone who has done nothing to him;
- or he disobeys, but that means he will have to revolt against the respected authority and fear the possible consequences.

According to the work of Milgram (1974), placed in the impossibility of escaping from authority and not wishing to commit acts they condemn, some men and women will end up fleeing from this situation of submission, but 65% of subjects prefer to obey to the point of bringing about the death of an innocent person as a result of their action, rather than revolt and confront authority and its symbols. It must be noted that if the "ridiculous" order brings about negative consequences, not just for someone unknown, but for a representative of authority, the refusal to obey is practically immediate (in Milgram's experiments, the university professor, in a white smock, himself sat on the "electric chair").

▶ An organizational practice, common these days, is the use of trainees in enterprises. In certain cases, the hierarchy orders the trainee to commit some reprehensible act on the pretext that, if discovered, they could say it was the trainee that did it.

▶ "A student, finishing up his work study internship with an organization, called me to let me know that he just refused to follow an order: he was asked to do something illegal, under the pretext that he would be exonerated – in case it was discovered – if it was established that the action was taken by a student. The call was motivated by strong emotional production that was linked to the dread of submitting to the pressures, and devaluing the internship. The student calmed down as soon as I said I backed up his decision to refuse."

▶ In 1998, the management of an insurance company for students was questioned because, among other things, there was some damaging testimony from someone who had been fired. It was possible that – worried about the hierarchical authority – this person said nothing before, either out of solidarity or fear. Once fired, the respect or fear turned to hate, with all its consequences.

---

10. Passive Resistance to Authority

In a laboratory experiment, subjects asked to do a task they don't approve of, will choose between submission or resistance. Only 35% of the population make the choice to resist, actively or passively. This type of conflict is always provoked by an order or an obligation to accomplish a task that is completely unbearable. We will now look at the different forms of resistance.

10.1 Derision

A work foreman asked me one day to advise him on the following problem: each time he arrived on site he found that one of the workers had done his work poorly and he reprimanded him. The worker would make a joke and start giggling ridiculously, a sort of weird, jerky, nervous laugh the whole time he was being reprimanded … This behavior so upset the foreman that he never found a way to confront the worker.

10.2 Passive aggression

Aggression can take the form of a general mode of passive resistance to demands to perform adequately. It can result in total and long-lasting professional inefficiency even when more efficient behavior is possible. These individuals become sullen, irritable and argumentative when asked to do something they don't want to do. They often complain to others of the unreasonableness of the things they are asked to do and take offense at suggestions …. For no reason, they criticize or scorn the superiors who are initiating these orders …. The subjects see a sad future for themselves, but aren't aware of the fact that their own behavior is responsible for their difficulties …. This oppositional disorder, stemming from childhood and adolescence, apparently leaves the subject predisposed to this disorder (DSM III-R, 1992):

1. They avoid obligations saying that they forgot them,
2. They believe that they work much better than other people give them credit for,
3. They hinder others' work and don't do their own part,
4. Without reason, they criticize or scorn people who occupy posts with authority to give orders.

QUESTIONNAIRE 16

Are you passive–aggressive?

Put a check in one column for each question using the key below:

1: I completely disagree

2: I mildly disagree

3: I'm not sure

4: I mildly agree

5: I completely agree

Connect the checks. The more your profile appears on the right-hand side, the more you have responded positively to the question.

	1	2	3	4	5
1. I am better than others.					
2. Management is really worthless.					
3. They always ask me for too much.					
4. I don't easily let others use me.					
5. At work, I don't hesitate to criticize those I don't like.					
6. It's always the same people filling their pockets.					
7. I am misunderstood.					
8. I do enough for what they're paying me.					
9. Yeah, sure, I'm listening …					

Positive consequences of declared aggression

Laborit enclosed rats, two by two, in cages with an electrified floor, the electric current being signaled by a bell. He showed that with no exit, when the current passed, the two rats would fight. Compared to those who took part in the same experiment, but were alone in the cage, and therefore had no outlet for their aggression, the two rats, when returned to the shelter, ate, drank and slept well and showed no hypertension. In brief, they were fine …. It was as if the expression of aggression, even useless in relation to the problem, allowed them to handle the situation better. We can look at another curious fact in this light: in times of war, a period where aggression is expressed everywhere, "shrinks" make much less money. It's as if, in this situation, everyone is feeling much better and no longer feels the need to see a psychologist!

Negative consequences of declared aggression

Aggression is the result of a combination of a too low level of serotonin, and a high level of noradrenalin. Serotonin acts as an inhibitor.

In the same way, if the neurotransmittors created by the serotonin are strengthened, aggression is reduced and more social behavior is favored. (Damasio, 1995, p. 108)

Various research programs, without a doubt financed by pharmaceutical labs, have consisted of giving a serotonin activator to volunteers who, according to their own standards, lacked self-control. Certain treated subjects reported to have experienced stronger self-control and better relationships with their entourage. Others, incapable of keeping jobs due to aggressive behavior, state that they have become professionally more stable. They testify that they have undergone no personality changes, but, confronted with threatening problems, now have the choice among several strategies, instead of feeling prisoner to automatic aggressive reactions. These experiments have been a profitable source of publicity for certain medicines (Cantor, Survector and Prozac®) the last of which has been dubbed the happiness pill by the public ...

10.3 The lie

The lie is a strategy that is rarely used as it has an instinctive repugnance for most and it demeans one's self-image. This strategy is only employed when its inconveniences are small when compared to the problems it would avoid. It is the direct product of a situation with no exit, a sort of psychological trap, in which the subject lets himself get caught and as a last resort, lies.

▶ *The family lie*: one of the cleverest cases ever reported to me concerned a young, 8½ year old girl confronting her military father who had the habit of doubling the contents of his daughter's plate the moment she said "I don't like that". Quickly, the child learned to adapt and when she saw the dish in question – mushrooms – on the table in front of her, she would exclaim "Mmm, great. Mushrooms!" and would eat them without a word. About a quarter of the way through her plate, she would finally say "these are great, but I'm just not hungry anymore". She thus avoided the usual punishment of being served another full plate. Thirty years later, when ordering a pizza, she always says "no mushrooms, please!"

▶ *The legal lie*: a lawyer has the right to lie, the defendant doesn't, so in a difficult court case, a lawyer is automatically needed. It is not the one who is right who will win, it's the one whose lawyer presents the best arguments. It's for this reason – even if you are in the right – that going to court should be a last resort, after all other avenues have been explored.

▶ *The systematic lie*: an adult has made lying a weapon, systematically used in case of danger. As a child, he was brought up in the strictest of conditions and has, without a doubt, experimented with lying as the only possible way out of his prison. I have often found myself in the situation where it was his word against mine and I have always been defenseless. Over time, both he and everyone else knew that when he said something, it was impossible to know if it was true or false. *(interview, October 16, 1998)*

▶ *The exceptional lie*: I remember having flagrantly lied twice in my life. The first was in 1956, the second, in 1967. The circumstances were identical. My signature was on a document and the question was "Is this your handwriting?" I answered no, and looked the person straight in the eyes while I denied it. It was clear that I was lying. He knew it, and he knew that I knew it, but there was absolutely nothing he could do. The objective was the same in both cases: block my opponent, and while I was fundamentally right, my means were not. *(interview, November 11, 1998)*

10.4 Religion

Yesterday, authority was a given, unquestioned and clearly established. Today this authority is no longer automatic and depends on personal adherence or commitment. If the subordinate decides to no longer play the game, the only thing the superior can do is to try to make his life miserable. If the subordinate is strong enough to handle this, due to his religious, familial or personal culture, the struggle will go no further.

▶ A Maghrebian foreman goes to the construction site each morning, gives his orders and, in chorus, the workers reply "Inch Allah!". He comes back at noon, becomes angry because the work hasn't been done and the workers again say "Inch Allah!". He lets them know that he wants all the work to be finished by that evening. When he returns to the site, nothing is done. He throws a fit and the workers, once again in chorus, reply "Inch Allah!"

10.5 The law

August 26, 1789, the Declaration of the Rights of Man and of Citizenship states "All citizens stopped or arrested in the name of the law must obey immediately: if not, they will be guilty of resisting arrest" (article 7). The declaration specifies "in the name of the law", but article 4 states that "the law only has the right to defend the public against acts harmful to society ... and no one can be forced to do what the law doesn't specify". That's where the difficulty lies, to know – before obeying or resisting – if the authority is legitimate and if the order given conforms to the law. Article 7 specifies that "those who solicit, expedite, execute or have executed arbitrary orders, must be punished" and article 2 includes "the right to resist oppression" as "the natural and indefeasible rights of man". Article 9 confirms that "all men are presumed innocent" and the "all harshness that is not necessary will be severely reprimanded by the law".

▶ Boukovsky, committed in a psychiatric hospital in Russia, obtained his freedom by strictly conforming to the law in the following way. He got a hold of the list of camp rules, a pencil and paper – which was in itself a feat – and complained – up to 10 letters of complaint a day – for each element in the camp not strictly adhering to the rules. Very quickly, the administration of the camp was overwhelmed with complaints and could no longer handle them. In the USSR, statistics are fundamental. A commission was sent to investigate, and the director was fired for incapacity to perform. Another director was named who, one year later, was subjected to the same letter-writing campaign. Finally, Boukovsky was expelled to the West ...

---

11. Active Resistance to Authority

If you want to understand the behavior of a "traitor", try to find the cause which he obeys and which to him, seems superior to the authority that he is betraying.

- They disobey the police.
- They don't respect the justice system.
- They sometimes will assassinate its representatives[5].
- And, at liberation, they are national heroes, as their behavior defined them, de facto, as loyal defenders of France when it was invaded[6].

The same can occur in other conflicts: Algeria with the F.L.N., Ireland with the I.R.A. Men who possess power and authority, possess them within a framework. If this framework is transgressed, the authority is no longer legitimate and resistance becomes legitimate. These behaviors are those that most escape the logic of satisfaction. In order to stay coherent to themselves, and loyal to their idea of what they are doing for their country, these men are, for the most part, imprisoned, martyred, massacred, tortured, etc. This type of behavior is very rare, but it does exist, as you can see from history. The legendary model is Robin Hood, who stayed loyal to a legitimate but absent authority, despite all its inconveniences and with all its advantages.

Thus, active resistance to authority is simply submission to a superior authority or value.

Active aggression is defined by the quantity of kinetic energy capable of accelerating the entropic trend of the system that is the target of the aggression. Aggressiveness is the characteristic of the actor capable of applying this energy to an organized group in order to increase disorder and diminish information and the organization (Laborit, 1974). Aggression characterizes this fundamental disposition, through which we can obtain satisfaction of our needs. It is linked to frustration. Understood in a narrower sense, this term relates to the aggressive character of the person (Sillamy, 1989). It results in "combat, debate and games" at the end of which a hierarchy is established (Rapoport, 1967).

These games consist of abstract and ritualized "battles". The behavior, during the games, is not necessarily the behavior one finds in "combat". Most times, manifestation of this aggressive behavior is enough to discourage the adversary. The reputation of being aggressive is sufficient to make the potential adversary back off. In hierarchical conflict, fear of active aggression will condition a behavioral response of inhibition of aggression, anxiety or passive aggression:

1. two or more actors are in a conflict situation,
2. it is followed by ritualized "combat",
3. return to step 1, then in function of resistance to obstruction for each of the actors, move on to step 4,
4. an order will be established, respected by each of the actors, that will establish an implicit hierarchy amongst them, often the opposite of the official hierarchical structure.

Exhibit 34 Emotional attitude within the hierarchy		
Nature of the personality	**Occupied post**	
	Superior	**Subordinate**
Dominant	Rational logic	Risk of intrahierarchical conflict
Dominated	Risk of weakening the hierarchy	Rational logic

12. Adhesion to Authority

The principal source – if not the only one – of support of, and adhesion to, authority is mutual respect. This implies a series of reciprocal, and equivalent, obligations between the actors.

1. Criticizing behind one's back is avoided.
2. Repeating what has been told in confidence is avoided.
3. Reprimanding in front of witnesses is never done.
4. One remains consistent in all circumstances.
5. In case of difficulty, we quickly and systematically warn the other.

> ▶ At the end of 7 years of imprisonment, Johnson, condemned to a death sentence in Mississippi, was executed in 1986 at 1:01 a.m., after his lawyer had exhausted all appeals. After his execution, a witness was found, a woman who had gone to the police to say that at the time of the crime, Johnson had been with her. Neither this witness, nor others, had ever been mentioned. Johnson was innocent. The whole prison had been taken with this sweet and friendly young man. The director of the prison, against the death penalty, and persuaded of Johnson's innocence, would be the one to push the button. During a press conference, the director was shown in close-up. His face showed the extreme violence of the contained internal conflict and emotion which distorted his face and affected his voice, but only the rhythm of his speech really gave any of it away. The strength of the ritual, a veritable second-by-second program, conceived so as not to leave room for the slightest slip, would be carried out to the letter. *(Arte, August 7, 1998, 10p.m.)*

13. A Brief Overview of This Chapter

13.1 Emotional production at the top

We're only better off at the very top. At all the other levels, if you don't want to cause too many problems, you are obliged to create some type of inhibition of emotional production.

13.2 Blind hierarchy

No matter the level, most power that one possesses "inhibits" the level below, so that we no longer receive "raw" and exact information, either because those below have been censured, or because they are undergoing an "absorption" of uncertainty. In addition, the behavior of the lower level is geared towards pleasing or, at least, not to displease too much, and given that, we lie in wait for an error of judgment when evaluation is made based on feelings.

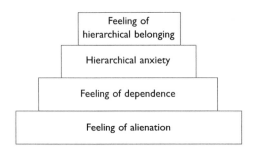

Exhibit 35 Emotional ladder of submission

13.3 Hierarchical anxiety

Going up the corporate ladder contains a series of anxiety-filled consequences. People who loved you begin to mistrust you; conflicts of power and authority are numerous amongst those whose responsibilities are similar. Competition is exhausting and worse are the true surprises, unplanned occurrences that destabilize previous plans.

13.4 Dependence, alienation and impotence

Resulting from the security that belonging to a system brings, dependence becomes the price to be paid. Pushed to the extreme in a hierarchy where a man considers himself just a pawn, he could feel despair in an alienating situation or impotence to do anything to prevent failure.

13.5 Submission to authority

In the spirit of obedience or respect, lower levels in the echelon have a tendency to accept everything, from the moment a respected authority asks them to do something.

13.6 Resistance to authority

Some people are capable of resisting intrapsychic conflict. This assumes strong aggressiveness. Other behaviors of resistance exist, humor or religion for example.

13.7 Adhesion to authority

This implies reciprocal respect.

CHAPTER 4

Situations of Failure: Disapprenticeship

Facing failure, the actor has two options: reject or accept the situation. Rejection will protect his emotional equilibrium, acceptance will question it. Failure could give rise to a feeling of guilt which will embitter the person to the point where psychological success will be near impossible. But having made a habit of success is also a serious handicap: when luck is no longer on your side, the disapprenticeship of success can be that much more painful.

It is unusual to deal with this subject – in any case, at least in management – but our observations concerning the careers of our students show that those that "make the difference" do not do so because of their appropriate behavior during success, but during their difficulties or failures. Those that succeed – according to their own standards – are those that get through difficulties better than others and are more open to change and therefore ready when favorable circumstances arrive. The way in which the experience of failure paves the road to success is a paradox. The principle of limited rationality explains that one decision is best only within a framework of choice that is limited in proximity to the decision-maker. Another limit to rationality must be specified: an action is only rational within the limits of the range of behaviors that is available, of which the actor is capable at the moment concerned. It is the emotional state of the subject that will define this capacity.

1. The Principle of Limited Behavioral Capacity

This principle is called the principle of **limited behavioral capacity**[1]. Behavior is not like a piece of clothing, chosen in the morning standing in front of a closet of behaviors, or rather, yes it is, but the choice depends on our emotional framework at the moment. It is imposed on us and we don't have the possibility to "change" ourselves every two minutes, if the weather changes. Yet, in a board meeting, certain files are considered good weather, others, storms, some are very hot, others freezing …. In other words, we can't resolve all situations successfully and it is important to learn how to integrate our failures …

2. The Feeling of Failure

2.1 Definition

The term "failure situation" is a misuse of the language, in that **failure is not a situation, but a feeling**, or more precisely, it is the psychological definition that we make of the situation. For a feeling of failure, there are three necessary conditions:

1. The existence of a deviation between the external situation and an internal norm.
2. The awareness of a link between the deviation and the actor.
3. A level of deviation that surpasses the personal norm, above which we experience feelings of failure.

For a feeling of failure to exist, the actor **must feel personally implicated in the process**, for example, believing himself to have been the source of the decisions or in judging himself responsible for not having stopped others' bad decisions. Failure represents emotional production resulting from the confrontation between the person's objectives, values, strategic choices and a unpredicted difficulty coming from the external environment that is in conflict with the outcome desired. Failure is essentially subjective. An organizational failure can be taken as a success by someone who had predicted it without being listened to.

> ▶ The success of a young man in an exam for an Ivy League school could be experienced as a failure by his friends. The marriage of a young girl could be felt as a failure by her mother who will lose her child. A young man's car accident could be felt as a terrible failure by the father who had bought the car for him …

2.2 Relation with other concepts

2.2.1 Failure and biology

It was found in 1968 that when animals experience failure, they show a drop in the concentration of cerebral NE and a release of a **high amount of corticosterone**, whereas the dominant animals show an elevated level of cerebral CA.

2.2.2 Failure and norm

Like a car breakdown or accident, failure comes from the gap between the situation and the norm that we have fixed and this norm is subjective. What makes us decide whether a situation is good or bad? The difference between what we hope for and what occurs? If our hopes are above what has really occurred, we will experience a negative sentiment, the intensity of which is situated somewhere between two extremes: the feeling that we could have done better and the feeling to have horribly failed. Reaching the norm doesn't produce any particular feeling. If the end result is higher than what we expected (can't believe my eyes!), the feeling of success could be very high.

2.2.3 Failure and error

Error is linked with a decision, a choice. It is related to an insufficient definition of the situation or a level of expertise that could be improved. A failure takes place on the downhill side in the process of resolution. It is both associated with the result obtained and is more global. It could come from errors in choice, but more often it comes from events that were not predicted and came as a surprise.

Exhibit 36 Logics of feelings of failure		
Internal environment	**External environment**	
	Negative deviation from the norm	**Positive deviation from the norm**
Feeling of failure	Appropriate emotional production	Lowered self-esteem, the subject is never self-satisfied
Feeling of success	Overblown self-image The subject is quickly satisfied with himself, even when the results are insufficient Puts blame on others	Appropriate emotional production

2.2.4 Failure and problem

The relationship between the "problem" and the "failure" is far from being simple. If you say that you have a personal problem what should be our response: "very good" or "I'm so sorry"? The answer depends on the circumstances. In the first case, the problem is positive, for it represents the beginning of a process of self-improvement. In the second case, it is prejudicial, as it represents a block somewhere in the process.

2.2.5 Failure and neurosis

The link between "neurosis" and "failure" is clearer. Neurosis is a deficiency disorder and not a personality attribute. It appears to be due to certain deprivations, as much as water or calcium deprivation can be the cause of certain illnesses. The deprivations related to neurosis concern security, ownership, identification, affective relationships, consideration and prestige (Maslow, 1968). Neurosis plays an active role in failure; it will be the source of emotional production that will multiply the problems but also can sometimes represent a source of motivation to exceed oneself.

▶ Example: this person has a very neurotic relationship with authority and what authority represents. At the end of her postgraduate studies, she doesn't obtain her diploma, because the orals for her specialization seem unmanageable for her. Pushed by a friend, she finally takes the orals and passes easily, but after having lost 2 years …

Exhibit 37 Failure and neurosis		
Internal environment	**External environment**	
	Failure	**Success**
Suffering	Appropriate emotional production	Success neurosis
Pleasure	Failure neurosis	Appropriate emotional production

In success neurosis, the person's success causes suffering. In failure neurosis, he seeks out failure in order to experience, in general, the pleasure of having the status of victim.

QUESTIONNAIRE 17

Do you have a taste for failure?

Put a check in one column for each question using the key below:

1: I completely disagree

2: I mildly disagree

3: I'm not sure

4: I mildly agree

5: I completely agree

Connect the checks. The more your profile appears on the right-hand side, the more you have responded positively to the question.

	1	2	3	4	5
1. Are you indifferent to the suffering of animals?					
2. Do household accidents (a fall, for example) make you laugh?					
3. Do you like morbid films, for instance, where the victims are buried alive or there is a catastrophe, to the point of finding them pleasurable?					
4. Do you have the tendency to cause your own failure by continuing inappropriate behavior?					
5. Do you vacillate between feeling all powerful and powerless?					
6. Have you ever done any anonymous small "acts of terrorism", like breaking a window or puncturing a tire for revenge?					
7. Is failure a means to get your parents' attention?					

3. Refusal of Failure: The Search for a Guilty Party

These mechanisms belong to the collective subconscious.

3.1 Supporters and followers, confronting failure of the cause

"It is impossible that our team lost!" "It the umpire's fault – or the fault of the other team's supporters!"

By "supporters" we mean the more fanatical people who embrace a cause whether it be sportive, familial, professional, religious, political or social. Examples abound that bring these people to commit murder. The film of Jean-Pierre Mocky, where Michel Serrault plays the role of a crazy supporter, and Eddy Mitchell plays an umpire, takes into account this collective madness when confronted with failure, and the incredible passion that invades the supporters of the losing team to search for and punish those responsible:

1. the supporter invests all he is in the supported Cause,
2. the Cause loses,
3. for the supporter, it is impossible, as his Cause is the best and thus there must be a conspiracy,
4. he designates a person, or group of people, as the origin of this conspiracy and thus responsible for the failure,
5. he takes it upon himself to revenge his Cause by attacking these people.

3.2 Status of scapegoat or the witch-hunt

From an ethical point of view, this is the oldest, most disgraceful and most scandalous of all collective emotional processes of problem resolution: disastrous events uniting the victims of the situation in uncommon violent and painful emotional states; action that would permit the disposal of the problem is no longer possible, the people must accept the unacceptable. The process of finding a scapegoat consists of seeking out the cause of the failure and transferring all hate and blame on this identifiable minority: the **enemy of the interior**. From an emotional point of view, this process is beneficial, as it does away with the feeling of responsibility and guilt, and the moving into action does away with the accompanying emotional violence by providing a modern version of a circus act. This process can be spontaneous: in that case, these people deemed responsible will be sufficiently fragile so as not to be able to defend themselves. But it could also be orchestrated by a political group: **the extreme right** often designates ethnic minorities (Jews for a decade before the Second World War in Germany). In France, the Communists were the first to be incriminated under the end of the Third Republic after the signature of the German–Soviet Pact. Freemasons would be directly behind Jews with the official publication of the 25,000 list of names during the era of Pétain: in the States, the Communists under Senator McCarthy in the 1950's; the immigrants in France in the period after the war. **The extreme left** are happy enough to more modestly designate bosses and politicians as responsible for all the world's ills. Today, there is a slight change of program as new witch-hunts are orchestrated by **the media**, searching for new audiences, designating highly placed "witches"[2] and organizing new witch-hunts[3]. To get to that point, the presumed scapegoat must satisfy certain criteria, for example be implicated as a witness in a case. In France, the pool is large. In 1999, thousands of heads of enterprises, and 700 elected officials went before the courts, drowning in inextricable situations as in the case of contaminated blood[4], or bribery scandals. Everyone is susceptible: the heads of companies suspected of bribing city commissions for building permits, the Olympic Committee, the European Commission, the Presidents of the Republic, the President of the State Advisory Board, and Elf among others. The fact whether these people are guilty or not holds absolutely no interest. To hell with the presumption of innocence. In fact, if they were innocent, the emotional process would be that much more violent, provoking strong reactions, between the "fors" and "againsts", it would involve many more people and the media would multiply their profits. Thus, the collective failure could permit those who gain by it to increase their wealth considerably.

▶ The United States, under McCarthyism – the red hunt; 130,000 Americans were called for questioning. Those who refused were condemned to closed prison terms. Media and film were particularly targeted. Charlie Chaplin would be called. Ronald Reagan was in charge of developing the black list. To be on the black list was a guarantee of unemployment. Julius and Ethel Rosenberg were not guilty but they had the perfect profile: activists and sympathizers. They were condemned to death in June, 1953. McCarthyism would increase and claim another victim: McCarthy himself. Attacking the army, television transmitted his declarations and Americans witnessed his unbalanced personality first hand. He was dismissed in 1954. Some 100,000 Americans were victims of this incredible collective madness. (Arte, February 11, 1999)

▶ In France, February 1999, there was an avalanche, followed by 3 meters of snow, something that hadn't happened in 50 years, destroying about 10 chalets on the opposite slope because of the strength of the avalanche. Almost immediately, the media began to implicate city officials.

▶ The discovery of the carcinogenic properties of asbestos and the thousands of tons of this material used in high schools, served as the basis to implicate high-ranking officials who were involved at the time asbestos was approved of as a means of fire protection. Under emotional public pressure, they tried to turn these decisions – whose object was to protect the public from fire – into a voluntary act of public poisoning.

---

4. Acceptance of Failure: The Feeling of Guilt

Guilt is the social cement that permits us to maintain cohesion among groups in a state of disintegration. (Meigniez, 1971, p. 90)

Making the distinction between that which we are responsible for, and that which we are not responsible for, is one of the greatest problems of existence. (Peck, 1978, 1987, p. 31)

4.1 Definition

This feeling of guilt has two distinct sources: first of all, **it is the product of the "superego"** (a sort of internal "cop"). An individual feels guilt when he lets a part of himself appear that he normally doesn't show or that he believes is not appropriate to show (Peretti, 1981). It is the state of reacting or of thinking of reacting in a way that the person considers morally unacceptable. For the most part, the person is unaware of the true set of values under which he judges or condemns himself, as he is also sometimes equally unaware of his own guilt feelings. We can say that **guilt is the product of the difficulty of distinguishing what we are truly responsible for from the rest**.

In this context, guilt is at risk of being the first price to pay when we take too many things personally.

The program of guilt is as follows:

1. I want (someone or something),
2. move on to 3 or 4.
3. I satisfy my need,
4. I feel constantly guilty and can't enjoy the satisfaction, go on to 6,
5. I don't listen to my wants, I am frustrated and have regrets,
6. I've lost, go back to 1.

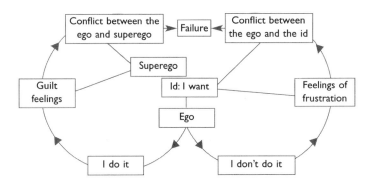

Exhibit 38 Feelings of guilt or guaranteed failure

It is the most developed form of a "system of double constraints" that leads one to failure. Whereas in the preceding schema there existed a way out, guilt prohibits all "winning exits", for no matter what the behavior chosen – action or inaction – there is negative production. For example, the individual could have the feeling of victory or success and, simultaneously, feel that this reaction is not legitimate. Guilt is not uniquely linked to success. It could be linked to having miraculously escaped a failure, an accident for example …

Interviews with survivors (concentration camps, plane or bus accidents) show the systematic appearance of the internal question: "Why me?"

Rithy Panh, the director of *One Night after the War*, asks himself daily, 10 years later, why the Khmer Rouge saved him …

4.2 The sources of guilt feelings

4.2.1 Judeo-Christian sources

The great religious systems have all assimilated this basic emotional mechanism and established symbols destined to be used as a tool of social order. The Hebrew tradition of redemption carries the most burden with these feelings of guilt.

1. God is good,
2. sin exists,
3. so man is guilty[5].
4. God is merciful. Through redemption he offers man the possibility of a new life.

▶ Katherine Pancol testifies to her guilt as follows: "I no longer know how to pray. As for religion, I've kept only the feeling of guilt which helped me when I did wrong, helped me weigh the pros and cons. The certainty that I would be punished and that it would be good for me … the pro is the pleasure felt from cheating on someone, the con the problems I would have if caught."[6]

4.2.2 Islamic sources

The transcendental tradition of Islam is different as it presumes the impossibility of redemption, and insists instead on respecting the letter of the law:

1. God is all powerful,
2. sin exists,

3.   it is committed by infidels (as written by the law),
4.   "Surely those who disbelieve, it being alike to them whether you warn them, or do not warn them, will not believe" (Koran, Chapter II, The Cow, line 6),
5.   "Allah has set a seal upon their hearts and upon their hearing" and there is a covering over their eyes, and there is a great punishment for them (Koran, Chapter II, The Cow, line 7).

Religion creates a representation of the world which replaces one's personal perception of reality.

▶"Given that the individual has appropriately 'adapted' to his entourage, the greatest madness, even the worst infamy committed by his group will not disturb him or, at least outwardly, trouble the tranquility of his soul, as long as the majority of the members seem to believe in the high moral certitude of the reigning social organization." *(Jung, 1933, 1964, p. 77)*

4.2.3 Buddhist sources

We will pay a little bit more attention to Buddhist logic, as it represents the only model presuming **100% guilt** for everything that happens by going beyond the notion of God and sin. Let's clarify what we mean by that. In rational logic, action is divided into two opposed sequences: **decisions and events**. The precise characteristic of an event is its independence in relation to the decision: the actor submits to it, he cannot cause or cancel it. If he can, it is not considered an event, but a decision. If something happens in his life, the subject is totally responsible in the sense of **causality**[7]. In other words, it is what the subject had wrought in a previous life that is the cause of the present event[8]. Buddhism sends the actor back on himself throughout his life. Alone, this closed loop permits him to manage without Divine concepts[9]:

1.   Something aversive happens to the subject.
2.   This fact is a consequence of programs previously executed.
3.   The subject is totally responsible for what happens to him.
4.   He must purify himself.
5.   He must avoid generating other aversive programs in his future lives.

The process of cause and effect from (1) to (12) (see note 7) represents the way of suffering. The road from (12) to (1) represents the cessation of suffering. From that moment on, those wishing happiness and not wanting to suffer must, by practicing meditation, try to cancel out, for example, the initial ignorance (3), that by the series of ideas, will cancel out aging and death (12). This is what constitutes the process of purification that will remain for all future lives.

4.2.4 Organizational sources

At the level of political or military organizations, Milgram showed that the primary objective of all totalitarian systems wanting to organize crimes is to assure that conditions exist that will inhibit guilt in its executors:

1. Division of the criminal process into several small parts so that each actor has only one part to execute and has only partial vision of the process to avoid his global understanding of the process.
2. Total control of information and establishment of a censor that favors specialized press over general.
3. Recruitment of perverse, sadistic or simply completely submissive individuals to ensure that the final phase of the process will be impossible to cover up with a positive act.

▶ High school final exams (the "orals" part in France). The math teacher had suffering written all over his face: a sharp profile with deep lines etching a path from his nose to his mouth, deep-set eyes with a piercing look, extremely thin and wrinkled lips. For this type of man, the only nourishing emotion came from suffering; what he suffered or the suffering he inflicted on others. He gave me the exam topic: "Limit of dx/x"! Not only did I like math, but I did very well in it (second prize in elementary math the following year). I went to the board and developed the limit, very quickly, like a student who knew his work. Then I stopped. The general method didn't work, it was a particular case that demanded a type of treatment I didn't know. He sent me back to my seat and I felt close to tears. He bent over to begin writing, then looked at me, saw I was crying, and I saw him hesitate. The verdict was announced: 60%???? The French teacher, without a doubt accustomed to his colleague's game, asked me if it went okay in math, and I told him what happened. The next year, I was taking elementary math and one fine morning, the math teacher wrote on the board: limit dx/x ... I leapt out of my chair and cried: "that's what I had in the orals last year!" The teacher became very angry, started to verbally abuse his colleague, who it appeared was a big troublemaker who would get his revenge every year at the final exams. Today, I preside on the exam jury every year and I sign off on hundreds of diplomas. When there is a student who is missing out by 5 or 6 points on his score, it is clear that things haven't changed much: one gets the impression that the teacher would lose his soul by increasing his grade by 1/4 point in order for the student to pass. Yet the instructions of the Department of Education are clear, take into account the year's behavior above that of exam day's performance, which is always a bit uncertain. *(interview, February 4, 1999)*

The decisions taken by an enterprise, especially the most difficult ones, are subject to pressure from several systems of criteria because in order to win, the enterprise must sacrifice the interests of some of its partners. The boss's guilt – above all in family businesses – "pushes" the decision-maker towards accepting demands that will put the organization under a great financial burden and eventually accelerate its demise.

5. The Neurosis of the "Guilty"

Feelings of guilt could be understood using an analogy between its archaic religious form and its modern psychoanalytic form. In psychoanalysis, guilt is a product of an affective deficit – a deficit of "affection". It is possible to avoid the beginnings of guilt feelings in early childhood if parental love is abundant and freely given – i.e. not negotiated. Negotiation, when introduced very early, will have a lifelong effect. We find it again in one's love life in the sense where a large part of one's love life is emotional regression. We find it again in enterprises, where the old childhood reflex can be revealed in the "paternal" relationship one has with the hierarchy – a confusion between father and manager.

1. mother is good,
2. if mother doesn't love me, or if I don't feel loved by mother,
3. I must have done something to deserve that …

5.1 Guilt and omnipotence

We don't feel guilty about things that are not our responsibility. If a person feels guilt about everything, it's because she feels responsible for everything. Guilt represents one side of the coin – the other side being omnipotence. Guilt is linked to the feeling of responsibility which can only be overcome by the involvement of the superego and the feeling of omnipotence.

▶ To illustrate the relationship between omnipotence and guilt, Salomé conducted the following exercise with an intern: he asked him to carry another student on his shoulders, then a third student was asked to lie down by the feet of the first student and pretend to be in pain. Then he said to the first student: "if you want to stop feeling guilty (and he pointed to the student on the floor), give up feeling omnipotent (and he pointed to the second student on his shoulders)."

5.2 Guilt and loyalty

Guilt feelings and the need for security are also two powerful loyalty motivators within the hierarchy. These two emotions are, without a doubt, painful for those who experience them, but they make for very loyal subordinates; it is one of the most sought-after qualities by managers. Someone who usually feels guilt will always be on time and will always make deadlines. In the case of delay, he will do everything to warn the manager and to avoid any inconvenience to this colleagues, as he will do all he can to lessen the interior pain he will feel. In addition, these people are hard workers, as work itself diminishes the pain of guilt feelings. It will act as a sort of tribute, a personal redemption that is for the profit of the organization. If they are loyal towards their superiors, they are also strongly attached to rules and could be considered very demanding by the people who work under them.

In summary:

The conditions for the **appearance** of guilt are:

1. the more the person has lived with a large affective deficit in his childhood,
2. the more he will experience a security deficit if, for example, love has been a negotiable commodity,
3. the more he has had a religious upbringing or something else founded on good versus evil,
4. the more the person will feel responsible for everyone around him,
5. the more the person feels the desire to direct and control his close domain,
6. the more he will have the tendency to be loyal and a hard worker,
7. the more he will feel guilty over his acts and behavior.

The conditions of the **inhibition** of guilt are:

1. the more the person had been unconditionally loved in his childhood,
2. the more religion has led him to feel that all that arrives is God's will and not the person's fault,

3. the more he profoundly respects the organization that employs him and gives him orders,
4. the less this organization provides him with the means to see himself in the total picture,
5. the more he will feel loyal or submissive,
6. the less he will feel guilt over his acts and behavior.

Exhibit 39 Different logics of the guilt complex

	Situation with strong personal responsibility	Situation with weak personal responsibility
Guilt feeling	Appropriate emotional production	Guilt feeling: familial, religious, organizational or personal
No guilt feeling	Inhibition of possible sources of guilt: religious, familial, organizational or personal	Appropriate emotional production

QUESTIONNAIRE 18

Do you tend to feel guilty?

Put a check in one column for each question using the key below:

1: I completely disagree

2: I mildly disagree

3: I'm not sure

4: I mildly agree

5: I completely agree

Connect the checks. The more your profile appears on the right-hand side, the more you have responded positively to the question.

	1	2	3	4	5
1. You've had a strict religious upbringing.					
2. Your mother preferred your sister(s) and/or brother(s).					
3. It's very hard for you to say "no".					
4. You almost never lie.					
5. It's painful to have to disobey.					
6. You feel very responsible towards your entourage.					
7. You really want to increase your efficiency in as many areas as possible.					
8. Sometimes, when you have a sexual encounter, you think it's wrong.					
9. In order to decrease your score a little, you lied on the previous question.					
10. You've told yourself it's dishonest to lie, and you feel ashamed of yourself …					

6. Emotional Collapse

A gap, itself a source of frustration, results from the difference between a situation and a norm. The situation being what it is, the actor has two ways to adapt: change his norm or tolerate the situation of frustration. The tolerance of frustration is not, in general, infinite and the person tries to react on these two levels if he wants to adapt. He can reduce the norm in such a way as to leave a tolerable level of frustration. We will see that norms are generally as flexible as a brick wall. Finally, if neither of these two acts are successful, it will result in "emotional collapse." We call "emotional collapse" the process by which behavioral capacity is momentarily reduced to its bare essentials.

The diagnosis of emotional collapse:

1. Self-confidence, and confidence in others, breaks down.
2. The person is no longer capable of reasoning.
3. He is not even capable of understanding what is said to him.
4. It's as if there was an "interior noise" so intense that it confuses understanding.
5. Or he understands what is said but is not capable of integrating it. The speaker could repeat the same thing five times and he still won't get it.
6. The pain becomes intolerable.
7. Something internal renders all psychic activity inoperable.
8. Even if consciously the person wants to escape the situation, and say something, he cannot, as if his words have gotten stuck in his throat.

Emotional collapse follows a gap that is too large in relation to the norm.

▶ A young woman is living happily with a man who has just been divorced. One morning, given the relationship of the two women with the little boy, she gives a type of self-help book to her boyfriend, telling him to give it to his "ex" for her, when they meet at the child's school. Later on in the morning, the "ex" calls, the young woman answers, and in the absence of the "husband", asks that she tells him "thank you for the gift". At that moment, the gap in relation to the norm is not very large. The young woman merely said to herself "He gave her the book, but didn't say it was from me." The husband comes home and the young women tells him what happened and he responded "Well! She didn't have to tell you that I gave her flowers ..." The young woman collapses into tears and the next three days are very difficult, as the realization that the gift in question was not a book but flowers, the gap in relation to the norm, taking into account the added aspect of surprise, was intolerable for her.

In the language of proximity, a manager's personal norms define the amount of blows he can take "before being knocked out". We could put it more scientifically: a personality defines, more or less consciously, the norms that identify, on the one hand, the areas in which the person is capable of accepting frustration and, on the other hand, the intensity of frustration, producing emotional production that, at the level of the psyche, the person can handle without reaching that level which will destroy, partially or totally, her "information structure"[10]. In other words, a "solid" manager is capable of tolerating large gaps in relation to their own norms, without entering into a crisis of self-confidence or doubt, wanting to quit or any of the many variations of possible reaction that could arise from the same range of emotions. The notion of "solidity" is culture dependent. For example, for a Japanese manager in a "superior–subordinate" relationship, saving face and not being questioned in front of others is of primary importance. If the opposite occurs, he could have feelings of revenge or suicide and his culture will "support" his reaction. For a French manager, short-cutting and "backstabbing" represent a lack of respect, for an Italian manager, it simply represents rapid and efficient management and for a British manager, a test of politeness. A solid manager is capable of "flexibility" in those areas where a more fragile one would show extreme rigidity, either vis-à-vis himself or vis-à-vis others. In other words, the ensemble of internal norms defines the point where defenses will be called into play, defenses that play a fundamental role in problem resolution. We have spoken of tolerance to illustrate the elasticity that a person has in relation to their norms. It measures the capacity (or incapacity) of one person to live through situations that are in strong opposition to their own norms. Concentration camp imprisonment, prisons, or animal zoos represent places that favor observation of the solidity of a person and his capacity to free his emotional production from the environment in which he is simultaneously shut in and overexposed. The company, family or couple can also represent those areas where personal fragility linked to rigid norms can cause great difficulties. Being stuck in a full-time job chosen because it will satisfy the obligations of a student loan, a civil wedding ceremony, finding out you have an incurable disease, all represent situations that necessarily require a strong and solid personality.

7. The Growth of Emotional Resistance

Deciding to change one's norms is extremely difficult, almost impossible in the sense that it is done unconsciously, only noticed afterwards and it is most always done after everything else has been tried. It is truly the last possibility, and still, in some cases, the person would prefer to fall ill rather than modify his norms.

7.1 Increase of norm level if the situation is simple

In simple situations, we are actually very intolerant of things that are banal or repetitive. Thus, we change our rationale as it is not a particularly serious situation that "causes a problem". A man who tolerates a thousand responsibilities in a day, could literally explode when he can't find his car keys, or is stopped on the road for a routine car check. There is a very weak gap between the situation and the norm, yet he can't tolerate any gap in these very simple and repetitive events. Thus, in this very simple situation, the norm could be placed so high that any gap surpasses the manager's tolerance and he explodes. This behavior at first seems incomprehensible, as he has no problem handling much more difficult trials, yet falls apart at what appears to be nothing …

▶ November 1998. A cyclone in Central America that caused thousands of deaths. We read about a British helicopter that saved Isabelle Ariola, a 36-year-old teacher, who had drifted on the ocean for five days, after having lost her three children, her husband and her entire village. She didn't fall apart for an instant. Impressed, the commander and the British rescue team wrote her a letter: "It is an honor to have rescued someone like you. … " Searching for some explanation, it was reported that she was a descendant of Darifuna slaves, liberated from the Ile of Saint Vincent. Against all expectations, it was only when she had her mother on the telephone that she let herself go, and broke down, live, in front of the entire world.

▶ In continuing education, my day began at 9:00 a.m. I needed a VCR. The secretary, who had access to it, hadn't yet opened the room. I installed the computer, and the connections. I brought the copies and the C.D. The room had to be locked between 12 and 2:00 p.m., because the night before, we received an e-mail warning us about increasing theft and suspicious characters in the building. I went up to the secretary to ask her for the key. I had prepared for every eventuality: for the copies that couldn't be delivered on time, for the room that had to be locked, the video that we had to finish the night before … everything but the key. The one that I was given was not the right one. 12:20 p.m., in a panic, I went up to the fourth floor, and bumped into the financial director, who had all the keys, was in a good mood and came down with me to lock the room. It was a very simple problem, but it caused me to panic, because this mix-up was totally unacceptable for me. A question of norms ...

We usually refer to this as "the straw that broke the camel's back", an explanation that implies a question of additional stress and not an explanation of situation-norm. It is easy to show that this explanation doesn't take into account the reality when you examine what happens when the situation becomes much more serious.

7.2 Increase in norm flexibility if the situation becomes more serious

An English proverb has put it another way: "the best way to forget your troubles is to wear tight shoes".

In this case, the gaps don't necessarily add up to produce a "break", for the norms become more flexible in response to the complexity of the situation. Below is an example that illustrates this problem. It's as if the more serious the event (in relation to the person's own norms), the more it erases the others.

> ▶ Because of a report he has written, a manager has just learned that his work is being seriously questioned by his director. He is on the edge of having a breakdown. The telephone rings, it's the hospital ... His son was in a car accident. Seriously hurt, but out of danger. Curiously, his morale immediately improves, he is calm again, goes to the hospital and kisses his injured son, forgetting all about the report in question ...

If there was a process of accumulation, the psyche would have broken down at the appearance of a new problem, but the opposite occurs. A problem that seems overwhelming is put into perspective when confronted with another problem. An Albanian proverb repeats this popular wisdom: when a person has a lot of problems, one says to him: "Mos e harrofsh[11]", which means that we wish that nothing more serious happens that would put his current – small – problem into perspective. Simon's principle specifies that norms decrease when the situation becomes complicated. What we don't know for sure, is why certain managers will easily agree to lower their norms and survive the problem, while others refuse to adapt their norms, exhaust themselves trying to resist this adaptation and would rather accept the inevitable business failure.

▶ An economic example concerns the evolution of prices during the Depression. Understanding more quickly than others the nature of the crisis, store owners accepted lowering their retail prices below the wholesale prices they paid (not very high – wholesale prices were also dropping, as they were buying in larger and larger volumes). Those that did continued to do well. Those that were determined to keep to their retail prices, refusing to lower them, quickly closed down ...

7.3 More serious situations tend to reorganize the norm hierarchy

Another proverb, of unknown origin, says: "If your God is small, your problems are great, if your God is great, your problems are small ... " Several "experiencers" – meaning those rare people who have experienced the worst of problems[12] and have come out okay – plane accident, for example – testify to the modification of their internal norms. As if, having lived through this "supreme accident", they have come out stronger, as if the experience has strengthened their psyche, as if nothing else could touch them. Their tolerance, in relation to the gaps between their norms and results, has become infinite, or maybe it's their norms that have been lowered? The second hypothesis has to be, at least partially, retained. In effect, these people testify to the inversion that followed in the value that they give to each problem that arises. Things that were once considered of primary importance (to attain a certain quantitative level, money, comfort and power) appear, after the Experience, ridiculous, and those things that were considered ridiculous *ex ante* (giving of oneself, time spent with children, seeing a flower, the flight of a butterfly, the feeling of wind on your face) is now considered primordial. Under the influence of a near-death experience, certain values, formally in or near first place, have fallen to last place, while those, originally placed low on the list, have risen to the top. But given that context, can one still be a good manager and worry about the survival of his/her company?

7.4 Avoid giving rise to useless conflicts

A gap that surpasses the norm tolerance will provoke a procedure to rectify the gap. These are procedures that have been described in our work on "Managers' relational strategies". If this procedure, in correcting the problem, causes other, more serious, conflicts, the situation, far from being simplified, becomes possibly inextricably more complex. The essential task of a manager is to decide between rigor and "mercy"[13]: to increase the flexibility of his norms and avoid remedies that he believes are worse than the problem, or maintain his norms – maybe as a result of his fragile personality – taking the risk of worsening the problem.

8. The Disapprenticeship of Success

Failure is the product of a program that is not appropriate for a given situation. The person who experiences failures can benefit from a potentially large acquisition of new programs: all depends on the way in which he "unlearns" from this experience … Failure is the occasion to simultaneously discover a limit – most execution programs become obsolete over time – and the opportunity to surpass this limit and make new sense out of the results. "Experience" is often the sum of all the failures that have shaped us. Success is the product of actions that have been adapted to the situation. The person who has experienced a number of successes lessens his potential capacity of apprenticeship. When the successes stop, he must "unlearn" and that operation will be much more difficult than just reaping the rewards of success. In this way, disapprenticeship is closely aligned with overcoming success, as apprenticeship is closely aligned with overcoming failure.

8.1 The object of disapprenticeship

The classic theory of apprenticeship was first conceived as a theory of need satisfaction – the apprenticeship of the means to satisfy a need or to respond to a situation (Simon, 1974). For this reason, it is very limited and insufficient to take into account disapprenticeship. The theory of disapprenticeship is, in fact, a theory of the acceptance of the disappearance of success. Apprenticeship targets success. Disapprenticeship targets relearning to live when the same level of success is no longer possible. While apprenticeship has a strong positive valence when it is accompanied by success, disapprenticeship will be slow and painful.

▶ All his life, Vincent Van Gogh, maintained his art and his style. It is said that his butcher, who was paid in paintings, was, at one point, tired of all the paintings he had of Van Gogh's in his attic and burned them. Van Gogh hardly sold any paintings during his lifetime. Another story is that of the prostitute who refused a painting as payment, and Van Gogh, in a rage, tore off his ear as payment. A misunderstood and repressed genius, he was never "forgotten". Even though the generations to follow would seize upon his work in order to speculate on its value, was his life, loyal as it was to his own values, well lived in such poverty and emotional misery?

8.2 Disapprenticeship is more difficult than apprenticeship

Laborit put a Wistar rat in a box with a bell that was followed by electrical discharges. The behavior of the rat followed two phases: the first is characterized by escape, even if the accompanying electric shocks are few – we call it the **escape phase**. The second phase, the **avoidance phase**, begins when the rat anticipates and escapes even if there is no electrical charge. The rat takes a certain amount of time, about 20 tries, before reaching the second phase. If it had been previously submitted to conditioning where there was no bell without electrical charges, it took him much more time to unlearn (Desor, 1994).

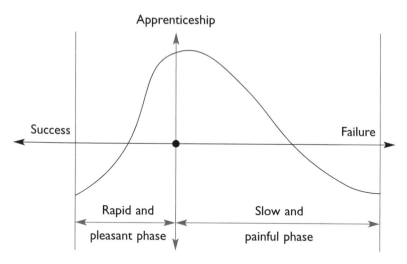

Exhibit 40 Disapprenticeship of success

The more rapid, numerous and long-lasting the success, the more the disapprenticeship will be long and difficult. We soon regard as a "has-been" someone who has been very successful, but who is now incapable of unlearning previous behavior in order to handle a less pleasant situation. We can cite cases of athletes or famous actors, incapable of continuing to live, once their "hour of glory" has passed.

▶ "In 1975, I acquired one of those first small financial calculators, the H.P. 80. The system used Polish notation that corresponded to a particular logic: You enter the data and work from the base of this data. Later, I had to buy a conventional calculator and I had constant problems with it., as the original Polish logic had been imprinted on my brain from the first experience. Fortunately, in 1986, the first P.C.'s arrived on the scene."

8.3 The relationship between disapprenticeship and irreversible situations

"Unlearning" or disapprenticeship is what must occur when we've lost, and the situation has become definitive. The approach towards retirement must be prepared for with a disapprenticeship of work, for a separation, the disapprenticeship of life as a couple, for death, the disapprenticeship of life to cite only a few of the more dramatic events:

1. The person, used to success, experiences failure.
2. Move on to step 3 or step 4.
3. She denies this failure, sets off her defenses and reinforces her behavior, go back to 1.
4. She becomes aware of the new character of the situation and the limits of her behavior,
5. She unlearns and adapts.

Grief theory has been primitively expressed in Jungian analysis and more generally in psychotherapy. It comes from the observation that psychotherapeutic help begins with a promise that one can overcome the impossibility of adaptation and ends as soon as the person has definitively renounced its symbolic protection. We speak of "grieving". We can define this theory as a process that allows one to be rid of defense mechanisms as soon as they become more of a hindrance than a help. This theory made decisive progress with Elisabeth Kübler-Ross, who attacked this "small" piece of reality – death – that had been neglected by medical researchers. Elisabeth Kübler-Ross analyzed the psychic transformations that the terminally ill made in their close relationship with death. She discovered that the "disapprenticeship of life" occurs around five distinct phases. We can observe similar phases in most disapprenticeships, though sometimes phases 2 and 3 are reversed. We have also observed the succession of these phases for persons engaged in long negotiations where they are deeply involved, but which are headed for failure. We will discuss this in the following chapter ...

9. A Brief Overview of This Chapter

9.1 Limited behavioral capacity

We can't know how to do everything. No matter what the personal capacity, behavioral range is "marked off". And in unknown or high-risk situations, it may be even more limited by strong emotions.

9.2 Gap in relation to the norm

In fact, our emotional life is organized around norms in the sense that what is produced is always different from our norms.

Exhibit 41 The emotional ladder of failure

9.3 Refusal of failure

This gap, in certain specified conditions, is experienced as a failure. It will be refused if the norms persist. It will be accepted if the norms permit it.

9.4 Guilt feelings

Failure always sets off a full production of reproach towards oneself and this level of reproach is increased if we were brought up with principles that made us believe that we could resolve anything, that we were "omnipotent".

9.5 Who fails?

Failure is fundamental for it is there that we either learn, or dig in our heels and become even more maladjusted. However, in order for learning to occur, the gap must not surpass certain of our limits.

9.6 Emotional collapse

If such is the case, we "fall apart". In general, the element of surprise helps to reduce behavioral capacity to nothing. It is even very probable that we will engage in inappropriate behaviors and thus, aggravate the situation ourselves.

9.7 The increase of emotional resistance

At that point, the fundamental problem is one of flexibility of the norms and that varies considerably with the situation. One "loses it easily" for a relatively small gap in a simple situation, while we may "hang in there" in situations that are very difficult.

9.8 The disapprenticeship of success

The most seriously affected are those that have had success too early or too easily, as they don't understand – on a psychological level – when success is no longer their own rendezvous with destiny.

CHAPTER 5

Irreversible Situations

*Failure is not definitive. An irreversible situation is. Most of the time it is maladapted emotional production that aggravates the situation of failure, a series of bad decisions that eventually makes the situation irreversible. The individual usually reacts "blindly", but can also take on an attitude we call "Attila", where the actor behaves in an inappropriate way on purpose. Once **the point of no return** is passed, the actor must go through **a grieving process** and the internal psychic acceptance will be accompanied by a rich and diverse emotional production that we will describe in this chapter.*

> Happiness is like a slipstream, it faithfully follows those who don't pursue it. If we stop to think about it, it immediately vanishes. (Origin unknown)

Among the **human** phenomena studied, the (almost) perfect example of irreversibility is death. Cancer that reaches the level of the ganglions and lymphatic system, being HIV positive in the 90's, a fall into empty space … all these can be considered irreversible. Cosmetic surgery is also irreversible. You have to be sure not to be making a mistake in taking that decision – afterwards there is no turning back.

At the **physical** level, we can admit without great risk that throwing a computer into fire or water is an irreversible process as far as getting the computer to work again. The same for a vase that has fallen and broken, an indelible spot on a piece of clothing, a cup of coffee that has spilled on a computer drive, etc.

At the **sports** level, a parachute jump is irreversible. Once you've jumped, it is no longer possible to get back in the plane. Pulling the trigger of a gun is also irreversible; nothing can stop the bullet after that.

An **organizational** model of irreversibility is company liquidation by the courts, loss of employment, work accident or a definitive sick leave …

At the **mathematical** level, it is the theory of graphs that gives us the concepts to define the irreversibility of a state. It defines states[1] and changes in a state[2]. A "final" state is irreversible, that is to say, once achieved, there is a 100% chance that it will stay that way.

At the **emotional** level, we qualify irreversibility as an autonomous process that affects us, for which we must grieve instead of trying to change it or avoid it. This state is called "letting go".

1. the less the actor has control of the situation,
2. the more the situation will evolve autonomously,
3. the less it will be possible to escape,
4. the more the actor must grieve over his lost ability to escape the situation, if he wants to conserve his mental health.

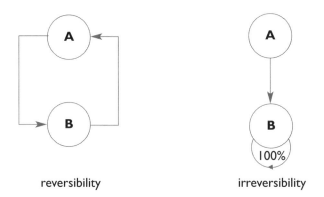

reversibility   irreversibility

Exhibit 42 Irreversible situations

1. The Permanence of Irreversibility

In action management, we define irreversibility as the process by which the deterioration of the situation is such that it is impossible, with the means and energy that we have at our disposal, to go back to a previous state. Irreversibility is the situation that comes after a confrontation between the external and internal environment The actor no longer possesses the means to turn the situation to his advantage, as the situation has inexorably evolved along its own logic, perceived by the actor as unfavorable in relation to his own norms. If the actor has no means to react and if, in addition, he cannot escape the situation, we say that it is irreversible in the sense that he must live through it and adapt to it. Winning the lottery is an irreversible situation. These processes are rarer than ones concerning situation degradation.

1.1 The principle of the permanence of irreversibility

The permanence of irreversibility is established in mathematics by a theorem that states that from the moment a situation[3] is in its final state, the probability that it will not continue on to the end is zero. There is only a difference of rhythm. Certain situations very quickly become irreversible, others take much longer.

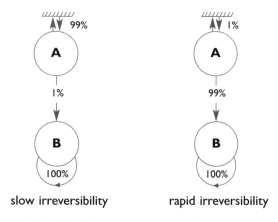

slow irreversibility   rapid irreversibility

Exhibit 43 The permanence of irreversibility

In *The New Alliance* (1979), Prigogne (Nobel Prize winner) and Stengers established the irreversibility of phenomena involving energy. The irreversibility of time was established by Reichenbach, Popper, Mehlberg, Bücher, Adams, Penrose and Percival (Costa de Beauregard, 1963). In emotional logic, Robert Blondin (1983) updated a series of principles one of which, "never go back", is a sine qua non, not only for happiness but very simply for personal balance. Psychotherapists warn that beyond the risk of the psychic destruction of the personality, there is a risk of suicide for people who, under pressure from their environment, choose to go back on a decision they had paid dearly for. A large part of the activity of Jacques Salomé (1984) consists of stopping his patients from trying to turn back the clock while going through the grieving process. Elisabeth Kübler-Ross (1985) cites the danger that the dying risk when their family tries to hold on to them. In order for death to occur in an atmosphere of serenity, the process requires that you accompany them through their process, without trying to hold them back.

1.2 The principle of entropy of exchanges between the internal and external environments

Costa de Beauregard speaks about the degradation of the universe following information production: "If someone learns something, the entropy of the universe increases." In effect, when a situation deteriorates and becomes irreversible, it produces information for the decision-maker concerned. This "transformation" translates simultaneously into both a degradation of the external environment and an enrichment[4] of the internal environment. But the psyche obeys the principle of entropy: the energy of degradation is superior to the information produced. Entropy and irreversibility are often associated, at least in our research domain. The degradation of the external environment enriches the actor with know-how that allows him to economize energy and leaves him capable of adapting.

2. The Scientific Exception: The Disappearance of Aversive Situations

With this exception to the principle of irreversibility, we enter a "forbidden zone". Are we in the presence of delirium or denial of actual, unexplained facts, or, on the contrary, is it a new paradigm questioning the validity of the old?

2.1 Momentarily reversible death

Scientific progress has put the community of researchers in confrontation with a new fact: people declared clinically dead are brought back to life later and later thanks to more and more complex procedures. Up to this point, no real problem, except they are finding that they are playing witness to intense emotional activity during those few minutes when they are midway between the two states, otherwise correctly defined as life and death. The 102 witnesses selected, using an extremely strict method[5], then studied with all scientific rigor by Kent Ring, professor of psychology at the University of Connecticut, allows us to establish consistency in which this is emotionally experienced. What cannot be defined, on the other hand, is if the experience is purely emotional or real. In other words, are the witness reports a product of coherent cerebral activity – which seems a little ironic – set off probably by the massive production of natural, highly euphoric substances freed by the brain at the moment of death, or is it an experience truly lived within the other universe that is awaiting the subject upon his death?

Situation definition	The situation	
	Dream (internal environment)	Reality (external environment)
Dream	Rational logic	Emotional logic or denial
Reality	Emotional logic and delirium	Rational logic

Exhibit 44 Denial or delirium

If what the witness reports is reality and he qualifies it as a dream, we are in the presence of denial[6] in the face of troublesome facts. If what the witness reports is a dream, while he qualifies it as reality, we are in the presence of delirium[7]. The choice poses an interesting problem, as it forces us to deepen the notion of testimony from the moment a fact is reported by the human brain and not recorded by a machine. What is troubling in this type of testimony is the extreme precision with which the witnesses describe the situations concerned as if they were experienced from the outside, from another angle, from some distance[8]. We can establish with certainty today that the state of being clinically dead can be reversed in the few minutes that follow a cardiac arrest, and that represents a great blow to the definition of irreversibility.

2.2 "Incurable" illness reversible?

Rigorous scientific accounting has established the existence of inexplicable healing in our current state of medical knowledge. Irreversibility being the essence of the human species, its disappearance has always been considered either as inexplicable if we adopt the scientific point of view, or as divine, if we adopt the religious point of view. Both points of view admit that these inexplicable facts have a tendency to occur within a particular structure: they do not seem to be produced at random, but often within cults, or within some sort of religious symbolism or in the presence of children, women or men engaged in religious testimony. On the other hand, they can concern anybody including nonbelievers. These facts completely overwhelm those who were the objects or witnesses of this phenomenon and it changes their emotional life by bringing them much more serenity and peace than they had before the experience[9].

▶ July 1973. Telling the story of the circumstances in which hundreds of pulmonary lesions, due to his tuberculosis, had healed in one night, Father Emilien Tardiff (Canada) explained that a group of Christians had visited him the night before and asked him to pray for himself. This good man, not wanting to hurt those "visionaries"[10], but also not wanting to appear foolish in front of the hospital personnel, asked them to close the door behind them. The next morning, he said – not without humor – to the doctor who was looking at the incredible healing showed by the X-rays: "You see, Doctor, I told them to close the door, but it was too late, Jesus had already entered …"[11]

2.3 Intuition and the point of no return

We also have testimony today reversing the arrow of time "facing the imminent point of no return". It occurs just before an accident, some microseconds before, as if the actor concerned has put into place behavior that allows him to avoid that point. Several stories that we know of seem to revolve around two tendencies. There are those that say: "I don't know why I did that; usually, I never do it, but it saved my life … " and there are those that were conscious of having obeyed a little voice in their heads. If we take the scientific point of view, we are confronting what we call "intuition", meaning a type of detection of a dangerous situation, by a reflexive action, from microinformation that is hardly audible in normal situations. Those who take a religious point of view consider that the actor perceives, in his internal environment, information coming from his external environment that is communicated to him by a protected force that can be referenced in the Bible[12].

▶ "C. is very allergic to bees. He's been studying for a test and has been reading for hours. A bit tired, he gets up, goes into the kitchen and takes a small bunch of grapes, was just about to put one in his mouth, when, mechanically, he felt pushed to wash them, which he normally never does, much to the chagrin of his girlfriend. He turns on the faucet and lets the water run over the grapes. Then looking out the window, lost in thought, he eats them. He looks down into the sink, and at the bottom of the sink, he sees a bee, soaked, trying to climb back up the sides of the sink. He crushes it, then becomes as white as a ghost … He realized that the bee was in the bunch of grapes … A simple jest, following his intuition, had saved his life …"

▶ "It must have been summer, because all I had on was a tee shirt. I was sanding with an electric sander that was fitted with a disk of heavy sandpaper, when a little voice in my head said: "Stop, there's going to be an accident." I cut the power and thinking about protecting myself from any sparks from the machine, I put on my protective glasses and – fatal error – started up the machine again, without taking off the disk to see what shape it was in –

several seconds later, the disk exploded! A piece cut into my right index finger and another lodged itself in my stomach."

▶ An afternoon in January in Fremont in the heart of Silicon Valley. Pierre Jovaniovic tells the story of how he had just left the Griol portable assembly factory and was on the highway, in a rental car driven by his friend. It was very calm when, all of a sudden, he threw himself towards the left, at the second when a bullet shot through the windshield, exactly where he would have been had he not moved. During the police investigation, the Highway Patrol told him that there were snipers in the area. He asked himself why he had thrown himself towards the left BEFORE the impact and not after?[13]

Today it is clear that there are three types of existing observations, and while we are no longer in the phase where the recognition of these phenomena immediately results in thoughts of witches, the controversy over their interpretation is far from finished.

3. The Increase of Aversive Situations

3.1 The principle of the chain of bad decisions (C.B.D.)

We can caricature this emotional process as **danger increases danger**.

This process is at the core of deterioration. From unfavorable, the situation becomes irreversible. It is the product of emotional production that panics the actor caught in the brutal deterioration of a situation. It presents itself in three ways, the first of which belongs in the external environment of the actor, the other two belonging to his internal environment.

1. the more the actor is in a dangerous situation,
2. the more his intense emotional activity will interfere with his decisions,
3. the more he will have the tendency to increase danger, by the inappropriate character of his actions.

Readers who have been trained in security measures know that the essential thing to do in an accident is, first of all, insure that a second and even third accident is avoided:

1. An aversive event occurs.
2. The more the person is shaken up emotionally by the event,

3. the more he will try to quickly do away with the event,
4. the less he will take precautions,
5. the more he will hide what is happening,
6. the less he will face the situation,
7. the less he will be aware of what is happening around him,
8. the more risk there will be to aggravate the situation by a chain of bad decisions.

▶ The Airbag is a system illustrating perfectly the struggle against the process of aggravation: this system is capable of receiving information when there is a sudden and violent deceleration, and then inflating in less time than it takes for a human being to be crushed against the dashboard of the vehicle.

▶ The morning-after pill is also a good example of clinical invention targeted to reverse an irreversible biological process.

▶ Once, during my first ULM flight return, I found myself virtually out of gas, almost at the runway, but this "almost" happened to be a forest that separated me and the machine from the runway. You have to have experienced this personally to understand the irresistible attraction of being confronted with the alternative, albeit fatal, that consisted of asking yourself if taking the risk to cross the forest to get to the runway was not possible. The risk of being totally out of gas would be the result of a bad decision and wasn't too serious, but would be very upsetting to a beginning pilot who would have a high level of respect for the rules in order not to risk his life by taking a second bad decision.

▶ We are very familiar with the battle that security has – in the parking lots of large companies – with cars that are parked illegally. We are less familiar with the reason why, which comes from the fact that if there is a serious fire, the firetrucks would not have access to the building due to these illegally parked cars. In effect, aggravation of a fire is proportional to an exponent of the time that has lapsed before intervention. Specialists say: "One minute delay and you need a thimble full of water, 2 minutes and you need a pail …"

▶ In a financial company, the transfer of an order by computer on a Friday afternoon had an error of a comma which would change absolutely everything about the purchase and its consequences in case of a drop in index. The author didn't take the time to warn his director, and it was someone less informed that became aware of the error. Terribly shaken up, she reported it to the management. It was an exhausting end of week for the staff and an anxious wait before Monday morning, but in reality the error was really nothing.

▶ The principle behind short-term economy is also a cause of C.B.D.: in 1995, Marie-Claude was president of a students' association for her graduating class, and when she asked, the secretary lent her the keys to the office, giving her her entire key chain. Why did the secretary give her the key chain instead of just taking off the key that Marie-Claude needed? When asked, she said she just didn't think of it. She wanted to avoid the annoying task of taking off one key from a key ring, but, without realizing it, she was setting off a chain of bad decisions. The secretary called her family to tell them that Marie-Claude would be coming back with the keys and that she would wait at a neighbor's. After having come from across town, Marie-Claude arrived at school, learned what had happened and became very upset, very agitated …. The risk of a car accident was considerably increased and she only just avoided one. It is interesting to note that the secretary also made a "C.B.D.": upset by the absence of her keys, once at her house, she didn't even ring the bell, and her brother, who was inside the whole time, could have let her in …

When something happens that could be serious for your company, and you are involved, it is indispensable to acquire the reflex to warn your hierarchical superior so that those susceptible to the consequences can be warned. For a director, there is no such thing as a good surprise. Confronted with a telephone call from the outside concerning the event, he must be able to say that he is aware of the situation.

3.2 "Hiding your head in the sand"

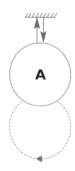

Exhibit 45 Hiding your head in the sand

Concerning the second dimension of C.B.D., there is a much more colorful and more descriptive expression to illustrate this process of the chain: "hiding your head in the sand". We often use this to describe the emotional "approach" of a gambler or a lover who loses time and time again, and again plays his luck, without having the psychological energy necessary to perceive that he is facing a situation that he cannot master and that will become irreversible if he persists. More commonly we say "I can't help myself". At the level of family, Milton

Erickson stated that if a couple are on the point of breaking up, they often react by deciding to have just one more baby or to buy a bigger and more beautiful house. Another example of a chain of bad decisions destined to create irreversibility by using "magic" is given by people who, badly shaken by a divorce, remarry immediately without giving themselves the time to step back.

3.3 "Blocking"

This is a sort of "stop!" that allows you to block the continuation of the preceding mechanisms. It is discovered in computers where, because of an error in programming, two "if" and "go to" instructions keep turning back on each other and block the following program from taking place. The actor, in a situation that is apt to transform into a catastrophe can, by a "sifting" procedure, and by putting all his energy into it, day and night, try to "force" the discovery of a solution that would permit him to impede the degradation of the situation.

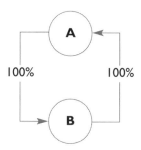

Exhibit 46
The emotional block

This procedure consists of psychological exaggeration – imagining the worst of the situation – giving weight *ex ante* to certain events in order to block the real aggravation *ex post*.

QUESTIONNAIRE 19

Are you at risk of C.B.D.?

Put a check in one column for each question using the key below:

1: I completely disagree

2: I mildly disagree

3: I'm not sure

4: I mildly agree

5: I completely agree

Connect the checks. The more your profile appears on the right-hand side, the more you have responded positively to the question.

	1	2	3	4	5
1.　I make choices based exclusively on my emotions.					
2.　I panic easily.					
3.　I don't listen when others tell me to do things differently.					
4.　People say I'm immature.					
5.　I have a lot of sexual partners, I abandon myself impulsively to the moment.					
6.　When I fail at something, I don't think about tomorrow.					
7.　People say I'm carefree.					
8.　I like to scare myself.					

3.4 "Attila the Hun"

"Where my horse has trod, grass no longer grows." This attitude has two opposing origins: narcissism and despair. Narcissistic people (Lowen, 1987) are those who break up the "game" after having taken advantage of it, who are simply desperate, and for whom others and particularly those who come after them have absolutely no importance in comparison to the seriousness of the situation they have just been through. These people have the commonality of playing out the end of the game in such a way as to destroy the game itself. They burn the field so that others who come afterwards have nothing left:

1. at the moment of an event or an agreeable situation,
2. the more the actor arbitrates his choices in relation to himself and the short term,
3. the more he extracts from the situation without any "ecological worry" to preserve it.
4. the more he will leave behind a deteriorated situation, at risk of becoming irreversible.

▶ The Attila approach was also used by the Russians facing a Napoleonic invasion. In face of the French troops, they burned everything that could be at all used by the invading troops.

▶ Within organizations, this attitude could be that of the director who is being asked to submit his resignation and sees himself being used as a bargaining condition for help for his ailing company. It is rare that he will accept to do this, and the society will go down along with him. This process occurs with egocentric persons, or people who do not bother with morality and ethics, who do not accept their failure, or who will try to take advantage of their leaving to transform the situation into a collective catastrophe, a situation that they have finished taking advantage of or that has become unfavorable for them: a member of a political party having lost its majority, a fired employee, etc.

▶ In the 80's, France installed a chain of two-star hotels. A well-known team in the business had taken an "Attila" approach, having so "burned" their bridges that they were forced to escape abroad. The professional world in France is small. Everyone knows everyone.

▶ There are also renters, who having been expelled from their homes, literally destroy their apartments before leaving. Without having to go that far, we see on highways, a car that had stopped in an open, green, clean space, for a picnic, and leaving it a mess, filled with their garbage. Even at the micro-behavior level, one can adopt an Attila attitude. A smoker in a car lowers his window to throw out his cigarette butt or his empty pack, instead of using the car's ashtray …

▶ We have seen student associations, who, before leaving and giving back their "keys", had used the venue without respect for the rules. The process is the same for our century – the problem of gas – that burns and pollutes the planet, without having any concern over the state of our planet or the generations to follow. For real estate owners, this attitude also exists, where generations have profited by their renters without maintaining the apartments, so that the generations that follow must reinvest in the renovation of this inheritance.

▶ At the Lorrain Center of Management, where we teach, there is a good quality, low-price cafeteria. The other side of the coin to this good quality/price relationship is that each one must clean up after themselves when they have finished their meal. After 12:45 p.m., you have the impression that someone had dropped all the garbage cans of the building onto the dining tables, as so many of the students behave like little Attilas, without worrying about those who follow them and must sit down at these tables: spilled coffee, cigarette butts everywhere, dozens of dirty glasses and empty sandwich bags.

QUESTIONNAIRE 20

Are you Attila the Hun without knowing it?

Put a check in one column for each question using the key below:

1: I completely disagree

2: I mildly disagree

3: I'm not sure

4: I mildly agree

5: I completely agree

Connect the checks. The more your profile appears on the right-hand side, the more you have responded positively to the question.

	1	2	3	4	5
1. If I'm caught, I'll just leave town.					
2. People are stupid, they only want to just get along.					
3. I don't want kids, they're a pain in the neck.					
4. I like to make my opponents think they're winning, and then I destroy them at the last minute.					
5. One lost, 10 found.					
6. I change my car every 2 or 3 years.					
7. I earn enough, but I spend more.					
8. I am completely indifferent to the opinions of others.					
9. I throw my cigarette butts out the window.					
10. I throw my empty cigarette packs on the floor.					
11. After me, the deluge …					
12. I do not hesitate to badmouth my last employer.					
13. I don't really care about leaving the toilet seat dirty.					
14. I use diesel oil that burns.					
15. I leave the water running.					
16. I throw bleach down the drain.					

4. The Point of No Return

4.1 The principle of no return

While in the course of a situation's evolution, **the idea** of the possibility of going back on a risky decision diminishes the anxiety linked to the risk of failure, you must be careful not to believe that it is the **act** itself that diminishes anxiety.

▶ Frank, 34 years old, manager in training:

"First of all, you have to be able to imagine the atmosphere of a desert. Imagine intense heat, predominance of sand, a horizon that is sometimes perfectly uniform and identical as you make a 360 degree turn. Add in a certain amount of anxiety, ever-present and necessary, in the form of a small knot in your stomach. I had traveled about 100 kilometers, and here it's been almost two hours since I'd seen anything but sand. No longer anything to indicate that the objective, a water source, is in this direction. No longer anything to position me vis-à-vis my point of departure, which was by now totally outside of my horizon. Needless to say that in this void of indications, doubt is born. Was it normal to see none of the indicators that I was sure to have crossed by now? In other words, was I on the right road? Was I on a road at all? If I wasn't on a road, then no one would be able to find me, if I ran out of gas or water. Again, in other words was I (and here we have the mental pronunciation of the word which is taboo) lost? I noticed that it was probable that I would be if I didn't act now. Stop. Two possible solutions:

1. continue, in the hope that I was going in the right direction, which, having just one compass, I realized was only a hope as soon as I voiced the question,

2. Turn around and go back towards the point where I last felt safe.

It was that that really positioned the danger. At that moment there was no longer any certainty. The compass wouldn't help me like a sextant or a GPS to discover my geographic location. So I took the decision to continue, which was based on an uncertain hypothesis from the start. The point of arrival was just as uncertain and hypothetical. If I opted for this decision, it meant that I opted for another 300 km of doubt and anxiety justified by the fear of not reaching my important objective. On the other hand, if I chose to turn back, I was closing off the possibility of resolving my mental position. In effect, the hypothesis of the immediate security of finding my point of origin with certainty by retracing my steps, was predominant. But I "knew" because the wise men of the desert told me that I may not refind my steps for a long time as they would have been rapidly erased and confused with other older markings that went out in all directions. If I lost this lead, without having found my objective, I would once again be in the same situation. A call to reason, against my emotion, against my fear, was the only way to assure the validity of any chosen solution and the quality of the endeavor. Therein lay my chance, the chance to be still sufficiently far from panic, even though I felt it approaching, that I could still think things through. Reason forced me to listen to the precious advice I had been given and to retrace my past route in order to envision the future. I started up again and continued on my way." *(interview, February 16, 1999)*

In looking at the danger of trying to go back, we can isolate certain material decisions regarding actual product purchases for which the possibility of being able to go back effectively reduces angst (Jarrosson, 1994). Anxiety linked with purchase is well-known to the marketing community who make sure to put the following reassuring phrase on the top of their instruction pamphlets: "You have just bought a 'Brand X' vacuum cleaner. Congratulations, you have made the best choice." Anxiety linked to the irreversibility of a purchase is known also by Darty (chain stores selling household and electronic products in France), who offer an immediate replacement of the machine if it functions poorly. Concerning **human situations** of the "on-the-job failure" type or within a couple, we observe attempts to believe in reversibility. For example, Christiane Collange[14] shows numerous examples of divorced couples who chose to try a new life together. The possibility of going back on the decision makes the person feel safe about going ahead with the process, but the actual going through with it represents a powerful factor within the decomposition of the personality that can block the individual in a definitive situation if the point of no return is passed …

4.2 The point of no return (P.N.R.)

There are **decisions of no return** (D.N.R.) and **events of no return**, and in practice the two follow each other very closely.

On the rational level, transgressing a work or highway security rule, jumping off into space in bungee jumping is a D.N.R.

On the emotional level, when we know things will never be as they were before, and that we are firm in our decision to leave the job or the couple, we have reached a P.N.R.

In human situations of proximity, belonging to the realm of maintenance of the group or the collective, the point of no return designates a symbolic limit that must not be passed if we don't want to personally take the consequences of a deteriorating situation. From the moment this limit is passed, it is no longer possible to avoid the consequences.

Emotionally speaking, when is it no longer possible to retrace our steps? Beyond that limit is it still possible to stop? Where exactly is the limit in a process that has already been engaged: in front or behind us? I have, like everyone else, experienced several points of no return and I believe that its emotional characteristic is its own proof: objectively undefinable, the P.N.R. is subjectively clear when one has reached it:

1. A reversible, but risky, situation is produced,
2. the actor acts, but does not take into account the risk,
3. the actor loses control in the sense that the follow-up has escaped his control,
4. the point of no return is passed,
5. go on to 6 or 7.
6. Nothing happens.
7. An irreversible accident occurs.

▶ In a plane, a propeller plane, the point of no return represents the geographical place in the path where no matter what the consequences for the pilot, he must continue, because there isn't enough gas left to allow him to make a U-turn back to the airstrip given the direction of the wind.

For someone in a glider plane, there is an altitude of no return (A.N.R.). For a given aerodynamic efficiency α the more a glider distances himself from his base, the more he must increase his altitude in order to be able to go back.

If a pilot is facing the wind, he has an increase in aerodynamic efficiency. All travel in the darkest area represents an obligation to land in a flat area, not being able to return to base.

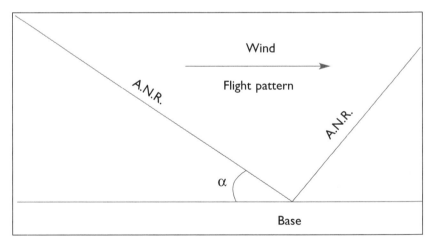

Exhibit 47 Illustration of the danger linked with no return

▶ Sexual intercourse without protection represents a P.N.R., vis-à-vis the risk of being HIV positive. As for pregnancy, the P.N.R. occurs around the tenth week[15], beyond that abortion is prohibited (in France). In psychoanalysis, it is symbolically the level of engagement where it is more dangerous for the psyche to stop than to continue. Within groups, as an example, in masonic rituals of initiation (Bayard, 1982), there is a P.N.R. within the process. At several different moments before that point, the candidate is told he could stop now and pull out if so desired. Afterwards, irreversibility is acquired through modification of the informational and emotional states of the candidate. Social situations involving a factor of authority (law or boss ...) moving from thought into action[16] is prohibited and will be sanctioned by a judicial procedure. In the teaching of negotiation, the dilemma of prisoner "AX-BY" occurs in 12 stages, containing a P.N.R. that will definitively close the situation to the advantage of the "cheater" if the act occurs in the ninth period. There is also a P.N.R. in those situations of professional negotiation that turn into conflict, because the personal nature of the attacks, as well as their violence, indicates that no matter what is done, there is no other solution other than confrontation that will result in the termination of the negotiations. Even if the culture of the society defines how far one can go, this point is variable and the act of sequestration represents a P.N.R. for most managers in most organizations.

5. The Status of Victim

The status of victim represents almost perfect resistance to grief. It seems that the victim is one of the most solid reactions that oppose the healing grieving process. An "emotional status" is conferred on the person by the feelings that his colleagues experience towards him. In the absence of a losing situation, the person that wants to benefit from such a status can create a hierarchical conflict when there is an organizational change; he has everything to gain, for even if he loses he will benefit from the number of advantages that the victim status confers upon him, notably consideration from others. The appearance of an illness can also produce a veritable turnaround in a situation. From dreaded persecutor, the person can become a respected victim. Illness following anxiety can be a very expensive, but very efficient "strategy". Of course, all illnesses are not the product of the unconscious operating as a savior of the cornered "ego", but in certain cultures, illness could represent the ultimate winning strategy, as the psyche finally obtains, thanks to the illness, the gratification that it seeks. The preceding elements in the analysis of the victim status in the extreme case of illness can also be found in everyday behavior. It is important to note, however, that the claiming of the victim status, without the presence of a real victim situation, attracts the most suspicion, at least in our Western culture. The tendency to seek out the benefits of this status resembles the tendency to seek out a mother figure, expecting the organization or others to help and protect:

1. the more the employee complains about the situation without acting to change it and without fleeing it,
2. the more the situation is described as unjust by those who know about it,
3. the more the employee benefits from the sympathy of others without having to account or pay for it,
4. the more his superiors hesitate to put pressure on him or even to demand normal results,
5. the more the employee benefits from increased tolerance,
6. the more those who know about the problem, come to him to find out how he is,
7. the more the employee will feel free to be disagreeable, even terribly so, the more one could think that the employee is acting within the emotional production of the status of victim.

QUESTIONNAIRE 21

Do you tend to play the victim?

Put a check in one column for each question using the key below:

1: I completely disagree

2: I mildly disagree

3: I'm not sure

4: I mildly agree

5: I completely agree

Connect the checks. The more your profile appears on the right-hand side, the more you have responded positively to the question.

	1	2	3	4	5
1. Do you tend to drive yourself in a self-sacrificing manner?					
2. Do you expect recognition for what you do?					
3. When you're ill, do you feel you have the right to be unpleasant?					
4. Do you like it when people speak kindly of you, admire you or complain about you?					
5. Will you sacrifice your choice of T.V. so that the others can watch their programs?					
6. You prefer that your companion chooses the restaurant.					
7. Do people listen to you easily when you talk about your problems?					
8. Your superior always speaks kindly and carefully to you.					

6. The Status of Substitute

This represents the ultimate resistance to grief: the lost subject – a child, a person, an animal – is replaced by another child, another person, another animal. They take the same name. Ludwig van Beethoven, Vincent Van Gogh and Salvador Dali are in this case (Cyrulnik, 1997, p. 133). When a dog is replaced by another dog, it has been shown that the suffering of this second animal could render the subject ill. The spouse who has left is replaced, very rapidly, by someone else who physically resembles him/her and from this we have the theory of the second couple, a most difficult one to succeed in.

7. The Grieving Process

For most members of an organization, the image that they have of themselves depends quite a lot on the system to which they belong and the place that they have succeeded in obtaining in this system. Certain people have dedicated months, sometimes years, in trying to make a place for themselves in the organization, to obtain a place that gives them a positive self-image. Change is a permanent given within an organization; changes that succeed are a continuous process arrived at by small successive changes. They respect the internal rhythm of people's ability to adapt. Sometimes managers impose more brutal changes on their organizations, no doubt because it has either become imperative, because they don't know how to pilot these evolutions day by day or because they didn't see the transformations of a market in full mutation. There can be great upheaval that will effectively modify the affective relationships within the organization. Psychologically, all change that results in a loss necessitates a process of "digestion": grieving.

7.1 The object of grief

Grief is the process by which the gap between the real situation and the situation definition made by the actor is slowly reduced in order to arrive at a final acceptance of things and the gap no longer exists.

Self-image destroyed: the object of the grief is a certain image we have of ourselves. "We manufacture **masks**; if, at a given moment, we have the opportunity to burn those masks, we can only do so by going through a tragic mourning process. All mourning is painful; but more so by the esteem that others give to us: parents, friends, children, colleagues, professors, who have seen us struggle towards the top, without worrying about the valleys we must cross…. Everyone will be disappointed, sad, unhappy to have to see that their admired subject was stupidly crushed by the difficulties of existence" (Donnars, 1982).

This complex process is accompanied by intense and astonishingly rich emotional production. In general, we can classify this production into five approximately distinct steps, that, also in general, follow each other. If the process is about to enter phase 5, there has been psychological success, in all other cases, failure. Each one of these steps corresponds to the putting into action of defense systems that are targeted at deforming information in order to protect the "ego". Little by little, the irreversible nature of the situation is clear, and in the best of cases, the individual accepts the situation as it is.

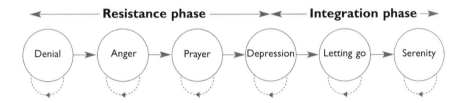

Exhibit 48 The grieving process

1. The irreversibility of the situation is at first denied.
2. The situation is, at first, treated as a simple problem (that causes anger).
3. It is then treated as a conflict (which necessitates negotiation).
4. It is then felt as a failure (which causes depression).
5. It is finally accepted, facing the failures of previous procedures of mitigation (which permits the feeling of peace and serenity).

The situation is at first exterior to the individual. The defense mechanisms will play their part, one after the other, to block the situation from being assimilated and integrated.

The very new appearance – in this millennium – of the situation where a man knows, years in advance, how he will die (AIDS), has given birth to further testimony of the grieving process and on the changes in values (4.6) that operate in these situations.

7.2 The denial phase

"I only thought it could happen to others!"

During the second chapter, we established a schema that represented the deterioration of a situation and showed that this deterioration is accompanied by more and more informational production. Faced with the irreversibility of a situation, denial is a mental operation by which the human brain becomes incapable of comprehending this information. It is obliged – in order to maintain the ego structure intact – to pretend as if this information was illegible or inexistent. Denial constitutes a program of mental flight from a situation. As flight results from an analysis of the situation, denial erases its existence. Behind all denial of reality, there is often the inappropriate feeling of being all powerful.

> ▶ "Crossing the street, a pedestrian hurries to avoid a car that is moving too quickly? It's a program of avoidance. On the contrary, the pedestrian who slows down his pace, because 'car drivers can go slowly like everybody else', that's a program of denial!"

> ▶ A car driver sees a large truck in front of him that is beginning to move to the side. If he moves to the right, it's a program of avoidance that is perfectly appropriate. He moves to the left, and it's a program of denial.

> ▶ The head of an enterprise is asked to come in to see his banker (he has greatly exceeded his credit limit). He adopts a low profile. He doesn't understand, and acts as if it was nothing at all. That's a program of denying reality.

7.2.1 Denial of situations

Denial is the most powerful of all the defense mechanisms. Consisting of a denial of reality, it often appears as psychotic behavior. It testifies to the highly fragile mental health of those that employ it.

> ▶ The film *Furyo* by the director Nadisa Oshima, produced by Jeremy Thomas (1982), shows David Bowie playing the role of an English officer imprisoned in a Japanese camp. Each morning he goes through the motions of washing up and shaving even though he has no water, no razor, no towel. The game is to deny reality in order to survive.

> ▶ The most characteristic of industrial denial is powdered milk. It is estimated that about 1.5 million children have died in non-developed countries after being fed on bottles prepared with powdered milk and non-treated,

non-sterilized water. At the beginning of the 80's, an internal code of ethics was put into place that prohibited advertising for breast milk substitutes. When questioned, the international Swiss conglomerate replied: "Nonpotable water is a danger for all alimentation and not uniquely for powdered milk", and continued to push young mothers to stop breastfeeding early. The market was estimated at 250 million dollars with an annual growth rate of 6%. *(Canal +, February 28, 1999)*

▶ Certain families, stuck in the denial phase, keep a place at the table for someone who has departed. There are other rituals also destined to defeat irreversibility, like leaving a candle burning, or a lamp lit, that show that we are waiting for the departed to return. Certain families, on the other hand, determined to completely erase the person in the collective memory, someone who has put the family at risk for example, will prohibit anyone from saying that person's name aloud.

▶ I was present at the most flagrant example of denial ever. We were on a ULM field at Delme (in France) when an unknown pilot joined us for a month's vacation. According to his papers, he was a pilot monitor. Friendships formed, a local pilot lent him a "three axes", whose sensitivity at slow speeds was well-known. He took off, went around the field and in his last approach, which was too slow, plunged and crashed. The pilot wasn't hurt. I saw this man yell about the machine, the weather, the wind but at no point did he admit the cause might have been with himself. One year later, again during vacation, he came back. We were wary of him. There were several new machines, one of which had to be broken in. He offered to do that, without taking off. The owner pilot wasn't aware of what had happened last time and he agreed. The former went out, took off and crashed again, but this time it was very serious and he only just escaped being killed. I went to see him at the hospital, after he had had several operations and after the police had taken away his license. He hadn't changed a bit. His explanations were still the same: it was again the fault of the machine, the wind, etc. Absolutely no question of his piloting.

7.2.2 Ostracism towards others

▶ Unable to get rid of someone considered as an "outsider", the famous West Point military academy practices *ostracism* (pretending that the undesirable person doesn't exist, destroying his things and anything else that concerns him, his mail, for instance) towards those recruits whose will has resisted all attempts at bending. Most leave, some commit suicide, and only one has resisted: James J. Pelosi, who became famous. How did he do it? "I read, I trained in sports, I started conversations with the Military Police." He lost 13 kgs during this reign of silence. *(Steinberg, 1975)*

7.2.3 Negation of one's own death

Certain psychiatrists feel it is reasonable to consider the hypothesis that senility is the last burst of energy with which the actor's brain puts itself out of service, because his life has resulted in a series of bad decisions that have distanced him, little by little, from his center and he must become aware of this in order to go into this last process with serenity.

QUESTIONNAIRE 22

Are you fond of denial?

Put a check in one column for each question using the key below:

1: I completely disagree

2: I mildly disagree

3: I'm not sure

4: I mildly agree

5: I completely agree

Connect the checks. The more your profile appears on the right-hand side, the more you have responded positively to the question.

		1	2	3	4	5
1.	Classes are OK, but it's a shame that the teachers aren't good, I would do much better.					
2.	I like my spouse. He does what he can.					
3.	People are very stupid and that annoys me.					
4.	I often have stomach aches, but I don't see doctors, they're incompetent.					
5.	Police would do better spending their time going after criminals, instead of giving me warnings.					
6.	I vote extreme right, because everything would be better with them.					
7.	I never use a condom when making love – it's useless.					
8.	Nazi camps only exist in the imagination of certain people.					
9.	I am eternal.					

7.3 The phase of anger and revolt

It's as if you are physically being pushed with a rush of adrenaline that you can't stop – you must let it continue and do its work. The exterior nature of the situation remains, but it becomes the object of violent attacks that could be directed at the person's loved ones, or at the "bearer" of the bad news, or anything else. History is filled with situations where the bearer of the bad news is subjected to the wrath of the prince. In the process of commercial negotiation, this phase will appear when it becomes clear that you must accept that the negotiation is lost.

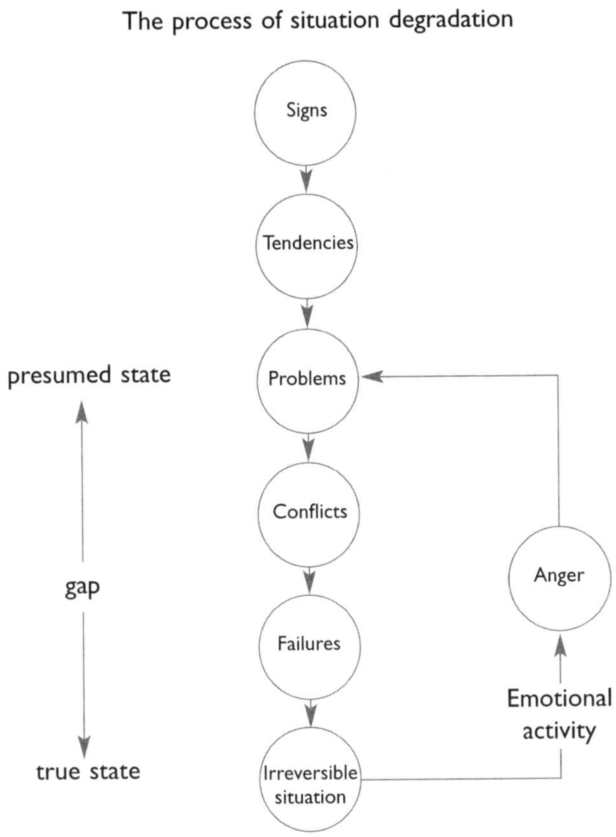

The process of situation degradation

Exhibit 49 A fit of anger. Irreversibility brought to a simple problem

A lawyer lost a grand jury case and was very angry: "If this is the law", he cried, "I'll burn my books." The judge responded, "It would be better if you read them."

7.4 The phase of negotiation and prayer

"When God wants to punish us, he answers our prayers."[17]

This curious proverb summarizes the danger inherent in using prayer to interrupt the grieving process. It is a phase of negotiation of "magic", in which the prayers are addressed to destiny[18]. The situation, in which we have sensed irreversibility, is "personalized". Bargaining occurs between the actor and the situation, or with any other divine intervention, or symbol, like a doctor, who is asked to act upon the irreversibility: "Doctor, one eye is better than nothing, no?" Often this bargaining consists of a request, a sort of payment. "If you heal me, Lord, I promise to … " and is followed by an act, or series of acts, that represent a large amount of symbolic spending, but is clearly less serious than irreversibility …

> ▶ "The story of the ring of Polycrate, tyrant of Syracuse, magnificently illus-
> trates the ritual of the gift. All was success for Polycrate: strong fleet, pros-
> perous village and Sicily was happy under his government. During an ocean
> voyage, wary of this happiness (in reality, he was very unhappy) he decided to
> make a sacrifice. He took off a magnificent emerald ring and threw it into the
> sea, thinking he was giving God proof of his obedience and faith. He returned
> to Syracuse. Everything seemed fine, but three days later, a great fish was
> brought to the palace. Upon opening the fish, they found Polycrate's ring! The
> gods had refused his gift. Polycrate went on to make a series of errors and
> finally his village was taken and destroyed."

If, having gone through this phase, the actor notices an inexplicable postponement of the irreversibility of the situation, he will associate the bargaining – the magical process – and the disappearance of the irreversibility, as an objective process. Certain people remain forever touched by this and profoundly change their lives; others will quickly forget their promises. The most impressive, when observing the latter, is to observe how human dignity will fly out the window in such situations. At first, the actor is overwhelmed by fear and his behavior becomes weak, imploring, and in this sense, he becomes kind, open or just simply different than before.

Several weeks after the disappearance of the irreversibility, the actor has forgotten everything; he once again becomes hard, closed, takes up his old habits and quickly forgets the warning he had had. The fervor of his prayer *ex ante*, is not equivalent to his impatience to forget, *ex post*, destiny's lessons. This actor, face to face with destiny, will react as if he had conquered it and is equal with the gods … but there is a risk …

> ▶ Father Tardif[19] tells the story of a paraplegic, who was miraculously healed
> following a pilgrimage to a sanctuary where all the crutches attached to a
> wall paid witness to this tradition of inexplicable healing. Following this tradi-
> tion, the Father asked the man for both his crutches, so he could hang them
> on the wall with the others. But as these crutches belonged to a very rich
> man, and were plated with gold and covered with jewels. the ex-paraplegic
> refused to give up his crutches and sat himself down. Later when he wanted
> to get up, he could not. *(Buisson, 1995)*

▶ If we take a religious point of view, we see that the Bible[20] rigorously defines the conditions of a divine gift: it is free[21], it comes from a request[22] but it is preferable that it be a collective request[23] and thanks is rarely given for it except by a non-believer[24]. Still referring to the Bible, we can also ask ourselves why Ieshoua ben Iosseph[25] would accept such an attitude of negotiation, when as a child he had been through what was probably a traumatic experience, given, from the first, his fierce reactions to the businessmen who "confused" business and religion on the Temple's esplanade?

▶ Continually fighting various battles for years (end of short-term job contract, impossibility of renewing it, serious illness of a loved one, not covered by medical insurance, an exhausting personal project, raising a baby with health problems), this young manager tells the story of one time when he was making the daily commute of some 60 kilometers between his home and his work. This was in January, and feeling at the end of his rope, he said the following prayer: "God, if you exist, have pity on me and show me a sign …" This had never happened to him before as he was not a believer. It was raining heavily on this three-lane highway – a highway that he unfortunately knew by heart – and night was falling, reflecting the headlights on the wet road. He passed the other cars, one after the other, at least ten at a time, by moving forward in his seat in order to better see the road, in spite of the light that was reflected on his windshield. He was in a hurry to get where he was going. Once again, he started to pass another car, believing it was OK to do so because the vehicle approaching appeared to be a motorcycle, when in reality it was a truck missing two headlights on the left. When he realized his mistake, he turned the wheel violently to avoid a collision, but his car, unbalanced, swerved a few times, crossed the road and finally crashed into another truck. The car was totaled, but he, himself, had absolutely no injuries …

QUESTIONNAIRE 23

Do you pray?

Put a check in one column for each question using the key below:

1: I completely disagree

2: I mildly disagree

3: I'm not sure

4: I mildly agree

5: I completely agree

Connect the checks. The more your profile appears on the right-hand side, the more you have responded positively to the question.

	I	2	3	4	5
1. Do you ever ask God to help you or to relieve you of your suffering?					
2. Have you ever had a little voice warn you of danger, on the highway for instance, so that a second later, it's obvious that you've avoided the danger?					
3. Have you ever felt, a few seconds before an accident, that you had the feeling it was about to happen?					
4. Do you know anyone who has been inexplicably healed during a mass for the ill, for example?					
5. Have you ever felt that your prayers have been answered?					
6. Prayer can only be useful if it is sincere, that's why children's prayers are the most listened to.					
7. Are you a believer?					
8. Do you find it normal that atheists can be inexplicably healed?					
9. If unexplained "healings" are of divine origin, they are primarily witness to divine presence.					
10. Do you think that someone who has benefited from divine intervention should give testimony to the intervention, even at the risk of looking silly?					
11. Do you have the feeling of being protected by a "guardian angel"?					
12. The intermediary between God and man is the Holy Ghost.					

7.5 The depression phase

All, or almost all, that has been said or written on this "illness" (Bergeret, 1975; Prigent, 1978) has stated that we still don't know how to eradicate it. We can identify, however, two aspects that clarify the situation. The first concerns its gravity. Depression is the most serious of human illnesses, as even death is not considered by the depressed patient as a complication, but rather as a "favorable" evolution; in effect, in other illnesses, the patient seeks to regain his good health in order to escape the illness, as death is the worse thing that can happen to him. In depression, the patient views death as an eventuality that is for the better, a sort of liberation. This thinking represents the principal symptom of the depressive state (Guelfi, Criquillion-Doublet, 1992). The second aspect is positive. For an actor who is getting more and more distant from his "center", depression represents the sole thread that still connects him to this center. It is a thread of pain, certainly, but it is the only indication for the actor that he is leaving a situation that has been deeply intolerable. "Depression is in the end, the art of the failure that saves! Those who are depressed are already on the mend, they just don't know it yet! In the meantime, they've produced a system of letting go, a renouncement that is grief. This grief has to do with the lost image,

The process of situation degradation

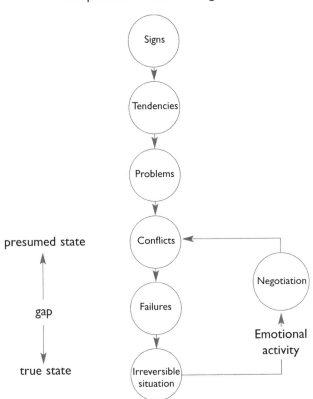

Exhibit 50 Irreversibility perceived as simple conflict

the lost esteem given him by any number of people – his superintendent, the owner of his apartment, his teacher" (Donnars, 1982).

The depressive phase is represented by the abrupt appearance of this illness – which normally takes several months to take root in the person's mental health – and doesn't last more than two or three days. Taking into account what was just said, it is clear that this phase is essential in the preparation of mourning, which is either about symbolic or real death. Biological analysis of neural phenomena has updated the brain's adaptation: the new situation – provoked by irreversibility – necessitates, in order to adapt, that thousands upon thousands – we don't really know how many – of neural connections weaken or disappear to leave room for new connections, better adapted to the new situation. This complex situation is accomplished by the variation of level of catecholamines stocked at the synapse

The process of situation degradation

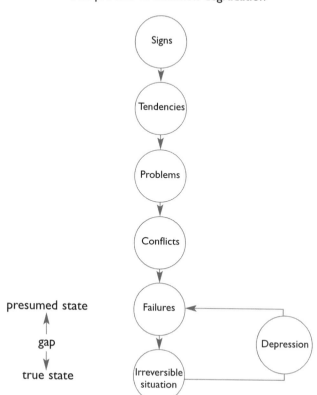

Exhibit 51 Irreversibility assimilated as a simple failure

level. From 12% in a normal individual, the level is reduced to 7% in an individual in the depressive phase. This reduction is accompanied by a feeling of suffering that is especially painful.

> ▶ "A person manages a medium-size firm, and after having fought for 22 years to keep the company afloat, she fails, becomes depressed, but at the same time experiences a sort of peace. To live being beaten, but to live anyway. The analysis showed that this small family-run operation had been given over to her as a mission from her father on his death bed, and after having kept her promise, she experienced her failure as a kind of liberation and found the serenity in finally having accomplished her mission." (Donnars, 1982)

QUESTIONNAIRE 24

Do you have episodes of depression?

Put a check in one column for each question using the key below:

1: I completely disagree

2: I mildly disagree

3: I'm not sure

4: I mildly agree

5: I completely agree

Connect the checks. The more your profile appears on the right-hand side, the more you have responded positively to the question.

		1	2	3	4	5
1.	I sometimes sit for a long time without doing anything.					
2.	I often think of death.					
3.	I can be sad in a situation that is otherwise very happy.					
4.	Life is long, I'll be glad when it's over.					
5.	What good is it?					
6.	I never want to make love.					
7.	I can't fall asleep.					
8.	It's hard to wake up in the morning.					
9.	The world is in bad shape.					
10.	Anafranil is an antidepressant.					
11.	Prozac is a very useful medicine for thousands of people.					

7.6 The phase of acceptance, letting go and serenity

Letting go is renouncing wanting total control, wanting only the best from others, to renounce having to constantly prove yourself, to accept that someone else is someone else and that you are yourself, I am who I am and not just someone I dream of being. Letting go is to trust, it's being able to sign a blank check on the future, on this life and that which follows. Letting go is to stop going after those who haven't given us what we expected. In fact, letting go is to begin to be truly happy, as happiness is like a slipstream, it follows faithfully those who don't pursue it. If we stop to contemplate it, to catch it, it immediately vanishes. From the moment where we can let go, where we no longer have the desire to be happy at all costs, we discover that happiness, is the acceptance of our human condition, it is the capacity to keep our hands open rather than clenched onto what we believe is indispensable. (unknown source)

The process of situation degradation

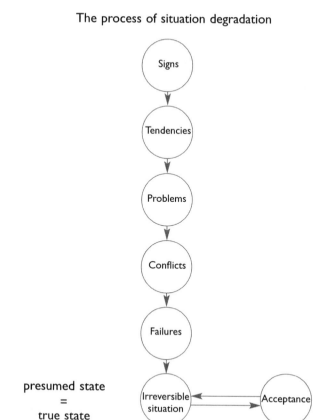

Exhibit 52 Irreversibility accepted

In summary:

1. the manager finds himself facing a challenge,
2. he takes inventory of the programs he has at his disposal to resolve the situation,
3. the execution programs judged to be inoperative are rejected and those that are used fail,
4. the manager employs resolution activity that results in intense search activity,
5. the resolution activity fails,
6. return to 4 then move on to 7, more or less rapidly in function of his **resistance to obstruction**,
7. he inventories the programs that he has to escape the situation; in case of success, go to 1, if not, go on to 8,

8. the escape programs are judged to be inoperable or those that are used fail,

9. return to 2 or 4 or 7, then move on to 10, more or less rapidly as a function of his resistance to obstruction,

10. he goes into inhibition of action, no longer knowing what to do,

11. return to 2 or 4 or 7 then move on to 12, more or less rapidly as a function of the degradation of the situation,

12. the situation becomes irreversible,

13. he moves into a phase of denial, the defense process fails,

14. he enters the magic phase, the defense process fails,

15. he enters the anger phase, the defense process fails,

16. he enters the phase of depression,

17. there is a letting go and an acceptance of his limits.

QUESTIONNAIRE 25

Have you finished grieving?

Put a check in one column for each question using the key below:

1: I completely disagree

2: I mildly disagree

3: I'm not sure

4: I mildly agree

5: I completely agree

Connect the checks. The more your profile appears on the right-hand side, the more you have responded positively to the question.

		1	2	3	4	5
1.	I rarely give it any thought.					
2.	I clearly see what my errors are.					
3.	I hope to be happy.					
4.	We lunch together from time to time.					
5.	We have become true friends.					
6.	I like his/her new companion.					
7.	I never feel the need to speak about him/her to my new companion(s).					

8. A Brief Overview of This Chapter

8.1 The irreversibility of the situation

In the long run, all is irreversible. Prigogine demonstrated that. Human activity can only slow down irreversibility. But on an individual level, very few events are irreversible, and it is up to us avoid causing one.

8.2 The chain of bad decisions

Risk-taking can be broken down into good and bad risks. In a serious situation, the risk is to aggravate the situation even more, either because you are "hiding your head in the sand" or because a certain line has been passed, or willingly, because we can escape the situation and don't care about leaving behind a worsening situation.

8.3 The point of no return

At some point, the degradation increases and an accident, physical or psychological, ensues.

8.4 The status of victim

This last system of logic allows us to regain some ground on the emotional terrain, on the condition that we can convince the "spectators" that we are only victims of events or of men. We can regain some general respect and positive emotional production.

8.5 The replacement

To flee from suffering and grief, the lost subject is replaced by another. The false relationship is based on need and not on desire.

8.6 The mourning process

There is nothing left to do but grieve, but it is not so simple, as often the victim's situation has a particular psychology that pushes away any possibility of grieving, and the resistance to grief by denial will appear. When the impossible reality is imposed, anger and/or negotiation will take over before the breakdown into depression that will bring the actor to eventual acceptance and peace.

The processes that we have just described concern perception. Grieving over your illusions and errors, accepting your failures as coming from yourself and not others, is to slowly reduce the gap between the situation and the definition that we have given it in our internal environment.

It is thus the road to success. In denial, the individual denies the facts, he is not lost, he is not impoverished, or, at least, if that is the case, it is not his fault, he blames it on others … In anger, the situation definition begins to integrate the unacceptable, but it provokes violence. In negotiation, the situation is defined, and we ask that it be changed, as if someone had the power to do so. In depression, a biological process takes over. Millions of neurons weaken, and many new ones take their place, giving rise finally to a feeling of serenity.

Exhibit 53 The grieving process

CHAPTER 6

Successful Situations

Succeeding is not winning. Winning is a product of a fight against others, succeeding is the product of self-harmonization. Feelings of success could come in the shape of a feeling of existence, a feeling of competence, of confirmation or of identification. Success depends on the choices involving personal beliefs and not stagnation. There is an ensemble of success factors, the essential of which is the capacity to find sense in one's existence.

Success is within reach for absolutely anyone and everyone, you just have to work 24 hours a day to achieve it. (unknown source)

An intelligent being who is happy to live unintelligently, will see himself inevitably overtaken by a deterioration of self-image. (Sybil Géhin, 1999)

1. The Paradox of Success

In **rational logic, success** is expressed, for the most part, by the priority given to the access of resources (information, budget, space and energy) which are situated in the external environment of the actor. **Winning** implicitly refers to a situation of a win–lose game, where it is the **loser who creates** the winner. In effect, personal and professional life is represented by a succession of alternating wins and losses. Psychotherapists stress the fact that "loss" represents an occasion to reconstruct one's internal environment, to better understand one's behavior and to develop inner strength. Lowen (1987) takes it farther, and, in calling his book *To Win to the Death*, he highlights the fact that the fight for dominance of resources distances the actor from his "center". Dozens of former students have told us that it is not in the phases of success, but in the phases of failure that they have had the feeling of progressing the most. Several managers in training, finding themselves unemployed after years of fighting to win, have told us that this is the richest and most fulfilling period in their lives.

The introduction of **emotional logic** profoundly modifies the process of success. It is also the result of a process of prioritizing access to resources, but it is **internal resources** this time: self-strength, personal development, know-how and apprenticeship, the capacity to extract sense from experience, etc. To **succeed** refers to a sentiment that appears when the interaction between the internal and external environment results in a process of personal and professional construction, the achieving of potential and the use of innate or developed talents, in order to achieve your objectives and remain in line with your own norms, values and capacities. In order to have the feeling of having succeeded in your life, of having driven your life, a sense of self-harmonization must exist. This harmonization doesn't result from combat with others, but it often results from an attitude of an interior letting go of the attitude of combat. The feeling of harmonization is above all subjective, for it depends on the subject (self-image and idealized self, among others). It results in the preeminence of the person's values over those of society (or of others) in the choices that preside over one's development. The **feeling of success** is represented by emotional production that is felt as durable and long-lasting. It has practically nothing to do with **winning** which is something more ephemeral and often linked to defense mechanisms rather than the depths of one's soul (Lowen, 1987). Succeeding is nothing more than being **happy with oneself**.

The feeling of success will be felt if:

1. The person pursues his own goals and, for decisions that affect his life, keeps to his path, independent of pressures that could push him in other directions.
2. Goals remain clear and conscious despite pressure from his entourage (external environment) and his superego (internal environment).
3. The person doesn't stop or interrupt the growth process, even if it results in long and painful emotional production that is notably linked to phases of grief particularly difficult to manage.
4. During this particularly difficult growth phase, he forbids himself from turning thought into action, no matter what the feelings.
5. He achieves satisfaction, according to his personal standards.
6. The feeling of success is even stronger than the satisfaction, which itself is more than imagined or thought possible.

▶ The famous character in *Starmania* – the rock opera by Michel Berger and Luc Plamondon – "January Zero", successful in business, had his office at the top of a skyscraper where he contemplated his universe feeling proud, but not successful as he "had wanted to be an artist". According to his own criteria, his life had passed him by. Young Olympic champions, having known glory early in life, are examples of the necessity of having to go through a long and painful psychological process in order to return to a normal life. We can also use movie stars or models as another example who fall into despair when their beauty or youth is gone. Winning is not succeeding ...

▶ In fact, C.G. Jung tells us that any attempts at differentiation using imitation will end up being false and counterfeit; it almost always fails and the person finds himself stuck in an affected attitude; he finds himself once again where he began, the only difference being a worsened state of impotency ... The powerful collective weight of society, clearly discernible, makes us pay careful attention to this delicate plant called "individuation", lest you get totally crushed under its weight.

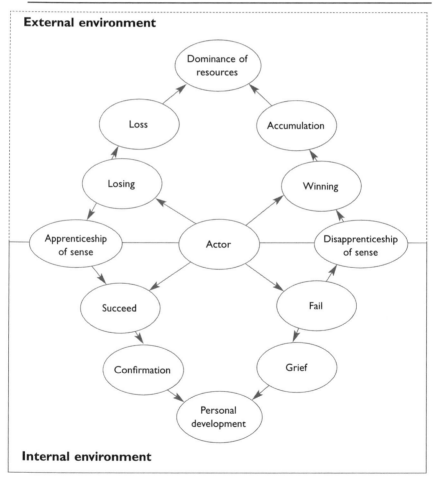

External environment

Internal environment

Exhibit 54 The rational and emotional logic of success

Exhibit 55 To win or to succeed?		
Internal environment	**External environment**	
	Win	**Lose**
Feeling of success	Integrated professional life and personal values	Professional life similar to personal values
Feeling of failure	Professional life far from personal values	Integrated professional life and personal values

2. Positive Emotional Production

Being happy with oneself isn't felt immediately, it is the product of a long path, each step being one rung on the ladder.

2.1 The feeling of existence

This is the first rung on the "ladder". It is what we feel when after having a serious problem or have succeeded in finally leaving a bad situation, we've found our potential again.

QUESTIONNAIRE 26

Do you feel you exist?

Put a check in one column for each question using the key below:

1: I completely disagree
2: I mildly disagree
3: I'm not sure
4: I mildly agree
5: I completely agree

Connect the checks. The more your profile appears on the right-hand side, the more you have responded positively to the question.

	1	2	3	4	5
1. I make sure that my work leaves me enough time to do what I love.					
2. I love my work.					
3. I love to take care of myself.					
4. Nothing's better than a good bath or a relaxing sauna.					
5. I love the feel of wind on my face.					
6. I love the sunset, it fills me with happiness.					
7. Seeing a bird eating fills me with joy.					
8. When I am happy, I smile easily – on the street, at work.					
9. It shows on my face as soon as I am unhappy.					
10. A smile fills my heart.					

2.2 The feeling of competence

According to White (1959) and Argyris (1963), the feeling of competence is the most important of human feelings. All individuals, without exception, need to experience competency in their relationship with their environment. Argyris underscores the difference between intellectual competence and interpersonal competence. It is the latter that has the principal influence on the feeling of competence.

2.3 The feeling of validation

According to Buber, "there is a double foundation to human relationships. The desire in all men to be validated by others for what they are, or what they can become, and, on the other hand, the innate aptitude in man to bring to another this validation" (1957).

QUESTIONNAIRE 27

Do you feel validated?

Put a check in one column for each question using the key below:

1: I completely disagree
2: I mildly disagree
3: I'm not sure
4: I mildly agree
5: I completely agree

Connect the checks. The more your profile appears on the right-hand side, the more you have responded positively to the question.

		1	2	3	4	5
1.	I easily tell someone when things are good.					
2.	If I see someone who is worried, I reassure them.					
3.	I make sure to do something nice whenever possible.					
4.	I accept a compliment, on my clothes or my work, with pleasure if it is justified.					
5.	"Keep going, you'll get there" is my favorite expression.					
6.	My father encouraged me in all that I tried.					
7.	It was rare that one of my parents would criticize me without reason.					
8.	I love taking care of my pet.					
9.	No one says that I spend my time complaining.					
10.	I don't hurt all over.					
11.	I don't have too many basic health problems.					

2.4 The feeling of identification

Simon (1974) formulated six fundamental factors that facilitate identification.

2.4.1 Prestige

The greater the group prestige, the stronger the tendency will be for an individual to identify himself with the group and vice versa. The situation of a group in society is determined by its possession of success symbols in any given civilization. Three such symbols are fundamental for identification:

1. success in the accomplishment of its goals,
2. an average socioeconomic level,
3. the more the group is known, the higher the status of the group in society.

2.4.2 Goal adhesion

The larger the boundaries within which the goals are seen as shared by the members of the group, the stronger the tendency will be for an individual to identify with the group and vice versa.

2.4.3 Frequency of interaction

The more frequent the interactions between an individual and the members of a group, the stronger the tendency will be for the person to identify with the group and vice versa. The more the occasion for contact, the more frequent the interactions. The stronger the cultural pressure for participation, the more frequent the interactions.

2.4.4 Homogeneity of individuals' pasts

The greater the homogeneity of the individual's past, the greater the frequency of interaction. On the other hand, the larger the community, the less frequent the interaction.

2.4.5 Need satisfaction

The greater the number of individual needs that are satisfied by the group, the stronger the tendency for the person to identify with that group and vice versa.

2.4.6 The absence of internal competition

The weaker the amount of internal competition existing between members of the group and an individual, the stronger the tendency for the person to identify with the group and vice versa.

2.5 The feeling of independence and of controlling your own life

▶ "As far as I'm concerned, experience is the supreme authority; my own experience has become my touchstone for all validity. It deserves all the more confidence exactly because it is so basic. It is at this most basic level, that the hierarchy of experience has the most authority." *(Rogers, 1978)*

▶ The person who pursues self-realization, and who has, by definition, gratified his elementary needs, is much less dependent, much less attached, is freer and more autonomous. While far from needing others, the individual motivated by growth could be bothered by others ... but since he depends less on them, he is less ambiguous in relation to them, less anxious and also less hostile, less eager for their kindness and their affection ... This independence vis-à-vis the exterior world also indicates that there could still be the possibility of unfavorable circumstances such as failure, bad luck, hardship, or accidents." *(A. Maslow, 1968)*

▶ But the risk is to be rejected by society if the road taken is too different: "As much as those who drown themselves in dignity appear banal to us, we are just as devoid of all comprehension of those who leave the mainstream, looking for what most do not look for, carried away by aspirations that are far from commonplace. If one of these subjects is, by chance, a true genius, we will only become aware of that fact one or two generations later." *(C.G. Jung, 1933, 1964)*

QUESTIONNAIRE 28

Test your interpersonal competence

Put a check in one column for each question using the key below:

1: I completely disagree

2: I mildly disagree

3: I'm not sure

4: I mildly agree

5: I completely agree

Connect the checks. The more your profile appears on the right-hand side, the more you have responded positively to the question.

		1	2	3	4	5
1.	I like having lunch with people I don't know.					
2.	I never hurt others.					
3.	I know how to listen.					
4.	People like my company.					
5.	I like meetings at work.					
6.	I like having guests.					
7.	I like being a guest.					
8.	I'm good at questioning someone's point of view without seeming to.					
9.	I have a lot of friends.					
10.	I prefer collective sports over individual sports.					
11.	I'm good at getting what I want from others.					
12.	Seduction is not choosing words over weapons, but choosing words as weapons.					

3. The Dynamic of Growth Choices

3.1 Different types of pleasure

We can differentiate between pleasures linked to consumption or the status of being a consumer, which can give rise to the pleasure of relief, and those pleasures linked to production in relation to "Funktionlust", a sort of state of ecstasy or serenity that is known in creative activities or personal development. Relief is much less stable than the pleasure that results from personal development.

3.2 Second choice

Personality is submitted to great number of forces, organized around the desire for a full life. These forces push the person to use all his capacities, to trust in the exterior world and the future.

The mechanisms of personal development can be summarized as follows:

1. Strengthening of impulses for development.
2. Increase of the lure of novelty and creativity.
3. Decrease of impulses towards security.
4. Refusal of positions of certainty, of defensiveness, of pathological regression.

Maslow (1968) considered the development of the person as the result of choice processes at various moments in their lives. Security has, of course, its own pleasures, whereas growth has its own anxieties, in the same way that security has its own anxieties and growth its pleasures.

Exhibit 56 The process of choice		
Internal environment	**External environment**	
	Security	**Change**
Anxiety	Case 1 Driving forces of change	Case 3 Inhibiting forces of change
Pleasure	Case 2 Inhibiting forces of change	Case 4 Driving forces of change

There is personal growth when the pleasure of life and the anxieties of security are greater than the anxiety of life and the pleasures of security. Pleasure as well as frustration are experienced subjectively. The neurotic aspects of the person are the results of old events that have reduced or erased the present capacity to experience pleasure in the "here and now".

There is personal growth if:

case 1 + case 2 > case 3 + case 4

Life at its best is a process of shifting, of changes where nothing is fixed.
(Rogers, 1968)

QUESTIONNAIRE 29

How open are you to life's experiences?

Put a check in one column for each question using the key below:

1: I completely disagree

2: I mildly disagree

3: I'm not sure

4: I mildly agree

5: I completely agree

Connect the checks. The more your profile appears on the right-hand side, the more you have responded positively to the question.

	1	2	3	4	5
1. I prefer a house with large French doors and lots of windows.					
2. I love traveling to new places.					
3. I avoid vacationing in the same place twice.					
4. I avoid confining myself to my small circle of friends.					
5. I like to meet new people.					
6. I like to dress differently whenever possible.					
7. I prefer to watch free birds rather than to have a caged one at home.					
8. I move houses easily.					
9. I prefer to take a walk rather than gardening.					
10. I link up easily with new acquaintances.					
11. With a camping car, you're sure to meet someone new on vacation.					

4. Factors Resulting in Successful Situations

4.1 Self-knowledge

Leadership requires the acceptance of one's motives, a solid identity, the consistency of reactions and a great capacity to be selective.

4.1.1 Self-acceptance

It's necessary to recognize and accept the diversity of our motivations. The control that someone has over his own actions and reactions supposes that he understands, rather specifically, his particular motivation. It would be nice to think that our interior world is filled uniquely with socially acceptable compulsions and desires, but that is not the case. It is useless to waste energy denying the existence of less benevolent, but just as human, feelings that we all have, such as rivalry, animosity, anger and suspicion. The operational criteria for self-acceptance is the aptitude to receive and emit information with the minimum of distortion.

4.1.2 The necessity to firmly establish identity

You have to know exactly what you are and what you are not; the myth that says you can adapt your leadership style makes things that much harder for the individual to truly center himself. To have self-esteem means to have value. Argyris (1970) established the conditions necessary to the growth of self-esteem:

1. the individual is capable of defining his own objectives,
2. these objectives are linked to his main aspirations,
3. he is capable of developing the strategies needed to achieve his goals,
4. the level of aspiration is realistic.

4.1.3 Consistency and continuity of reactions

This refers to the stability of the emotional situation in which we show ourselves to others. Frequent changes are particularly damaging to subordinates who need an atmosphere of security. This point is the inverse of that described by Fiedler who advocated variation in psychological distance as a function of subordinates' performances.

4.1.4 The necessity to be more selective in occupations and relationships

QUESTIONNAIRE 30

Do you know how to say no?

Put a check in one column for each question using the key below:

1: I completely disagree

2: I mildly disagree

3: I'm not sure

4: I mildly agree

5: I completely agree

Connect the checks. The more your profile appears on the right-hand side, the more you have responded positively to the question.

	1	2	3	4	5
1. My spouse wants to go out but I'm tired and I have a hard day tomorrow, so I say I can't go out tonight.					
2. One of my children does her best "acting job" trying to convince me to give her some candy before dinner. I smile, but firmly say no.					
3. My secretary makes a lot of spelling errors. I have refused to give her more than average on her evaluation.					
4. All my friends smoke, but I always refuse to have one in spite of their teasing.					
5. I admire Moslems who are capable of getting down on their knees to pray, no matter where they are.					
6. In France, to say no to someone is considered practically aggressive. Too bad – that's not my problem.					

4.1.5 The necessity of learning to communicate

- Try to know your reactions
- Avoid unexpressed reactions that will only simmer before boiling over; try to know your opinions

4.1.6 The necessity of adopting a cyclical lifestyle

The efficient use of energy appears to require a rhythmic style of alternation; work, leisure; speaking, listening; working alone, working in a group; waking, sleeping …

4.2 Facts are our friends

▶ "During my early lab experiments, I remember the anxiety I felt waiting for the first results to appear. And what if our hypothesis was wrong! And if we had made a mistake … ! I remember feeling at the time that facts were like potential enemies, bearers of bad news. The least light that could be shed on the subject might lead us to the truth. Seeking the truth is never harmful, it is neither dangerous nor uncomfortable. Even though I still hate to go back and revise my opinions and hypotheses, to have to abandon my way of perceiving things or of thinking, I ended up by recognizing that this painful reorganization is called learning, and that, as disagreeable as it may sometimes be, it always brings you nearer to a more satisfying perception, because it is a perception that is closer to the truth." *(Rogers, 1978, p. 23)*

4.3 The obligation to anticipate

By definition, to anticipate is to act without waiting for satisfactory information evaluation. The work of management consists of anticipating, to act in advance as much as possible, in the context of chaotic perturbation, and unstable sequences of events.

To feed this anticipation, the manager has less and less information that is clear and precise. If he waits for such information, the time for decision and profit will have been long gone. Rational logic supplies an adequate work tool for decision-making when the level of information is sufficient:

1. the individual confronts a new situation,
2. he employs search activity,
3. there is a large information deficit,
4. the individual moves into action anyway, in order to anticipate certain events
5. return to 1.

When the level of information is greatly lacking, emotional logic will supply the sole guide for decision-making. "If you 'feel' something, go for it! If you don't 'feel' it, don't do it!"

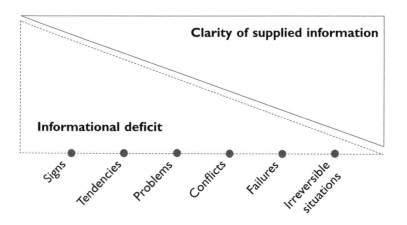

Exhibit 57 Deterioration of available information

4.4 The relationship between the brain and self-actualization

Ned Herrmann proposed a metaphorical model that has its origins both in MacLean's (MacLean, Guyot, 1990) three-brain physiological model and in the metaphorical "hemisphere" model of decision processes proposed by Henry Mintzberg (1976/77) to explain the quadruple complexity of the decision process. Mintzberg states the problem in the following terms: why are certain people so intelligent and so narrow-minded at the same time? How it is that certain of the most creative of thinkers are incapable of understanding a financial statement and certain accountants have absolutely no sense of the conception of a product?" (Ned Herrmann, 1996). In the Herrmann model, cerebral activity is classified in four different domains that result from the intersection of observations made on the left/right continuum and the noble/archaic brain. We can identify the A quadrant (left, superior) that represents logical behavior, the B quadrant (left, limbic) that represents organizational behavior, the C quadrant (right, limbic) that represents affective behavior and the D quadrant (right, superior), that represents creative behavior. For each of these cerebral activities, Herrmann's questionnaire allows us to establish if the subject is in "avoidance", "secondary preference", "primary preference" or "strong preference". The fact of being in avoidance or secondary preference should not be interpreted as if the subject does not possess the corresponding dimension, but that, the nuance being rather subtle, he avoids using it in his approach to problems, or only uses it occasionally.

► "The right brain (in particular quadrant D) is the only part of the brain that pushes for change. As essential as the left brain is for success in business, it is also the sign of a slow death when it is used without the involvement of the right brain." *(Herrmann, 1996, p. 141)*

► "The more one exercises responsibility in an enterprise, the more it is important to connect intuition and thought." *(D-J. Isenberg, 1985, p. 29)*

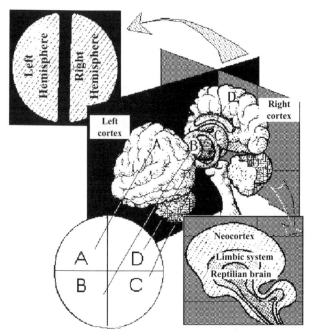

Exhibit 58 Ned Herrmann's four-brain theory illustrated

4.5 Sense research and symbolic function

Edward Chace Tolman in 1932 showed that in explaining decision-making, we could not ignore the notion of intent, aim, objectives and goals. The term "imagination" comes from "image", meaning "representation". This representation doesn't correspond to the sensations that are received from the exterior world by our nervous system. The nervous system gives rise to a memory of an old image. The multiplication of images thus received gives birth to symbols, a sort of abstraction of a concept that links the real and its representation. The multiplication of categories puts at the disposition of the brain a great capacity for comparison and creation.

> I have had the pleasure to be able to discern order in my experiments. It seems to me inevitable to seek out significance, order, and legitimacy in all accumulated experience. (Rogers, 1978, p. 22)

5. How to Develop the Symbolic Function

In his professional work, Professor Mintzberg never ceased trying to send a message to management training institutes to modify their teaching in soliciting the four-brain theory and not uniquely the superior left brain, as the hard management sciences do "as in finance or in the reformulation of financial theory, that has practically done away with the financial analyst as actor and decision-maker[1]". His criticisms against the training curriculum of M.B.A. programs are legendary. But why were such attacks needed to change the situation? **These mechanisms for the development of the capacity to draw sense from experience** had been described for almost 25 years under the term "paroxystic experiences" by Abraham Maslow (1968) who made it a central concept to "self-actualization". We find the same concept in Marilyn Ferguson's journalistic work, under the name of "consciousness expanding". There are other precursors, going back to the time where universities didn't exist and apprenticeships took the place of a pedagogy founded on the interpretation of experience.

5.1 "Off-site" seminars

If you close your door to all errors, you also close it to the truth. (Tagore)

Vehicles for training, directed at increasing the capacity to symbolize and to make sense out of what is experienced, have been largely developed within our school using not only written documents, course projects, internships, association activity, but also, more originally, by creating seminars that, for example, take place in a south Moroccan desert, or on a raft trip in the South of France. The "Outward Bound" approach, as described in the press, has been ridiculed by the Amado report (Amado, Deumie, 1990). This **amalgam** of several methods has contributed to masking its inherent interest and has also contributed to the inhibition of tentative attempts to create pedagogy, hesitant certainly, but uniting certain global situations where the process of "thinking-in-action", the objective of the Ottawa thesis, truly functions (Paquet, Gélinier, 1991). According to our observations, these seminars seem to result in a double acquisition: for the great majority, gratifying emotional production and for some, an occasion to discover a true key to understanding others, but most of all to understanding their own reactions to the unknown[2]. While visiting Professor Krafft's behavioral laboratory, Didier Desor showed me a box, "look at this, this is where intelligence is manufactured". He explained that even though basically conceived to prohibit all stimulation, by putting Wistars rats in this box filled with nooks and crannies and games the size of their cortex increases.

"Experience shapes youth" as the wise men say. It is probable that one day we will be able to show scientifically – as was done for the Wistars rats – that such experiences create millions of new connections within the brain – much more than a single university course – even one given at Harvard (Mintzberg, 1990).

5.2 Experimentation: the Boring picture

Our hypothesis is that teaching founded on experimentation engages the brain more completely than teaching that relies solely on listening. It provokes not only a simple modification of the available information, but a modification – however minimal – of the neural network that transmits this information. In lecture halls, we have demonstrated the existence of the association between emotional production and the expansion of cerebral perception with the help of Dr. Boring's drawing. Certain students stay blocked longer than others on the single vision of the image, and experience a veritable emotional explosion when their perception suddenly includes the double image. Older *training group* practices originating from the U.S. in the 1960's, also show the presence of emotional production in personality modification (Salomé, Gallant 1984). The systematic appearance of emotional production situated by Laborit in the limbic area of the brain permits the development of the hypothesis that the second perception is in relation to new connections that solicit the limbic area before, during and after the birth of this new symbol as perceived by the cortex.

This experiment supports several hypotheses concerning the establishment of neural connections:

- superior cortex (A or D) → limbic (B or C) → superior cortex (A or D), – superior cortex (A or D) → limbic (B or C)
- left cortex (A) → limbic (B or C) → right cortex (D).

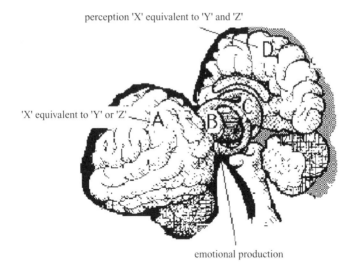

perception 'X' equivalent to 'Y' and 'Z'

'X' equivalent to 'Y' or 'Z'

emotional production

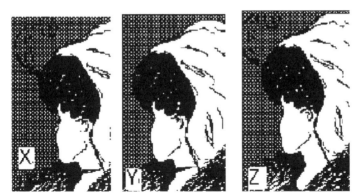

Exhibit 59 The hypothesis concerning the relation between emotional production and the acquisition of a new symbol

This last hypothesis can be strongly supported as it is the only favorable one if a subject treated pharmacologically with mood inhibitors cannot, or not without great difficulty, obtain perception of the second vision. In effect, the experiment establishes the existence of the concomitance of the two phenomena but doesn't allow us to decide on one order over the other. The double perception could very well be established first and then excite the limbic area with emotional production. Herrmann's original work, *The Creative Brain* (1988), established it is the right side, the creative brain, that acts as a mixer, while at the limbic level but still on the right, the affective brain, the producer of emotion, is found. It is what allows us to support the following supplementary hypothesis: superior cortex (D) → limbic (C). The right brain concept is being revived within the scientific community. Six thousand questionnaires (HBDI) completed by managers (Vuillemin, 1991) helped to develop a more complete understanding of human brain functioning. In fact, only the capacity to understand and interpret what happens to him will allow the individual to function on a level of learning and excellence. The symbolic function – if it exists – is in direct relation to emotion. All change, all learning, is in relation to that.

6. A Brief Overview of This Chapter

6.1 The paradox of success

"To succeed" is not "to win". "Winning" is preceded by an external struggle for dominance over the environment. "Success" is preceded by self-harmonization.

6.2 The feeling of existence

This represents the first step on the ladder towards success. It is felt by those who "take pleasure" from doing what they do or from being who they are.

6.3 The feelings of competence and of validation

These are preceded by integration into the human hierarchy where you are recognized by others. They cannot be obtained without the presence of others and are thus strongly linked to the norms of others. Those who have chosen a different path, one of innovation, where they are the pioneers, must learn to do without these feelings of competence and validation.

6.4 The feeling of belonging and of identification

These are the benefits for those in privileged positions of power.

6.5 The feeling of being independent and of controlling your life

If taken to its extreme you can do without others in your life.

6.6 The dynamics of growth choices

Decisions must be taken when climbing up the corporate ladder, and each change in itself brings anxiety, as the pleasure that security brings is erased. If, *ex post*, the choice seems clear, *ex ante*, it appears very uncertain.

Exhibit 60 The positive emotional ladder

6.7 Factors of success

There are certain factors which are the sources of success. They are organized around the establishment of a strong personality, communication and the acceptance of the facts which sanction one's acts.

6.8 The symbolic function

This function represents the tool that allows you to understand the sense that authorizes a decision. It can only be developed by a capacity to modify one's habits, and to increase the type of experiences that may appear difficult but are worth it for the competence they bestow.

QUESTIONNAIRE 31

Test your symbolic capacity

1. If you wanted to illustrate a "beginning"?
   a. a teaspoon
   b. a hammer
   c. an open door

2. If you wanted to symbolize the strength of a choice?
   a. an ashtray
   b. an anvil
   c. a mountain climber's carabiner

3. If you wanted to represent the desert?
   a. a dune
   b. a palm tree
   c. an empty water bottle

4. If you wanted to represent love?
   a. a knife and fork
   b. two nestled Russian dolls
   c. a loveseat

5. If you wanted to represent precision?
   a. an adding machine
   b. a pencil sharpener
   c. a tax return

6. If you wanted to represent resourcefulness?
   a. a tool box
   b. a Swiss army knife
   c. a computer

7. If you wanted to represent an increase?
   a. a weighted measure
   b. a petty officer's cap
   c. a diagonal line going from bottom left to top right

8. If you wanted to represent shame?
   a. a fence with barbed wire at the top
   b. a garbage dump
   c. a crying child

9. If you wanted to represent a decision?
   a. a knife
   b. a pair of scissors
   c. a wad of bills

10. If you wanted to represent memory?
    a. a fossil
    b. a computer disk
    c. a brain

11. If you wanted to represent art?
    a. a brush
    b. a trowel
    c. a piano

12. What does a chair symbolize?
    a. rest
    b. concentration
    c. friendship

13. What does a table symbolize?
    a. the kitchen
    b. foundation
    c. synergy

14. What does light symbolize?
    a. knowledge
    b. day
    c. night

15. What does a flower symbolize?
    a. beauty
    b. the ephemeral
    c. justice

16. How would you symbolize justice?
    a. a tape measure
    b. a scale
    c. a clock

17. How would you symbolize power?
    a. bank notes
    b. a mallet
    c. a measuring weight

18. What does a stone wall symbolize?
    a. a prison
    b. construction
    c. duration

19. How would you symbolize the police?
    a. a tape measure
    b. a police cap
    c. a flashing light

20. How would danger be symbolized?
    a. a red triangle
    b. an exclamation point
    c. a rope about to be cut with scissors

21. How would you symbolize duration?
    a. a block of granite
    b. a chronometer
    c. a yellow falling leaf

QUESTIONNAIRE 32

Test your symbolic capacity

1. *Find the common point among:*
   a. a block of granite
   b. an exclamation point
   c. a police cap

2. *Find the common point among:*
   a. a scale
   b. a note on a door
   c. day

3. *Find the common point among:*
   a. knowledge
   b. a carton of fruit juice
   c. a cap

4. *Find the common point among:*
   a. a computer
   b. a pair of glasses
   c. the ephemeral

5. *Find the common point among:*
   a. garbage
   b. an income tax return
   c. money

6. *What do the following items represent to you?*
   a. a digital lock
   b. a key in a lock
   c. a closed door latch

7. *What do the following items represent to you?*
   a. a brick
   b. a trowel
   c. a sack of cement

ANSWERS TO QUESTIONNAIRE 31

Question number	a	b	c
1	0	0	1
2	0	1	2
3	1	0	2
4	0	1	2
5	1	0	0
6	0	2	0
7	0	0	1
8	0	1	0
9	0	1	0
10	1	1	1
11	0	0	1
12	1	0	0
13	0	1	0
14	1	0	0
15	0	1	0
16	0	1	0
17	0	1	0
18	0	0	1
19	0	0	1
20	1	0	0
21	1	0	0
Total			

More than 20 points:
first rate creativity

Between 10 and 19 points:
good creativity

Between 5 and 9 points:
you need practice being creative

Between 1 and 4 points:
you didn't understand the exercise

ANSWERS TO QUESTIONNAIRE 32

1: impact
2: they carry or are carried by something
3: they all contain something
4: rapid aging process
5: feces, or its symbolic equivalent!
6: security
7: construction

From Emotional to Symbolic Man

Emotional logic introduces the interaction between two entities (external and internal environments) and is represented by two concepts: "the situation" and the "definition of the situation". These two concepts enable us to see the profound gap between rational prediction and behavioral reality, particularly during trials and difficult situations where emotional production is great.

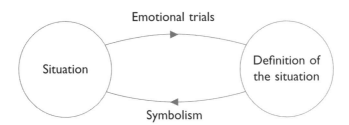

Exhibit 61 The interaction of apprenticeship

Recognizing the existence of emotional production as a product of the gap between the internal norm and the external situation, allows us to go much farther than theories using need as the basis would allow. This recognition takes into account activities focused on the external, whereas need – internal by definition – does not. Pleasure is witness to the positive gap whereas suffering shows a negative gap. A situation, because of its complexity, could give rise to both feelings simultaneously. A negative gap could be treated with creativity, if the actor searches for a solution to the situation. If it is a product of an unsuited or maladjusted norm, it is personal development that will take over. Thus, the double effect is positive: creativity enhances the actor with the acquisition of new know-how, whereas in the absence of a solution, the modification of his norms allows him to become more serene. Thanks to his neocortex, emotional man can create speech about his particular challenge, but the source of the meaning that he will give it resides in the archeocortex. To these two worlds – the internal and external – emotional man adds a third – the symbolic world (Ellenberger, 1970)[1], the only one truly capable of imagining new connections, new structures, and new solutions whose coherence will be submitted to the reality principle (Rogers, 1978; Laborit 1981; Donnars, 1991). It is following conflict, suffering and tribulations that the creative function tries to attain its heights. Challenge represents an archaic place for the clash between the external environment – the external world – and the internal environment – the internal world. It has its feet in both worlds. It is in the external that we are able to measure the gaps, and in the internal, the challenge becomes feeling, maybe even resentment though emotional logic. Thanks to this emotional energy, we can create a supplemental symbol, sketch out a solution, or question a personal belief. While the gratifying situation (Chapter 1) constitutes a victory of the tested over the test, the aversive situations (Chapter 2) represent above all, self-modification. Personal development is to the internal what creativity is to the external.

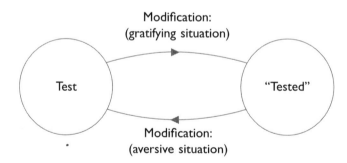

Exhibit 62 The interaction of personal development

Self-modification is filled with suffering, the heart of an internal environment in the middle of restructuration and change, and this suffering could be drawn out as long as the defense mechanisms powerfully resist "letting go"[2] (Chapters 4 and 5). The subject is not blind in his choices, he is simply an "emotional" prisoner. His decision and choice processes are witness to the collision between two incompatible "information structures" and of the search for harmony: the emotional part, dominated, suffering and unable to influence decisions, and the rational part, dominating due to defense mechanisms[3].

This conflict is essentially internal. It stops when the deterioration of the external environment forces the subject into a sort of truce in order to gather his energy for some conflict or external action[4].

Acting to guarantee survival, there is a norm for arbitration that affects the energy spent between apprenticeship and action. Interviews held with actors who are inundated with the turmoil of daily competition serve as proof: very little is said on internal preoccupations. But when a failure occurs the preoccupations of personal development are once again activated – like a computer whose program to clean up the hard drive, for example, has been "on hold" with instructions to start up only when a certain amount of "dead" time has passed. The time spent on learning and personal development becomes whatever time is left over, comparable to saving versus spending.

The heart of personal development is represented by the grieving process over imagined impossibilities. Observation of the last two or three days preceding death allows us to construct a sort of outline that could be applicable to a much longer period of time – a period of 30–40 years – and describes the process of assimilation from internal denial and attempts at scientific rationalization, to rebellion against authority before the intervention of interior negotiation with faith and prayer that represents the pivotal phases between depression and peace – signifying the end of the struggle for that which the subject is not.

Death is the only norm simultaneously approved by the scientific, emotional and the religious models. It represents the ultimate reality of life and its nonintegration in these models would constitute denial. This norm allows us to state the following rule: a life lived by the actor in such a way that there is little work left to be done to face and handle death, is superior to a life that has been based on the denial of this final test[5].

The Integration Process of Suffering[6]

The Kübler-Ross model allows us another look at cycles of humanity pointing out the slow and progressive integration of suffering across the different statuses that are simultaneously, alternatively or successively conferred on it.

In the first, humanity uses denial of the internal nature of happiness: its search is reduced to that of frontal assault, confused with military power and its corollary, war. By its very nature ephemeral, the feeling of victory requires other battles to be reborn. In this model, suffering and pain are attributed to defeat. The dominant psychological process for the reduction of suffering is the denial of defeat. By personalizing and attributing it to an easily conquered or exterminated minority, the losers share with the winners an easily acquired fleeting feeling of victory (Chapters 4 and 5). How often has civilization obeyed this model? In any case, we cannot date this paroxystic phase with any precision in the recent past.

The second process is marked by the hierarchization of subjects sharing a belief in the path to salvation. (Chapter 3). The objective is the same, but the rules have been changed. From the economic approach of Karl Marx to Stanley Milgram and Crozier's managerial approach, and above all to the biological approach of Laborit, it is power that represents the instrument of submission or liberation[7], according to whose side you are on. In this mode, suffering is attributed to inhibition, a product of submission. The struggle for promotion, even if it is ineffectual, temporarily erases the feeling of suffering and assures the maintenance of the biological balance of the structure. This model explains centuries of equilibrium and apparently stable coexistence, based on a feudal system that didn't die regardless of the strength of repeated revolutions. A revolution is condemned before it starts by the same criteria it attacks. It uses the same emotion that distances the actors from their center forcing them to commit the same biological error.

The third process, that of prayer, will be the theme of the third millennium, if one believes the prediction that is generally attributed to Malraux[8]. Requests being absent or present in the life of the actor, God – the subject of prayer – plays a different role depending on whether he is situated outside or inside the subject: outside, he is the vector of values based on fear; inside, he becomes the vector of values integrated in a new alliance with the person. In both these models, suffering[9] is attributed to man, to his lack of harmony with God and to his faults.

Finally, the fourth process will result from the total renouncement of solutions geared towards an external enemy. Suddenly deprived of all his usual archaic and ancestral supports, man "finds" depression[10], just as one finds religion; demonstrated at first by a panic within, an upset in the status of mental health knowledge[11], followed by the development of psychoanalytical thought and finally by the proliferation of new sectors – psychotherapy and therapists – taking on those functions long ago given away to sorcery or religion. Battalions made up of men and women who – sensitized by their own suffering – will dedicate their lives to helping others, accepting to end war, symbolically retaking, in the transfer, the place otherwise occupied by the victim, sacrificing their own defenses or driven by dominant intervention – paternal or divine[12] – in the hopes that having exhausted all interior combat, the subject will find serenity. In this model, suffering is attributed to the distancing of the subject from his center and to all barriers that block his way towards that center. This is somewhat the situation today, at least in northern Europe.

Given these facts, the study of the emotional logic of action has quite a future. But the secret, if it exists, lies elsewhere. It is in symbolic logic: first of all, we have to understand how the brain manufactures sense, then trace the entire education system for the development of these mechanisms – but for that, we have a long way to go, to abandon the object in favor of the subject as the center of apprenticeship.

Case Studies

Case Study 1

A consultant for a company already has too much work, and he has been asked to take on yet another assignment. He must decide whether he will once again reduce the time he spends with his family, or drop one of his other assignments, which happens to be a relatively small but basically more prestigious project …

1. What type of internal conflict will this manager go through?
2. The request to be dropped from one of his other assignments belongs to which type of behavior?
3. Accepting being overworked belongs to which type of behavior? What are the risks?

Case Study 2

D. is leaving his director's office and he is not happy. This is the second time that he has been refused a raise. His work results are excellent, he is the creator of several interesting innovations but the problem lies with the company. They, in fact, must control their spending down to the last penny and they don't have the means to give him a raise. At 33 years old, D. is at the top of his form and now has two children. He has been working for this company for the last 10 years and he has gained certain advantages over the years. His hours are flexible and he owns a number of work tools that were charged to the company.

1. What are his security factors? Are they satisfying?

2. What are his growth factors? Are they satisfying?
3. Should he:
   – ask again for the raise?
   – let the matter drop?
   – look for another job?

Case Study 3

A young lawyer is having a lot of marital problems during her summer vacation. A few days afterwards she loses her most important court case. In mid-October, due to recent heavy rains, she finds herself cleaning up the damage caused by a leak in the house where she now lives alone. She had also learned, a few weeks earlier, that her mother has a fatal disease. A little bit later, her heating system breaks down and she has to live in freezing temperatures for 12 days with her 4-year-old daughter. A problem with the pipes ended up cutting off the water and later that day she opened her mailbox to find a letter from her husband's lawyer outlining her husband's fight for custody for their 4-year-old. This person is obviously in a more fragile position than the average person, yet she doesn't crack under all the pressure.

Why?

Case Study 4

This morning, the managing directors of the company were informed that Mr. Dupont, an ex-employee of the company who had just been fired, had locked himself in a phone booth and called to say that unless he was reinstated he would kill himself. Information received about this young man described him as someone who was honest, fair and a good worker, someone who just didn't understand what had happened to him.

1. What is the nature of the situation?
2. What mental phase is Dupont going through?
3. In your opinion, is the threat of suicide serious?

Case Study 5

The STF company produces prototypes for limited production orders on a project-by-project basis. At a moment when his factories are fully employed, a salesperson accepts a very large order with staggered, but still rather close, delivery dates. The management gives the green light on this order as well as the OK for overtime. In the rush, the cleaning and preparation of the factories are overlooked in spite of warnings given by one of the union members in the factory. A young worker, about to be married, has an accident on the job and loses his sight. The investigations show negligence on the part of the company and the worker. In his personal life, the worker becomes very aggressive and his fiancée leaves him.

1. Identify the chain of bad decisions.
2. Where is the point of no return?
3. Why does the worker become more and more aggressive to his fiancée?
4. What would have been the best attitude for the fiancée to take to help accelerate "healing" on an emotional level?

Case Study 6

Claire is a second-year student. Last June, because of an internship she was doing, she neglected her classwork. On September 18 she was supposed to take a test at 2:00 p.m., and at 11:45 a.m. she was able to get in touch with the professor to discuss her grades. The conversation didn't go very well at all and she hung up on him.

Claire's point of view:

> Of course, I should have gone to get my grades in June, but with the internship and then the summer vacation, I forgot … Teachers don't correct papers very well. I had a D on the last paper and there was absolutely no corrections on the paper itself. If I had a D, that meant it was a terrible paper, I should have seen red marks all over the pages.

> I was able to get him on the phone by telling his secretary that there was a calculation error made on my grade, but the teacher didn't want to discuss it with me, even though he could have said he would meet with me between noon and two to discuss the grade so that I wouldn't have to retake the test. In addition, I hadn't studied at all for this test … With what we pay for these courses, I hung up on him and slammed the door shut on his secretary on the way out. I didn't take the test. They're all idiots!

The administration's point of view:

The program director: "Each time I explain that only teachers are able to change a grade and then only with a jury to approve the change – afterwards it is no longer possible. Only clear errors of calculation can be changed."

The teacher's point of view:

The secretary had called me on my portable phone just as I was going to pick up my kids at school, telling me there had been a calculation error in one of the papers from June.

I asked her to put the student on and it was then that I found out there was no such error concerned but that the student felt that the corrections should have been written clearly in red on the paper.

I explained the difference between mid-term exams, whose objective is peda-gogic and the corrections are noted, and the final exams where only the grade is given.

She argued that she was paying for this course. I told her that a teacher who has eight courses cannot possibly grade 200 papers individually, it would take ten times as long. She hung up! I didn't even have the time to give her an appointment to come in and discuss her grade!

This is a situation of failure that has become an irreversible situation.

1. What are the emotional events in this chain of bad decisions?
2. In your opinion, what was the point of no return?
3. It would have been easy to avoid this situation. How?

Case Study 7

A person, 59 years old, has just been found unconscious in the street. The ambulance brought him immediately to the hospital where examination showed the presence of Charcot disease. It is a rare and fatal disease with no known cure. The patient becomes more and more paralyzed until the moment where the life functions are impacted. Death generally comes from respiratory insufficiency. During an interview with a doctor, the patient asked, "Can I still drive?" Then he said to his daughter, "It couldn't get worse than that!"

1. What type of situation is this?
2. The patient is in which psychological phase of acceptance of his disease?
3. Do you think it would be better to tell him it's a fatal disease or to wait?

Case Study 8

A young director, just named to the post, finds himself facing his first hiring situation. In order to limit undue personal influence or pressure from himself, he decides to create two independent working committees. The interviews take place. The two groups unite to make their choice and the candidate who was chosen by both groups is hired. Less than three months later the new employee leaves.

Why?

Case Study 9

Case study of Marie-Claude Passagret-Panmark from the French National Training and Consulting Society (Société Nationale de Formation and Conseil, SNFC).

When she was hired by SNFC at 35 years old, Marie-Claude already had quite a lot of experience with them as a consultant. As part of the agreement, she promised to begin a Master's as soon as she finished her university degree (as most of their clients have at least a university level degree, SNFC requires that their employees have the same). She had been hired to bring in new business (training contracts) as a way to partially pay for her post. Her job was full-time, not freelance as was the case before (a freelance employee only prepares and gives the training courses, while someone on full-time status is at the agency five days a week and is responsible for other tasks involved in the day-to-day running of the office). Her training courses consisted of training managers in the human resources area and to help them in recruitment procedures. At SNFC, there are two different procedures for personnel evaluation. If the employee reaches his/her objectives, then the objectives are annually redefined based on the needs of the company. This is done during a meeting with the director, without the intervention of the department head. If the objectives are not reached, the employee will be seen by the department head in a series of meetings. These meetings are held with the goal of reviewing the objectives and progress of the employee, and resolving any problems that might be prohibiting the person from achieving the objectives. As for the first point discussed when she was first hired, Marie-Claude later refused to enroll in a Master's program at the end of her trial period when her contract became definitive. She pointed out that it was a fiduciary clause that wasn't written. She had only brought in one training contract, that the company lost at the end of the year, and following that the company gave her two more contracts that she handled in the same way, losing both of them. On the job, she conducted herself more as a freelance worker than full-time employee, refusing all tasks other than the production tasks specifically mentioned on her work schedule. It was clear that she went too far in this, with the other trainers ending up having to do her work (photo-copying all the materials – overheads, course outlines, etc. that she would use for her courses). She refused several times to take care of these tasks that were rightfully hers to do and she did this, at one time or another, in the presence of most of the other employees. She became sullen and irritable when someone asked her to do something that she didn't want to do. She often complained to others, infuriated by the demands that were being made on her, but bristled at any hint of suggestions or reference to the fact that these "demands" were simply part of the daily work as an employee of the company. She didn't show up for meetings and appointments, and when the secretary mentioned this to her she replied "yes, I heard about it but I wasn't sure it was still on."

As soon as she was hired, Marie-Claude was involved in a series of conflicts and began criticizing her superiors (never face to face) who had tried to work with her. In chronological order:

- the manager of continuing education
- the manager of pedagogic planning and coordination
- project managers
- and finally the department head, as soon as he asked her to report on her work.

At first, she is backed up by management and the department head to whom she brings her complaints; she is even offered the post of manager of continuing education. She refuses without explanation. As far as her teaching is concerned, it is submitted to a sort of evaluation where the students themselves are either consulted or asked to estimate their level both before and after a course. Marie-Claude's classes were one of the weakest in terms of individual progress. As soon as it becomes clear that the employee isn't handling her workload efficiently and not reaching her stated objectives, the company's evaluation procedure (usually adequate – an interview with the department head) is put into motion. During the first few years, there were interviews every six months and at that time Marie-Claude was having personal family difficulties (she lived alone with her children, one of whom had had a car accident which required a long convalescence). It was decided to postpone the objectives for evaluation the following year. The date for this second interview was for the following September. During the successive interviews, the same procedure was used – each time the objectives were postponed for the following year. The arguments for this decision were variously Marie-Claude's health and then the death of her father (her rebellious nature, nurtured from childhood through adolescence, was reactivated with the death of her father and she became more and more irritable). Throughout this period, all specific work requests went unanswered. In addition, Marie-Claude complained that she already had enough to do keeping up with all the rules and regulations of the department. Exhausted, the department head decides to initiate a **written procedure**, putting everything in writing as the interviews, meetings and verbal agreements of the preceding years had not been followed. On January 5, the department head demands, in writing, to have a written report of the state of progress of work on several of her objectives. On February 12, an evaluation interview took place, and the department head put the results of that into writing, making sure that it would no longer be possible to deny that these things were ever asked. During the year, Marie-Claude had refused practically all the points on her list of objectives and the department head decided that regardless of any excuses given, an appointment would be made for next September to discuss the group of objectives not reached during the three to four preceding years. In the meantime, during that year, Marie-Claude committed a professional misconduct (in France, professional misconduct is one of the few legitimate causes for dismissal) – she had given a course without having reviewed the contents of the case study that she was responsible for teaching. In September, the meeting took place as planned, but Marie-Claude, who had gotten used to her "temporary" status refused to change her behavior. During the first trimester she suddenly told her boss: "I'm going south next week" and handed him a doctor's note authorizing it. The company functions using a mission by mission or project management style. The project managers are designated by the top management, sometimes by recommendations from the department heads. The project managers are the "selectors". They are responsible for seeing the project through, organizing the course and negotiating with the teachers. Facing them are all the departments and the teachers of the

SNFC. The project manager is in complete control over the choice of teachers. In other words, no employee can assume to be permanently in charge of a task, and is at risk of being pulled off the project if his/her work suffers. In reality, the risk is in theory only – the employees usually work hard at fulfilling their roles and usually there is no reason to pull them off a project. Sometimes there are some failures and tasks may change hands: widespread student dissatisfaction during a course, poorly conducted intakes that sometimes allow poor candidates to take the courses, repeated teacher absences, personal conflicts, conflicts with the project managers, etc. Each task is assigned by the manager within the framework of the mission. The manager has complete freedom in organizing the project, and if it fails, he has complete responsibility. It is the manager and the manager alone who will be submitted to any and all criticism. The flip side is that he/she is also free to hire someone new or fire someone – within a restricted project budget. For the employee, there is a sort of internal marketplace: if the employee has an excellent reputation, he can literally drown under all the requests for his services, and even though flattered, he is obliged either to take it all on or learn to say "no", and thus risk alienating certain employers. If the employee has a weak or mediocre reputation or he arranges it so as to do as little work as possible, he may not have much work and is forced to actively seek work and is always under the risk of losing this or that particular project. The refusals of the "stars" forces the managers to be content with those less involved in their training roles. From the manager's point of view the employee who is working for him must continue to improve until their work is completely acceptable (the first year the employee is learning and refining the product, the second year the employee tests and rectifies his training course and method and by the third year it should meet all expectations). It would be an understatement to say that from the beginning when a mission was given to Marie-Claude, serious risks were being taken as far as its completion was concerned … In October, as all the other members of the department were busy, a manager asked the department head for someone to work on a new contract. When the department head said that he "only had Marie-Claude available", the manager answered "oh well, with her, at least you're sure the project will be a disaster". For several years, the department head had fought in vain for more involvement and preparation from Marie-Claude. He ended up deciding to give her only those jobs where she might have a chance of succeeding, specifically diagnostic tasks. The department head also gave up on the personal interview procedures and asked that the problem with Marie-Claude be treated in meetings with the rest of the staff. Marie-Claude continued to refuse all work

requests and brought in yet another argument: she verbally accepted to show up more often at work, but under the proviso that "it's the same for everyone". This new argument was based on the fact that one of the other members of the department (who had just undergone surgery and was still recovering) was on a more or less convalescent work schedule. Marie-Claude's remark was particularly unjust, as this "arrangement" of a few months was exactly the same type of arrangement that she herself had abused for several years. Worried about avoiding conflict, the management suggested a compromise whereby Marie-Claude would change her contract to three days a week, with the manager only being able to ask her to be in the office two days a week. She refused this compromise, which was actually understandable, as her contract was now four days a week with her presence required in the office only one day a week. No one was giving an inch, neither the department head nor Marie-Claude. Everything had been tried and failed and no compromise was reached. Marie-Claude started to spread rumors about her boss – rumors that "hit below the belt", her way of trying to continue her status as "victim" which had been to her advantage for the last three years. This slander came in different forms: Marie-Claude stated, in front of at least two witnesses, that her department head was out for revenge because she had refused his sexual advances ...
(This type of slander, of undermining, is not uncommon. In fact, some consultants had noticed Marie-Claude talking to clients, slandering the company. Responding to a request once made by a student, she answered " the company doesn't pay me enough to do what you're asking". Marie-Claude behaved in such an awkward manner that during a bid for a certain project with Parisian clients, the clients asked that she be taken off the project or they would go elsewhere.) After all this, her boss once again asked to see her, to ask if, in fact, she was spreading rumors about him. Not only did she confirm that she indeed had said those things about him, but she warned him that if he continued to ask her to account for her work, she would begin a systematic campaign of slander against him – both internal and external to the company. She specified that she had lots of friends that she could call upon to help her in this. She added that as of that moment she refused to work with him. Her aggressive behavior that day was in part explained by the fact that she had stopped smoking and was following a treatment that had her nerves on edge. From that meeting, the conflict left the organizational framework and became an interpersonal issue and the department head decided it was no longer within his domain to be responsible for this problem. He wrote this in a letter, saying he would no longer work in such conditions with Marie-Claude and handed the file over to management. It was then that Marie-Claude cried

"victory", letting everyone know that she had succeeding in pushing the department head to commit professional misconduct while she was exonerated, as she would make clear by the letter that the department head had written ... In fact, this letter could be taken as a rupture of her work contract and would allow Marie-Claude to attack the company and sue for damages and interest ...

1. Identify the different types of behavior employed by Marie-Claude.
2. Identify Marie-Claude's personality type.
3. What management errors were committed by the company and what problems allowed these errors to occur?
4. Do you think that the department head was right in waiting so long? Why?

What would you recommend?

Notes

Prologue

1 Beginning in 1958, Asch, supported by an important movement in parasociological research, questioned the rational model, stating a perfect equivalence between decisions and values, establishing that, in fact, interviews and surveys are the fruit of an unconscious "rationalization" intervening *ex post* to avoid living through cognitive dissonance, a painful source of emotional production.
2 Or rather emotion deemed unacceptable by the culture (American).

Foreword

1 Personal or organizational structure.
2 Nevertheless, in these periods, the rejection of the emotional dimension could give rise to individual (DSM 4) or collective deficits (Meignez, 1971; Bergeret, 1974; Kets de Vries, Miller, 1985), sources of pathology that could enter in as limits of the preceding processes.
3 Laborit defined four behaviors: consummation (drinking, eating, sleeping, copulating), gratification (doing that which will bring pleasure), punishment (flight or fight) and inhibition (doing nothing).
4 These determining situations will be the object of a complete work on the logic of decisions.
5 The most well-known is the LISREL model.
6 The prototype for this method is Stanley Milgram's Yale University study on submission to authority.
7 Stanley Milgram (1974).
8 Elton Mayo (1946).
9 It must not be forgotten that the school of human relations born of the skewed Hawthorne experiments was above all a product of a "remedial" hypothesis by the researcher, worried about making sense out of his very costly study whose variables had been poorly defined from the start.
10 Because, according to our research, it is the situation that determines the perseverance of the emotional processes.
11 Regarding the testimonies given in this text, a great number of facts have been gathered by chance from a survey conducted on the definition of life profile.
12 This method has been used by journalists in prison exposés, where journalists had themselves put in prison, and by ethnologists who, having lived a long time in their milieu, became a subject equal to the others under observation.

13 In this last case, the researcher also becomes subject, and as this is not looked upon favorably by science, it must be clearly stated in the study report.

14 This describes organizational conflict.

15 *Introduction to Psychological Type*, 5th edition, ECPA, 1995.

16 "Become what you are", *Le souffle d'or*, 1994.

17 Being ISTJ, ISTP, ESTP, ESTJ, ISFJ, ISFP, ESFP, ESFJ, INFJ, INFP, ENFP, ENFJ, INTJ, INTP, ENTP, ENTJ.

18 "How to say it"; *The Communication Process*, 1994, InterEditions, Paris.

19 Left brain, right brain; neocortex, archeocortex defining four processes; logic, organization, affective and creative, each one affecting a level of use; avoidance, dilettante, expert or first order (cf. www.herrmann-france.com).

20 The resolution of a situation supposes three conditions:
that the resolution is stable;
that the level of resources needed are reasonable in relation to the problem to be solved;
that the solution does not create other problems, at a different level, which would be more difficult to resolve.

21 This idea is developed in *An Open Letter to Executives of the Soviet Union*, Seuil, 139 pp.

22 Nizard considers retroaction to be the essential variable in his model.

Preview

1 Picked up by the exteroceptors.

2 Picked up by the interoceptors.

3 According to M.F. Hirigoyen, 10–15% of suicides can be attributed to professional causes.

4 "The quantification of the unquantifiable, for validation purposes is, in the best of cases, comparable to the Leibnizienne attempt to mathematically prove the existence of God". (Devereux, 1980, p. 29 cited by Chanlet, 1997, p. 8).

5 See also Lecuyer (1996, pp. 93–117).

6 Association Francophone de Gestion des Ressources Humaines (The French and French-speaking Association of Human Resource Management), 16, avenue de Verdun, 75010 Paris – Telephone: 01.40.35.40.00.

7 Herrmann Brain Dominance Instrument.

8 Boukovsky, V.; *This Shooting Pain We Call Liberty*. France Loisirs, 245 pp.

9 We cite the case of a woman who had been married for three years to a divorced man who, after his death, continued to pay the compensation that was owed to his widow, to his ex-wife, and worse, it was his ex-wife who was financially comfortable and his widow who was in a state of financial need.

10 To completely verify this hypothesis, a study must be conducted on adults who had been delivered by Cesarean section, and to establish if the rate of nervous depression (for example) is lower than that of the population who were delivered normally.

Chapter 1

1 In the course of this process, the actor will develop valences, that's to say that he will feel pleasure or aversion for the situations he experiences. These valences, in turn, will react by leading him to select those fields of action where he will do what is possible in order to bring together both work and pleasure. At the beginning, the family milieu supplies him with his first field of experience, and that could serve to attract him or to turn him away

definitively, depending on the experiences he had and the valences he developed in this initial milieu.

2 The late Maurice Castagné and his team, in Nancy, France.

3 This refers to knowing how to avoid errors that can cause problems. The classic example is the memo; a manager who has written a memo, even once, that dealt with a highly intense and emotional problem, will never do it again. He will use a personal interview if the problem is individual or a meeting if the problem is a group issue.

4 We have two stories that pay witness to this: an elementary schoolteacher that one day became director of 10 companies, and Alain Thirion, who having decided to become one of the leaders of the printing business, dabbled in a little real estate by selling the Grand Hotel in Gérardmer, in order to raise capital that he didn't have.

5 A person's competence is inversely proportional to the quantity of exterior information that is needed to confront a situation.

Chapter 2

1 Prigogine shows in *The New Alliance* that science is condemned to reconcile itself with data of this order.

2 In the Ottawa thesis, Paquet and Gélinier (1991), having noted this antagonism, launched a defense for manager training that leaned more towards action as a source of apprenticeship rather than "reflection *ex post*" as a source of knowledge.

3 At a reading of a dissertation committee, it was noticed that the doctoral candidates' search for certainty comes from the fact that they must concentrate uniquely on data that has been hyper-filtered and finally, deprives them of the analysis of the foundation of the observed phenomenon. We see, for example, theses seeking to establish results by equations that eliminate all psychological analysis in order to limit the results to quantifiable data. For the same reason, finance, much too easy to model, would be the preference of human resource management.

4 For this graph, think of a recent difficulty and position your level of fear and your capacity to confront it. In general, for the same individual and a given problem Y (curve y), the fear is maximal at the discovery of the problem (point A). It fades, little by little, as the manager's resolution activity allows him to establish a means to confront (point B). The change of curve depends on the personality of the actor. If the manager shows more and more self-confidence, he will move onto curve x. If he shows less self-confidence, he will move to curve z.

5 *La vie du rail*, 17-9-1997, pp. 8–10.

6 We say that the valence is positive when the person is drawn to the situation, in the opposite case, we say that the valence is negative.

7 A great deal of research states that subjects who avoid situations where success is almost certain and instead choose more difficult tasks also have superior I.Q.'s (Fraisse and Piaget, 1963).

8 Notably in the CRECI.

9 Median Forebrain Bundle; bundle for reinforcement and reward.

10 PeriVentricular System, bundle for punishment.

11 Are not two sparrows sold for a farthing? And one of them shall not fall on the ground without your Father. But the very hairs of your head are all numbered. Fear ye not therefore, ye are more value than many sparrows (Matthew 10: 29–31).

12 And he withdrew from them about a stone's throw, and knelt down and prayed, "Father, if thou art willing, remove this cup from me; nevertheless not my will, but thine, be done" (Luke 22: 41,43).

13 "You have heard that it was said 'An eye for an eye and a tooth for a tooth.' But I say to you, do not resist one who is evil. But if any one strikes you on the right cheek, turn to him the other also," (Matthew 5: 38, 39) and in Luke: "but I say to you that hear, Love your enemies, do good to those who hate you, bless those who curse you, pray for those who abuse you. To him who strikes you on the cheek, offer the other also; and from him who takes away your coat do not withhold even your shirt" (Luke 6: 27–29).

14 The Book of Job teaches us that Job was an irreproachable man, filled with life and loyal to God and there he stood – deprived of all. Three men wanted Job to be punished for a fault committed. The debate occupies the middle of the book (Chapters 3–37). Job defends God and declares his own innocence. Finally, God intervenes himself (Chapters 38–42). He gives back to Job the double of what he had lost!

Chapter 3

1 It is not rare that the salary of a director of a large group exceeds 3 million French francs per year.
2 Deloffre, G., *The Practice of International Negotiation*, ed. Eska, 1999.
3 Population density also intervenes.
4 Kleinbaum, N.-H. Livre de Poches, 1993, Paris.
5 In article 2 of the Declaration of the Rights of Man of August 26, 1789, it is written that resistance to oppression is one of the fundamental rights of man: "These rights are liberty, property, safety and resistance to oppression."
6 Article 7 of the Declaration of the Rights of Man states: "Those that solicit, expedite, execute or have executed arbitrary orders, must be punished."

Chapter 4

1 "The members of organizations … are limited in their knowledge and aptitude to learn and resolve problems" (Simon, 1970, p. 134).
2 Attacked for a long time in the United States, as happiness is a right as it is written in the Constitution, and it is that statement that pushes the more naive to think "if I'm not happy, it's because the politicians aren't doing their job".
3 See the book by Béatrice Majnoni d'Intignano, *The Unemployment Factory,* 1998, Plon, among others p. 14.
4 Blood donors are generous in prisons, where homosexuals and drug addicts are numerous and are at high risk of being HIV positive.
5 Genesis 3.6 "She took of its fruit and ate; and she also gave some to her husband and he ate."
6 *Les hommes cruel ne courent pas les rues,* 1990, Seuil, p. 29.
7 Buddhism explains suffering by a series of cause and effect:
   1. Because of this, that appears.
   2. Production of this, that is produced.
   3. Because of initial ignorance, karmic transformation occurs.
   4. Because of karmic transformation, the conscience appears.
   5. Because of conscience, name and form appears.
   6. Because of name and form, the basis of knowledge appears.
   7. Because of this basis of knowledge, contact appears.
   8. Because of contact, sensation appears.
   9. Because of sensation, need appears.

    10. Because of need, greed appears.

    11. Because of greed, change appears.

    12. Because of change, age and death appear.

8   "For the nature of the spirit is such that mental qualities developed from a strong base cannot be lost."

9   The Buddhist model belongs to science, in the sense that it gives causality a central place. It belongs to Islam in the position of fatality and to Christianity for its position that the person possesses the capacity to reconstruct his life, his life being considered as an eternal succession of lives.

10   According to Laborit.

11   That should be the worst of your problems.

12   Near death experience (N.D.E.).

13   In Hebrew, the words "mercy" and "maternal compassion" have the same root: *raham* and *rehenim*, that implies a choice between paternal and maternal attributes.

Chapter 5

1   By the summits, symbolized by the "rounds".

2   By the arrows, indicating a probability coefficient.

3   Modeled by a graph.

4   In the form of an increase of experience.

5   *Life and Death*, 1982, Quil, New York.

6   Probably of a scientific origin.

7   Probably of a religious origin.

8   The solution to this problem: to choose between an internal hypothesis and an external one is to enlarge the scope of the problem as – if scientists demonstrate the validity of the second hypothesis – it will put into question the impossibility of scientifically demonstrating the existence of God.

9   We cite the cases of scientists, so shaken by the convergence of testimony that they have "converted".

10   Quoting the testimony of another priest: "I don't know if all charismatic Christians have seen the light, but in my parish, all those who have seen the light are charismatic!".

11   Testimony of this type, found throughout the world, are recorded by Flores *"In the fire of love"*, 1993, Stock, 230 p.

12   In the Jerusalem Bible:
- Psalms 90–91: 9–12
- The Book of Kings: 19: 4–9; 11–13a
- Genesis16: 6–12; 19: 15
- The Book of Tobias: 3: 16–17; 5: 4–17; 11: 7–8
- Daniel: 8: 16; 9: 21–22; 10: 11–12

13   *Inquiry into the Existence of Guardian Angels*, 1993, Filipacchi, p. 13.

14   *The Divorce Boom*, 1983, Marabout.

15   The 10th week of pregnancy or the 12th week of no menstrual cycle (French Law No. 75-17, January 17, 1975, art. L.162.1).

16   Acting out.

17   Karen Blixen, *Out of Africa*; Sydney Pollack.

18   Mozzani E., *Le livre des superstitions*, ed. R. La Hout, 1995, 1822 pp.

19   Died June 8, 1999.

20   Bible, translated by Chouraqui, 1989.

21   Matthew 10: 6.

22   Matthew 6: 7.

23 Matthew 18: 19–20.
24 Luke17: 17–18 and Matthew 9: 13.
25 Jesus, son of Joseph.

Chapter 6

1 Laroche and Nioche, ICN conference, Nancy, France, 1992.
2 We went to see Professor Krafft's Laboratory for Behavioral Study (Nancy 1); by taking regular saliva samples from volunteers, he has been able to trace the emotional chronobiology of each one of them.

Epilogue

1 H.F. Ellenberger, *History of the Discovery of the Unconscious*, ed. Fayard, 1970; 1994.
2 The strongest prison that emotional man can experience is that of pathological fear coupled with a high level of success. It becomes so dangerous to face unhappiness for this man – prisoner in a double locked cell where letting go – the only source of serenity – will only occur when a serious and violent shock is experienced by the person – a shock strong enough perhaps to knock him out of his prison and give him back his heart and put him back on his true emotional path.
3 The appearance of dreams being the first sign, a sort of floating dialogue, full of warnings, and with all due respect from the dominated part trying to address the dominating.
4 As proof, the reduction of psychotherapists' revenue during times of war.
5 If this process takes place in 2-3 days for the dying – does that mean that the division of time has been so unequal that most of their lives have been spent in the "denial" phase and that it is only at the urgency of imminent death that this phase is very quickly accomplished. If you refer to other research on death, we can believe that actors, having allowed the day-to-day internal transformations to run their course without interference, live through this final phase, which is actually a very short and rapid transition, accomplished in a few minutes, between a perfectly constructed life and imminent death.
6 We speak of suffering and not of emotional production, as it is the part of emotional production that will play a specific role in what follows, according to the value that is accorded to it.
7 Scholars see the world in quite the same way: society's objective is to hide the exploitation of the dominated by the dominating; even love is nothing more than a form of domination.
8 "The third millennium will be religious (or spiritual) or it will not be".
9 This takes into account divine intervention as do the five phases of the EKB model: even while denying His existence, one can still find writers and poets who insult God, calling him a crook, before sliding into either depression or ecstasy.
10 Depression's emotional logic is not well known. It is often expected that national peace will bring about individual joy. Given this, we are usually surprised when the opposite occurs, yet, biologically, it's been shown that it is indeed the opposite that is produced: peace when it is filled with calm and inaction is a source of depression and of the doubling of psychotherapists' revenue.
11 As shown by the exorbitant cost of functional illnesses, aberrant consumption of tranquilizers, increase in suicides among the young, increase in work strikes, and widespread deterioration, rise in power of the extreme right, the development of the politically correct, modern expression of psychotic denial, and so on.
12 In the psychoanalytic model, the symbolic murder of the father and the feeling of definitive loss of the mother, constitute the sign of entry into the adult world.

Bibliography

This bibliography contains the list of studies, works, and articles that were a part of the research for this book, as well as other references that treat subjects and themes relating to the present subject.

ADEY W.-R., 1964, "L'élaboration et le stockage de l'information dans le système nerveux", *Actualités neurophysiologiques,* 50th series, Masson, pp. 263–95.

AFPLANE, 1991, *Management stratégique des PME/PMI: guide méthodologique,* Economica.

AGAZZI E., 1996, *Le bien, le mal et la science,* P.U.F.

AKTOUF O., 1989, *Le management entre traditions et renouvellement,* Gaétan Morin, Montreal.

ALLPORT G., 1950, *The Nature of Personality,* Addison-Wesley.

ALLPORT G., 1955, *Becoming,* Yale University.

AMADO G., DEUMIE C., 1990, "Pratiques magiques et régressives dans la gestion des ressources humaines", *R.G.R.H.* No. 1.

AMAURY de SAINT VINCENT, 1989, *Mobiliser par l'entretien individuel,* Edition du Moniteur, 256 pp.

AMIOT M., 1991, *Les misères du patronat: le monde des petites et moyennes entreprises industrielles et de leurs patrons,* L'Harmattan Logiques sociales.

ANASTASSOPOULOS J.-P., BLANC G., NIOCHE J.-P., RAMANANTSOA B., 1985, *Pour une nouvelle politique d'entreprise,* P.U.F.

ANHOKHIN P., 1975, *Biologie et neurophysiologie du réflexe conditionné,* Mir, Moscow.

ANSOFF I., 1989, *Stratégie du développement de l'entreprise, Les Éditions d'Organisation,* 5th revised edition.

ARGYRIS C., 1957, *Personality and Organization: the Conflict between System and the Individual,* Harper & Row.

ARGYRIS C., 1963, "Exploration in Human Competence", Roneo, Dept. of Industrial Administration, Yale University. Quoted by C. A. (1970) p. 31.

ARGYRIS C., 1970, *Participation et organisation*, Dunod, 325 pp.

AUBERT D., GRUÈRE J.-P., JABES J., LAROCHE H., MICHEL S., 1991, *Management. Aspects humains et organisationnels*, P.U.F. Fondamental, 2nd edn 1992, 656 pp.

AUBREY B. (ed.), 1985, *Les nouveaux guerriers: la quête de la maîtrise de soi*, Revue Autrement, 202 pp.

AVENAL M., 1990, *Des managers et des cadres prêts pour l'Europe de 93*, EME, 263 pp.

AXELROD R., 1992, *Donnant, donnant, Théorie du comportement coopératif*, Éditions Odile Jacob, 234 pp.

BACHELARD G., 1949, *Le rationalisme appliqué*, P.U.F.

BARDELLI-GODEFROID V., GROSJEAN P., 1992, *La motivation de l'individu dans l'entreprise: l'exemple des cadres*, I.A.E. de Nancy 2, D.E.A. de gestion, 46 pp.

BATESON G., 1980, "La double contrainte", in *Vers une écologie de l'esprit*, Vol. II, Seuil.

BAYARD J.-P., 1982, *La spiritualité dans la franc-maçonnerie*, Dangles, 430 pp.

BEAUCHARD J., 1981, *La dynamique conflictuelle, comprendre et conduire les conflits*, Réseaux.

BEAUVOIS J.-L., JOULE R., 1981, *Soumission et idéologies*, P.U.F. 205 pp.

BELLENGER L., 1984, *Être constructif dans les négociations et les discussions*, Entreprise moderne d'édition.

BENET M., 1987, *Toucher juste*, Le corps à vivre, 75008, Paris.

BERGERET J., 1974, *La personnalité normale et pathologique*, Dunod, Paris.

BERGERET J., 1975, *La dépression et les états-limites*, Payot, 358 pp.

BERLYNE D. E., 1960, *Théorie du comportement et opérations*, P.U.F., Paris.

BETTELHEIM. B., 1972, *Le cœur conscient*, Robert Laffont.

BLAKE R., MOUTON J., 1969, *Les deux dimensions du management*, Les Éditions d'Organisation, Paris.

BLAKE R., MOUTON J., 1984, Surviving arises through Participative Management, *International Management*, February.

BLAKE R., MOUTON J., 1987, *La troisième dimension du management*, Les Éditions d'Organisation, Paris.

BLANCHARD K., LORBER R., 1990, *Le Manager Minute au travail*, Les Éditions d'Organisation.

BLONDIN R., 1983, *Le bonheur possible*, Les Éditions de l'homme, Montreal, 329 pp.

BOITEUX S., 1998, *Le rapprochement entreprises–écoles de gestion: vers de nouveaux principes de formation*, HEC, University of Montreal.

BOLLE De BAL M., 1985, *La tentation communautaire*, Éditions de l'Université de Bruxelles, 261 pp.

BOLTANSKI L., 1982, *Les cadres*, Éditions de Minuit, 523 pp.

BOSTON CONSULTING GROUP, 1980, *Les mécanismes fondamentaux de la compétitivité*, Hommes et Techniques.

BOUDON R, 1979, *Effets pervers et ordre social*, P.U.F., 286 pp.

BOUILLOUD J.-P., *L'invention de la gestion, histoire et pratique*, L'Harmattan.

BOURNOIS F., 1991, *La gestion des cadres en Europe*, Éditions Eyrolles, 273 pp.

BUBER M., 1957, Distance and Relations, *Psychiatry*, vol. XX, May, pp. 101–3, quoted by Argyris, (1970, p. 32).

BUISSON M.S., 1995, *Lève-toi et marche!*, Éditions de l'Emmanuel, 261 pp.

BURKE M., 1982, *Les styles de vie des cadres et des entreprises*, InterEditions.

CALORI R., ATAMER T., 1989, *L'action stratégique: le management transformateur*, Les Éditions d'Organisation.

CANNAC Y., 1985, *La bataille de la compétence*, Éditions Hommes et Techniques.

CARLZON J., 1986, *Renversons la pyramide*, InterEdition.

CASTAGNÉ, COMBES, GAGNÉ, LANGEVIN, SARTORI, 1988, *P.E.P. : A chacun sa Propre Entreprise Performante au sein de l'entreprise*, Éditions Publi-Union, 340 pp.

CHALVIN D., 1971, *Auto diagnostic des dirigeants*, Hommes et Techniques, 297 pp.

CHALVIN D., 1977, *L'entreprise négociatrice. Le pouvoir peut-il se pratiquer?*, Dunod.

CHANDLER A.-D., 1962, *Strategy and Structure*, MIT Press, Cambridge MA.

CHANLAT J.-F., 1990, *L'individu dans l'organisation: les dimensions oubliées*, Les Presses de l'Univ. Laval, Éditions Eska, 842 pp.

CHANLAT J.-F., 1997, "Sciences sociales et management : plaidoyer pour une anthropologie générale", *Cahier de Recherche* No. 97–17, École des HEC, Montreal.

CHIFFRE J.-D., TEBOUL. J., 1990, *La motivation et ses nouveaux outils*, EME, 150 pp.

CHOURAQUI A., 1988, *La Bible*, Desclée de Brouver.

COLIN C., DESOR D., 1986, "Différenciation comportementale dans les groupes de rats soumis à une difficulté d'accès à la nourriture". *Behav. Proc.* 13, 85–100.

COLLANGE C., 1985, *Le divorce boom*, Marabout, 287 pp.

COSTA de BEAUREGARD, 1963, *Le second principe de la science du temps*, Seuil, 151 pp.

CRENER M., 1979, *Le management*, les Presses de l'Université du Québec, Montreal.

CRENIER M., MONTEIL B., 1971, *Principes de management*, les Presses de l'Université du Québec, 511 pp.

CROZIER M., 1964, *Le phénomène bureaucratique*, Seuil, Paris.

CROZIER M., FRIEDBERG E., 1977, *L'acteur et le système*, Seuil, Paris, 436 pp.

CYERT J.-L., MARCH J. G., 1970, *Processus de décision dans l'entreprise*, Dunod.

CYRULNIK B., 1993, *Les nourritures affectives*, Éditions Odile Jacob, 244 pp.

CYRULNIK B., 1997, *L'ensorcellement du monde*, Éditions Odile Jacob, 310 pp.

DAMASIO A. R., 1995, *L'erreur de Descartes, la raison des émotions*, O. Jacob, Sciences, 360 pp.

DEJOURS C., 1990, "Plaisir et souffrance dans l'organisation", see Chanlat (1990).

DEJOURS C., 1993, *Travail et usure mentale*, Bayard Éditions, Paris.

DEJOURS C., 1999, *Souffrance en France. La banalisation de l'injustice sociale*, Éd. Seuil, 192 pp.

DELAIRE G., 1985, *Commander ou motiver*, Éditions d'Organisation, 131 pp.

DELOFFRE G., 1999, *Pratique de la négociation internationale*, Éditions Eska, 224 pp.

DESOR D., 1994, "Différenciations comportementales dans les groupes de rats confrontés à une difficulté d'accès à la nourriture". Thèse d'État ès Sciences de l'Université de Nancy I.

DEVEREUX G., 1980, *De l'angoisse à la méthode*, Flammarion, Paris.

DIEL P., 1947, *Psychologie de la motivation*, reedited, Payot, 1991.

DIEL P., 1956, *La peur et l'angoisse*, Payot, 215 pp.

DONNARS J., 1982, "La dépression ou comment survivre?", conference, Le corps à vivre, Paris, 20 pp.

DONNARS J., 1985, "La séduction", conference, Le corps à vivre, Paris, 21 pp.

DONNARS J., 1986, "La trahison", conference, Le corps à vivre, Paris, 45 pp.

DONNARS J., 1991, "La tolérance", conference, Le corps à vivre, Paris, 28 pp.

DRUCKER P., 1969, *L'ère de la discontinuité*, Les Éditions d'Organisation.

DRUCKER P., 1976, *Vidéo sur la prise de décision*, Images pour la formation, Paris.

DRUCKER P., 1981, *L'entreprise face à la crise mondiale*, InterEdition.

DRUCKER P., 1985, *Les entrepreneurs*, Éditions J.-C. Lattés.

DSM-III-R, PICHOT P. (Président), 1992, *DSM-III-R*, Masson, 624 pp.

DSM-4, PICHOT P. (Président), 1996, Masson, 700 pp.

DUPONT P., OSSANDON M., 1994, *La pédagogie universitaire*, P.U.F.

DURKHEIM E., 1893, *De la division du travail social*, P.U.F., Paris.

FRAISSE P., PIAGET J., 1963, *Traité de psychologie expérimentale*, Fasc. V, Ed. P.U.F., 287 pp.

FRIEDMANN G., 1963, *Où va le travail humain?*, Gallimard, Paris.

FRIEDMANN G., 1964, *Le travail en miettes*, Gallimard, Paris.

GAULEJAC de V., 1987, *La névrose de classe*, Éditions H. G.

GAUTHIER C., TARDIF, M., 1996, *La pédagogie*, Gaëtan Morin.

GEHIN S., 1993, "La représentation mentale, élément qualitatif dans la prise de décision", Mémoire de DEA, sciences de gestion, I.A.E, Nancy 2.

GEHIN S., 1999, *Méthodes de communication interpersonnelle*, Éditions Eska, 200 pp.

GEHIN S., IVANAJ V., 1993, "Les valeurs des dirigeants et les stratégies de croissance des PME", I.A.E, Nancy 2.

GELINIER O., 1984, *Stratégie d'entreprise et motivation des hommes*, Édition Hommes et Techniques, 311 pp.

GENELOT D., 1993, *Manager dans la complexité. Réflexions à l'usage des dirigeants*, Insep éditions, 324 pp.

GHERTMAN M., 1981, *La prise de décision*, P.U.F.

GIBSON J.-L., IVANCEVICH J.-M., DONNELY J.-H., 1991, *Organization (behavior, structure, processus)*, Irwin.

GLEICK J., 1989, *La théorie du chaos*, Albin Michel.

GODET M., 1991, *De l'anticipation à l'action: manuel de prospective et de stratégie*, Dunod.

GOGUELIN P., 1989, *Le management psychologique des organisations*, Édition les hommes et l'entreprise, Vol. I: 134 pp., Vol. 2: 191 pp., Vol. 3: 229 pp.

GOLEMAN D., 1995, 1997, *L'intelligence émotionnelle*, Robert Laffont, 505 pp.

GOUILLARD F.-J., 1989, *Stratégie pour une entreprise compétitive*, Economica.

GROF S., 1983, 1979, 1975, *Royaumes de l'inconscient humain*, Édition du Rocher, 280 pp.

GROUPE L'EXPANSION, 1991, *Motivation des cadres: valeurs clés de l'entreprise*, Harvard l'Expansion, 127 pp.

GROUX G., 1983, *Les cadres*, Édition La découverte, Maspéro, 127 pp.

GUELFI J.-D., CRIQUILLION-DOUBLET, 1992, *Dépression et syndromes anxio-dépressifs*, Ardix Médical, 144 pp.

GUENDET G., EMERY Y., NANKOBOYO F., 1986, *Motiver aujourd'hui*, Les Éditions d'Organisation, 204 pp.

GUILLAUME P., *La psychologie de la forme*, Flammarion, Paris.

GUMPERT E.-D., BOYD P.-D., 1989, "Stress et solitude du patron de PME", in *Gestion et management des P.M.E. : Les valeurs clés de l'entreprise*, Harvard L'Expansion, winter, pp. 49–55.

HAGEGE C., 1986, *L'homme de parole*, Fayard.

HAMPDEN TURNER C., 1990, *Atlas de notre cerveau*, Les Éditions d'Organisation, 225 pp.

HENRIET B., 1986, *Leadership et management*, Éditions Liaisons, 149 pp.

HERRMANN N., 1988, *The Creative Brain*, Brain Books, 456 pp.

HERRMANN N., 1988, *Les dominances cérébrales et la créativité*, Retz, 368 pp.

HERRMANN N., 1996, *The whole brain business book*, McGraw-Hill, 334 pp.

HILLEL J. EINHORN, ROBIN M. HOGARTH, 1987, "La prise de décision; l'expérience et l'avenir", *Harvard l'Expansion* No. 47.

HIRIGOYEN M.-F., 1998, *Le harcèlement moral, la violence perverse au quotidien*, Éd. Syras, 212 pp.

ISENBERG D.-J., 1985, "Comment réfléchissent les dirigeants?", *Harvard l'Exp.* No. 37, p. 28.

ISRAËL L., 1980, *La décision médicale*, Calmann-Lévy.

ISRAËL L., 1989, *Boiter n'est pas pécher*, Édition Denoël, 314 pp.

JANKELEVITCH V., 1987, *Quelque part dans l'inachevé*, Folio/Essai.

JARROSSON B., 1991, *Invitation à une philosophie du management*, Calmann-Lévy, 225 pp.

JARROSSON B., 1994, *Réflexions sur le processus de décision*, Édition Maxima, 245 pp.

JOULE V., BEAUVOIS J.-L., 1987, *Petit traité de manipulation à l'usage des honnêtes gens*, P.U.F de Grenoble.

JUAN S., 1993, *Organisation et management en question*, Harmattan.

JUNG C. G., 1933, 1964, *Dialectique du moi et de l'inconscient*, Édition Gallimard, coll. Essais, 287 pp.

KAST F., ROSENZWEIG J., 1970, *Organization and Management: a System Approach*, McGraw-Hill.

KATZ D., KAHN R.-L., 1966, *The Social Psychology of Organizations*, John Wiley, New York.

KEPNER C,-H., TREGOE B., 1972, *Le manager rationnel*, Les Éditions d'Organisation, 215 pp.

KERNBERG O., 1979, *Les troubles de la personnalité*, Édition Privat, 287 pp.

KETS DE VRIES F.R., MILLER D., 1985, *L'entreprise névrosée,* McGraw-Hill, Paris, translated by the Neurotic organization, Jossey-Bass Inc., San Francisco.

KOENIG., 1990, *Management stratégique: vision, manœuvres et tactiques*, Nathan.

KOONTZ H., O'DONNEL C., 1973, *Les principes de management*, Marabout, 783 pp.

KORNHAUSER, 1977, "Mental Health of Factory Worker", *Human Organisation*, Vol. 21, pp. 43–6

KORZYBSKI A., 1953, *Science and Sanity*, New York, The International non-Aristotelician Library.

KORZYBSKI A., date not known (about 1954), "Le rôle du langage dans les processus perceptuels", conference text distributed by the Librairie non-aristotelicienne de Paris.

KORZYBSKI A., BULLAT de VILLARET, 1973, *Introduction à la sémantique générale*, Le courrier du livre, 187 pp.

KORZYBSKI A., FEJAN, "Fondements de la sémantique générale", Not dated, Édition Vie et action, conference, 19 pp.

KUBLER-ROSS E., 1975, *Les derniers instants de la vie*, Éditions Labor et Fides, Geneva, 247 pp.

KUBLER-ROSS E., 1985, *La mort, dernière étape de la croissance*, Éditions du Rocher, Monaco, 217 pp.

KUHN T., 1962, 1970, 1983, *La structure des révolutions scientifiques*, Flammarion, 284 pp.

LABORDE G., 1987, *Influencer avec intégrité*, InterEdition.

LABORIT H., 1955, *Réaction organique à l'agression et choc*, Masson, Paris.

LABORIT H., 1958, *Biologie et structures*, Coll. Idées, Paris.

LABORIT H., 1974, *La nouvelle grille*, Robert Laffont.

LABORIT H., 1976, *Éloge de la fuite*, Coll. La vie Robert Laffont, 234 pp. or Gallimard Coll. Idées, 186 pp.

LABORIT H., 1980, *Copernic n'a pas changé grand-chose*, Robert Laffont.

LABORIT H., 1981, *L'inhibition de l'action*, Masson, 214 pp.

LABORIT H., 1984, *La colombe assassinée*, Grasset.

LABORIT H., 1994, *La légende des comportements*, Flammarion, 317 pp.

LACAN J., 1973, *Le Séminaire*, Vol. IX, *Les quatre concepts fondamentaux de la psychanalyse*, Le Seuil, Paris.

LAMBERT P., 1968, *Management ou les 5 secrets du développement*, CLE.

LANDIER H., 1987, *L'entreprise face au changement*, Entreprise Moderne d'Édition.

LAURIN P., 1973, *Le management manuel*, McGraw-Hill, 765 pp.

LAWRENCE P.-R., LORSCH J.-W. 1974, *Organizations and their Members: a Contingency Approach*, with Morse, Harper & Row.

LEAVITT H.-J., 1958, *Psychologie des fonctions de direction dans l'entreprise*, Hommes et Techniques, 304 pp.

LEAVITT H., 1958, *Managerial Psychology*, University Chigago Press, translated in 1969, *Psychologie des fonctions de direction dans l'entreprise*, Hommes et techniques.

LECUYER B.-P., 1996, *L'invention de la gestion*, L'Harmattan, Paris.

LEFTON R.-E., 1987, *Motivation efficace par l'entretien d'appréciation*, McGraw-Hill, 306 pp.

LEGENDRE P., 1976, *Jouir du pouvoir*, Édition Minuit.

LE GOFF J.-P., 1992, *Le mythe de l'entreprise; Critique de l'idéologie managériale*, Découverte.

LEGRES J., PEMARTIN D., 1981, *Pratique des relations humaines dans l'entreprise*, Les Éditions d'Organisation, 197 pp.

LEMOIGNE J.-L., 1974, *Les systèmes de décisions dans les organisations*, P.U.F.

LENDREVIE, undated, *Encyclopédie du management*, Centre supérieur des affaires de Jouy-en-Josas, France Expansion.

LEVISON H., 1973, *Les cadres sous pression*, Les Éditions d'Organisation.

LEVITT T., 1991, *Réflexions sur le management*, Dunod, 194 pp.

LEVY-LEBOYER, 1993, *La crise des motivations*, P.U.F., 134 pp.

LEVY-LEBOYER, 1998, *La motivation dans l'entreprise*, Éditions d'Organisation.

LEWIN K., 1935, A Dynamic Theory of Personality, McGraw-Hill.

LEYGUES M., 1976, La motivation des hommes dans le management, Chotard, 210 pp.

LIKERT R., 1967, *The Human Organization: Its Management and Value*, McGraw-Hill.

LOWEN A., 1987, *Gagner à en mourir*, Hommes et groupes éditeurs, 307 pp.

MacGREGOR D., 1969, *La dimension humaine de l'entreprise*, Gauthier-Villars.

MacGREGOR D., 1974, *La profession de manager*, Gauthier-Villars.

MacGREGOR D., 1975, *Leadership et motivation*, Ent. moderne d'édition (EME), 198 pp.

MACHIAVEL, 1980, *Le Prince et autres textes*, Gallimard, 473 pp.

McKELVEY B., 1982, *Organizational Systematics*, University of California Press, Los Angeles and Berkeley.

MacLEAN P.-D., 1970, "Le cerveau limbique. À propos de la tendance paranoïde chez l'homme", *Confrontations psychiatriques* No., 6 pp. 45–64.

MacLEAN P.-D., GUYOT R., 1990, *Les trois cerveaux de l'homme*, Robert Laffont, 366 pp. (articles from 1970, 1978, 1982, 1983, 1984).

MAFFESOLI M., 1976, *Logique de la domination*, P.U.F.

MAIER N.-R.-F., 1952, *Principes des Relations humaines*, Les Éditions d'Organisation, 550 pp.

MARCH J.-G., COHEN M.-D., OLSON J.-P., 1972, "A Garbage Can Model of Organizational Choice", *Administrative Science Quarterly*, Vol. 17, No. 1, pp. 1–25.

MARCH J.-G., OLSON J.-P., 1976, 1979, *Ambiguity and Choice in Organizations*, Universitetsforlaget, Bergen.

MARCH J.-G., SIMON H.-A., 1958, *Organizations*, Wiley.

MARCH J.-G., SIMON H.-A., 1969, *Les organisations*, Dunod, 253 pp.

MARX K., 1938, *Le capital*, Imprimerie Floch.

MASLOW A., H., 1968 (1962), *Vers une psychologie de l'être*, Fayard, 267 pp. (1962), *Toward a Psychology of Being*, D. van Nostrand Co., Inc., Princeton, NJ.

MASLOW A., H., 1969, "A Theory of Metamotivation: the Biological Rooting of the Value Life", in *Reading in Humanistic Psychology*, edited by A. J. Sutich and M. A. Vich, The Free Press, Ltd, New York.

MAYO E., 1946, *The Human Problems of Industrial Civilisation*, Macmillan, New York.

MEIGNEZ R., 1971, *Pathologie sociale de l'entreprise*, Gauthier-Villard, 225 pp.

MICHEL S., 1989, *Peut-on gérer les motivations?*, P.U.F, 210 pp.

MILGRAM S., 1974, *Soumission à l'autorité*, Nouvelles Éditions Calmann Levy, 272 pp., latest edition, February 1993.

MINARIK E., 1987, *Motivation individuelle, clé du succès de l'entreprise*, Les Éditions d'Organisation, 204 pp.

MINTZBERG H., 1971, *The Structuring of Organizations*, Prentice Hall, Englewoods Cliffs, N.J.

MINTZBERG H., 1976, Planifier à gauche et gérer à droite, *Harvard l'Expansion*, No. 3, p. 74.

MINTZBERG H., 1982, *Structure et dynamique des organisations*, Les Éditions d'Organisation, 464 pp.

MINTZBERG H., 1986, *Le Pouvoir dans les organisations*, Éditions d'organisation, Paris and Éditions Agence d'Arc, Montreal, 678 pp.

MINTZBERG H., 1990, *Le management: voyage au centre des organisations*, Éditions d'Organisation, Paris and Agence d'Arc, Montreal 576 pp.

MINTZBERG H., "Formons des managers, non des M.B.A.!", *Harvard l'Expansion*, No. 51, p. 84.

MISSENARD B., *Savoir négocier face-à-face*, Les Éditions d'Organisation.

MONTAUD B., 1993, *César l'éclaireur*, Dervy, 239 pp.

MORENO R., 1990, *Théorie du Bordel Ambiant*, Livre de Poche, 350 pp.

NAISBITT J., 1982, *Les 10 commandements de l'avenir*, Sand, 346 pp

NAVRIDIS K. (ed.), 1997, *L'aventure psychosocio-logique*, Desclée de Brouver, Paris.

NIZARD G., 1991, *Les métamorphoses de l'entreprise; pour une écologie du management*, Économica, 281 pp.

NUTTIN J., 1991, *Théorie de la motivation humaine. Du besoin au projet d'action*, P.U.F.

ORGOGOZO I., 1988, *Les paradoxes de la communication à l'écoute des différences*, Les Éditions d'Organisation.

OLD J., MILNER P., 1954, *Positive reinforcement produced by electrical stimulation of septal area and other regions of rat brain*, J. Comp. Physiol. Psychol., Vol. 47, 419–27.

PAQUET G., GELINIER O., 1991, *Le management en crise pour une formation proche de l'action*, (the thesis of Ottawa), Economica, 162 pp.

PARSONS T., 1964, *The Social System*, The Free Press, New York.

PAUCARD A., 1988, *Éloge de la faiblesse et autres petites lâchetés*, Robert Laffont, 167 pp.

PAZ O., 1972, *Le labyrinthe de la solitude*, Gallimard.

PEARLIN L., 1961, *Alienation from Work*, The Free Press, Glencoe, IL, pp. 139–40.

PECK Scott, 1978, 1987, *Le chemin le moins fréquenté. Apprendre à vivre avec la vie*, translated from the American by L. Minard, J'ai lu, 374 pp.

PERNIN D., 1985, *La gestion des hommes*, Hommes et Techniques.

PERETTI (de) A., 1981, *Du changement à l'inertie*, Dunod, 247 pp.

PETERS Th, WATERMAN R., 1983, *Le prix de l'excellence*, InterEditions, 347 pp.

PETERS Th., AUGUSTIN N., 1985, *La passion de l'excellence*, InterEditions, 442 pp.

PETIT F., 1988, *Introduction à la psychosociologie des Organisations*, Privat.

PFEFFER J., SALANCIK G.R., 1978, *The External Control of Organizations, a Resource Dependence Perspective*, Harper & Row, New York.

POIRIER J., RIBADEAU DUMAS J.-L., 1978, *Le cerveau limbique, cerveau affectif*, Laboratoires Hœchst, Puteaux, France.

PONTALIS J.-B., 1994, *Aimé et être aimé, Nouvelle revue de psychanalyse*, No. 94, Gallimard, 239 pp.

POUCHENEL, 1993, Enregistrement public le 23/07/63 de J. Brel à Knokke, La collection, Vol. 1, limited edition No. 6456.

PRIGOGINE, STENGERS, 1979, *La nouvelle alliance*, Folio/Essais, 435 pp.

PRIGENT Y., 1978, *L'expérience dépressive*, Desclée de Broover, 266 pp.

RAPOPORT A., 1967, *Combats, débats et jeux*, Éditions Dunod, 309 pp.

REBOUL O., 1980, *Qu'est-ce qu'apprendre?*, P.U.F.

REICHHELD, 1996, *The Loyalty Effect*, Harvard Business School Press, Cambridge.

REUZEAU M., 1993, *Économie d'entreprise: organisation, gestion, stratégie d'entreprise*, ESKA.

REVAL A. 1945, *Baden Powell*, Société d'éditions modernes parisienne, 123 pp.

RICE A.-K., 1958, *Productivity and Social Organization, the Ahmedabad Experiment*, Tavistock Publications, London.

RINPOCHE S., 1992, *Le livre de la vie et de la mort*, Édition de la Table Ronde, 571 pp.

ROGERS C.-R., 1978, *Le développement de la personne*, Collection Organisation et Sciences Humaines chez Dunod.

ROJOT J., BERGMANN A., 1989, *Comportement et organisation: comportement organisationnel et théorie des organisations*, Vuibert, 352 pp.

SAINSAULIEU R., 1977, *L'identité au travail*, Presses de la Fondation Nationale des Sciences Politiques, Paris.

SAINSAULIEU R., 1982, *Les relations de travail à l'usine*, Les Éditions d'Organisation, Paris.

SAINSAULIEU R., 1987, *Sociologie de l'organisation et de l'entreprise*, Dalloz, Paris.

SAINT EXUPÉRY A., 1946, *Le petit prince*, Éditions Gallimard, 93 pp.

SAINT SERNIN B., 1979, *Le décideur*, Éditions Gallimard.

SALLENAVE J.-P., 1993, *L'antimanagement*, Les Éditions d'Organisation, 125 pp.

SALOME J., GALLANT S., 1984, *Les mémoires de l'oubli*, Le Regard Fertile, 493 pp.

SARTRE J.-P., 1948, *Esquisse d'une théorie des émotions*, Herrmann, Paris.

SCHEID J.-C., 1980, *Les grands auteurs en organisation*, Dunod, 239 pp.

SCHEIN E.-E., 1970, *Organizational Psychology*, 2nd edn, Prentice Hall, Englewood Cliffs, N.J.

SCITOVSKY T., 1976, *L'économie sans joie*, Calmann-Lévy, 294 pp.

SCOTT W., MITCHELL T., 1973, *Organisation des structures de l'entreprise: analyse des comportements*, Publi Union.

SELYE H., 1974, *Stress sans détresse*, La Presse, Montreal.

SERRES M., 1980, *Le parasite*, Grasset.

SFEZ L., 1974, *Critique de la décision*, Armand Colin.

SFEZ L., 1984, *La décision*, Collection Que sais-je?, P.U.F.

SIMON H.-A, 1970, *Administrative Behavior*, Milan.

SIMON H.-A., 1974, *La science des systèmes, science de l'artificiel*, Epi, 159 pp.

SIMON H.-A., 1983, *Administration et processus de décision*, Economica.

SIMON P., LAROSE R., 1976, *La gestion des organisations*, Thème 2, Université du Québec à Montréal.

SILLAMY N., 1989, *Dictionnaire de la psychologie*, Larousse, 290 pp.

SILVERMAN D., 1970, *La théorie des organisations*, Dunod, 213 pp.

STEINBERG R., 1975, *L'homme et l'organisation*, Time-Life International (Netherlands) 173 pp.

STINCHCOMBE A.-L., 1965, *Social Structure and Organization*, in J.-G. MARCH (ed.) *Handbook of Organization*, Rand McNally, Chicago, IL.

SULLOWAY F.-J., 1979, *Freud, biologiste de l'esprit*, Fayard, 595 pp.

TARDIF J., 1992, *Pour un enseignement stratégique: l'apport de la psychologie cognitive*, Éditions Logiques, Montreal.

TÉNIÈRE-BUCHOT P.-F., 1989, *L'ABC du pouvoir Agir Bâtir Conquérir ... et Sourire*, Les Éditions d'Organisation.

THEVENET M., 1992, *Impliquer les personnes dans l'entreprise*, Liaisons.

THOMPSON J., 1957, *Organization in Action*, McGraw-Hill, New York.

TOFFLER A., 1970, *Le choc du futur*, Denoël.

TONOLIO A.-M., 1994, "Variabilité inter-individuelle, contrainte de l'environnement et structuration de groupe. Une étude chez le rat Wistar". Thesis at l'Univ. de Nancy 2.

TOURAINE A., 1973, *Production de la société*, Édition du Seuil, Paris.

TOURAINE A., 1974, *Pour la sociologie*, Édition du Seuil, Paris.

TOURAINE A., 1978, *La voix et le regard*, Édition du Seuil, Paris.

TOURAINE A., 1984, *Le retour de l'acteur*, Fayard.

TOWSEND R., 1985, *Faites décoller vos hommes et votre entreprise*, Le Seuil.

TREPO G., 1973, *Les racines du centralisme dans l'entreprise, revue Management-Direction*, No. 37, in *Encyclopédie du management*, Centre Supérieur des Affaires de Jouy-en-Josas, France Expansion.

TURKAWKA B., 1999, *Méthodes de recherche d'emploi*, Éditions Eska, 133 pp.

VAES U., 1953, *La hiérarchie dans la structure de l'entreprise*.

VALLERAND R-J., THILL E. E. (eds), 1993, *Introduction à la psychologie de la motivation*, Vigot.

VATÉ M., 1976, *Le temps de la décision*, P.U.F.

VIDAL A., 1978, *Introduction à une science du réel indéterminé*, P.U.F, 427 pp.

VINCENT C.-P., 1993, *Du paradoxe à la contradiction. Pour une nouvelle approche du management*, ESF Editeur, 222 pp.

VUILLEMIN L., 1991, *Une enquête sur les préférences mentales de 99 managers français, Communication et langages,* Vol. 91, pp. 37–45.

WATERMAN R., 1990, *Les champions du renouveau,* InterEditions, 390 pp.

WATZLAWICK J., HELMICK-BEAVIN D., JACKSON D., 1972, *Une logique de la communication,* Le Seuil, Paris.

WATZLAWICK P., 1981, *La nouvelle communication,* Le Seuil.

WEBER M., 1964, *The Theory of Social and Economic Organization,* Freepress.

WEICK K.-E., 1979, *The Social Psychology of Organizing,* 2nd edn, Reading, MA, Addison-Wesley.

WHITE R.-W., 1959, *Motivation Reconsidered: the Concept Competence, Psychological Review,* Vol. 66, pp. 297–333.

WIENER N., A. ROSENBLUTH A., BIGELOW J., 1943, *Behavior, Purpose and Teleogie* (comportement, intention et téléologie) in *Philosophy of Sciences,* Vol. 10.

WILLIAMS L., 1986, *Deux cerveaux pour apprendre: le droit et le gauche,* Les Éditions d'Organisation, 204 pp.

WOLFGANG K., 1964, *Théorie de la forme,* Coll. Idées, N.R.F., Paris.

WOODWARD J., 1958, *Management and Technologie, Problems of Progress in Industry,* No. 3, H.M.S.O.

WOODWARD J., 1970, *Industrial Organization Behaviour and Control,* Oxford University Press.

WOOT de PH. A., 1984, *Profil de dirigeant,* Cabay-Economica.

ZALEZNIK A., 1963, *Les dilemmes du leadership, Harvard Business Review,* July–August, translation H.E.C. Montreal, in *Encyclopédie du management,* Centre d'enseignement supérieur des affaires, France Expansion.

ZALEZNIK A., 1966, *Human Dilemmas of Leadership,* Harper & Row.

ZALEZNIK A., KETS DE VRIES M., 1975, *Power and the Corporate Mind,* Houghton Mifflin.